HOW MAVERICK MOMS ARE CREATING THE
NEXT GENERATION OF EXCEPTIONAL MEN

RAISING
BOYS
WITHOUT
MEN

PEGGY DREXLER, PH.D.,
Assistant Professor of Psychology in Psychiatry,
Weill Medical College of Cornell University,
with **LINDEN GROSS**

RODALE

This book is for all the maverick mothers
I have come to know and admire.

Printed in the United States of America

Rodale Inc. makes every effort to use acid-free ∞, recycled paper ♺.

Book design by Christina Gaugler

Library of Congress Cataloging-in-Publication Data

Drexler, Peggy.
    Raising boys without men : how maverick moms are creating the next generation of exceptional men / Peggy Drexler, with Linden Gross.
        p.   cm.
    Includes bibliographical references and index.
    ISBN-13 978–1–57954–881–0 hardcover
    ISBN-10 1–57954–881–4 hardcover
    1. Boys.   2. Masculinity.   3. Single mothers.   4. Parenting.   I. Gross, Linden.   II. Title.
HQ775.D74   2005
306.874'32'0973—dc22   2005010098

Distributed to the trade by Holtzbrinck Publishers

2 4 6 8 10 9 7 5 3 1 hardcover

RODALE
LIVE YOUR WHOLE LIFE™

We inspire and enable people to improve their lives and the world around them

For more of our products visit **rodalestore.com** or call 800-848-4735

CONTENTS

ACKNOWLEDGMENTS

First and foremost, I owe a debt of gratitude to the families that participated in my research project. All the parents took time from their busy lives to meet with me or have lengthy phone conversations. Each family, parents and children alike, participated to the fullest, openly sharing their thoughts and feelings with me. I am thankful for their enthusiastic endorsement of this project.

Linden Gross, an extremely elegant wordsmith, helped to make this book what it is. Despite some trying times, Linden never wavered in her commitment to making this book the best it could be.

Gail Ross, my agent, was always there when I needed her. Gail is hands down the best!

I am privileged to have had Jane Isay, editor extraordinaire, on my team. Jane gave generously of her time, reviewing and shaping the book with her keen intellect and all the force of her critical and comprehensive knowledge.

Elizabeth Crane was immeasurably helpful in a multitude of ways.

Geneviève Van de Merghel's responsiveness, work ethic, and professionalism were invaluable in writing this book.

David Groff's lively intelligence stimulated many discussions that informed the book.

Steve Seligman graciously shared his creative mind with me and helped me to gain a fuller perspective of psychoanalytic theory, both traditional and contemporary.

William Damon permitted me to use his Social-Cognitive and Moral Judgment interview. That and his work with children have greatly enhanced my understanding of the nature of moral development in youngsters.

Many years ago Morris Peltz provided the creative spark for what ultimately is this book with his question, "I wonder how these children are doing?"

I had the good fortune to have had three editors at Rodale:

Mary South initially "got it" and bought the book.

Mariska Van Aalst's belief in the project and her expertise as an editor were invaluable in providing clarity to this project.

Amy Super added the important and necessary finishing touches to the book. I will never forget Amy's actual words when she gave the book her seal of approval.

Alex, my beloved son, graciously allowed me to use his stories.

I am indebted to my wonderful daughter, Katherine, who kept me loving and laughing through the entire process of writing this book.

Mickey's (devoted husband, best friend, and dragon slayer) steadfast determination in the face of obstacles has been an inspiration to me.

INTRODUCTION

Whenever I pick up a new book in psychology, I want to know something about the author, so let me introduce myself. I come to the issue of how mothers are raising children with a strong interest, both professional and personal. I was raised in a homogeneous, suburban East Coast community in an era when the *Father Knows Best* ideal of family life prevailed. When I was 3½, my own father died suddenly of a heart attack, leaving my mother a widow at age 33. So, like many of the children in this book, I was raised by a single mother. I had older sisters, which was like having three mothers. We were the only family in the neighborhood without a dad. This growing-up experience led to my lifelong curiosity about what it is like for children who, as I did, grow up without fathers in female-dominated households. I think that my interest in psychology and my determination to pursue a career that combines research with therapy also has deep roots in those years spent in a family that was then quite unusual.

I am also part of a long-married, heterosexual couple, but my family tree continues to sprout in ways that challenge tradition. My son, now 26, was conceived the "usual" way, but after waiting 14 years for another child, my husband and I adopted our daughter as a newborn. I'm an older mother with a young child. Many of my contemporaries have children in high school or college, or who are out of the house or married. Some of my friends are even grandparents. Having an elementary-school-age adopted child along with an adult son has helped me to understand firsthand today's school-age children, as well as those girls and boys whose places on their family tree are untraditional.

Being married so long to the same man paradoxically makes me part of a new minority. The U.S. Census Bureau recently reported that only 23.5 percent of households in the United States now contain families like mine—the *Father Knows Best* kind, the kind with a married mom and dad and their children. The definition of family that prevailed during most of my life and professional career is inexorably shifting because of new technologies for conceiving children and new configurations of familial relationships. Families are changing. Parenthood is changing. All you have to do is pick up the daily newspaper to see it. My version of family has even left our TV screens. Children NOW, a national child- advocacy organization that examines media messages to kids, reports that the nuclear family is disappearing from network television. On the six broadcast networks in 2001, only about 1 in 10 regular characters in prime-time series was a parent, and over one-third of those parents were single.

In a country in which one in two marriages will end in divorce, and 40 percent of babies are born out of wedlock, the mom-dad-and-kids version of family is now less than definitive. Moreover, ideas of how children are conceived and what kinds of relationships add up to a "family" are being redefined. More and more children in the Western world are being raised not in the traditional nuclear family but by single or divorced parents, stepparents in "blended families," adoptive parents, and grandparents. An increasingly large number are being raised by mothers who are single and who have not divorced a husband or been abandoned by a man; these mothers are single by choice and have made a conscious decision to have a baby and find a sperm donor to do it. Lesbian couples and single mothers by choice are pioneering new ways of getting pregnant via donor insemination. In the midst of the social upheaval and debate that has taken place about family structure, I became fascinated with the question: Can parents in nonnuclear families, without both a mom and a dad in the household, successfully raise children?

Years before I began the research for this book, as a professional mental-health worker, I was shocked to observe the level of prejudice against mothers, manifested in subtle and cruel ways. While studying for my first master's degree at Columbia University, I worked in a foster care adoption facility, where I was primarily responsible for the placement of children. One of my cases involved a white couple that had been foster-parenting two 3-year-olds: Mandy, a Caucasian girl with blue eyes and brown hair; and a Hispanic child, Ana, with mocha-colored skin and piercing dark eyes. Both were adorable. Though the couple professed to love each child, they could—or would—adopt only the Caucasian child, despite the fact that the girls had been raised as sisters in this foster home for over half their lives.

The agency worked long and hard to find a family placement for Ana. Finally they came up with what was in effect a two-mother family: a fairly affluent professional woman who was dying for a daughter and whose mother lived in the same home.

I had the unfortunate task of picking up Ana to take her to her new family. Needless to say, there were a lot of tears. Ana had met her new mother before, and there had been a transition period, but she was being taken away from the only home she knew. It was heart wrenching. Still, I knew that in the long run she would be better off with a single mother who desperately wanted her, and who had a family support system, than with the mom-and-dad family who had been ambivalent about her presence.

Over the following weeks, I visited both Ana's old foster family and her new mother and grandmother. Though Ana was still experiencing some real grief and sadness, in many ways she had started to grow pleased about her new family situation. On one occasion, she proudly showed me her new room, and on another, her special chair in the kitchen. She let me know that her seat at the table was in the middle, between her mother and grandmother. But she wasn't the only child who had to adjust. When I went back to check on the family adopting the Caucasian girl, Mandy, the little girl took one look at me and yelped to a friend who was visiting, "Quick! Hide your baby brother. Mrs. Drexler is coming." She saw me as the woman who took children away from their families. Such can be the cost of building any kind of family.

However, the situation of Ana's adoption possessed far greater enduring irony: If she had been a boy, she never would have been placed with the two women—nor would she have been placed with a single mother. As independent parents raising children without the presence of a father, mothers have long been treated with dubiousness, fear, and even contempt. Traditional theories contended that mothers who reared sons without the presence of an active father—or who were married but "overbearing" or raising "mama's boys"—instilled lifelong psychic disability, schizophrenia, or, worst, homosexuality in their sons. More recently, society's guardians have declared that single mothers—whether unmarried or divorced, poor or employed, straight or lesbian, or as white and prosperous as Calista Flockhart and Jodie Foster—are sending violent, drug-using hellions out into the world, boys who present no positive maleness, all due to the combination of Mom's presence and Dad's absence.

Since Freud, mothers have been inculcated with the idea that we need to cut our sons' cords to make them men ready to take on masculine roles in the world, from working toward worldly success to making war.

We have been further told by Freudians, social psychologists, and the popular culture that our sons need their dads in order to become upstanding male citizens. If not for Beaver Cleaver's mom and dad, June and Ward, where would Beaver and his brother, Wally, have been? Without Ward, wouldn't the boys have missed the supposedly crucial opportunity to separate from June by identifying with a very present father?

According to Freud and others who followed him, June alone could not have achieved everything required to bring up "the Beav" successfully. During the first 3 to 4 years of Beaver's life, he would have needed Ward to imitate, long for, and react to, in order to gain the prize of being like his father. This theory—that boys acquire masculinity only with an in-house male in the mother's bedroom—has prevailed to the detriment of both mothers and their sons. It presumes that the earliest relationship between infant and mother is simply a caretaking one. The assumption is that the mother is only a need provider for her son, while he in turn becomes physically and emotionally dependent on her. Eventually, assuming there is a present father in the home, the mother must withdraw herself from the child if her son is to become independent of her and escape the dire fate of being a mama's boy.

The deep emotional connection between a mother and her son has been demonized for generations. As a research psychologist, I have seen how mothers worry that they will emasculate their sons by loving them too much. God forbid that a boy suffer from "smotherlove."

Mothers of all kinds worry about smotherlove. Married mothers worry about the damage they might inflict by spending time with their sons, especially if Dad works long hours at the office or is often away from home. Newly single mothers worry about providing a solid foundation for their sons' masculinity, because most boys see much less of their fathers after a divorce. Single moms by choice are on the desperate lookout for male role models for their sons.

The 1990s began to see a cultural shift in these attitudes, with a spate of books alerting parents, and the culture at large, about the need to attend to boys' emotional needs in order to temper the violence and depression rampant among young men. Yet even the most thoughtful mothers continue to internalize the "Back off, Mom" rule that has applied for so long. They worry about their "smothering mothering" and consciously pull back from ongoing connection with their sons. I lived through these worries myself when my own son was growing up.

Although in today's world sons are placed in families with only a mother, concerns persist about a single mother's ability to raise a masculine boy without the presence of an in-house male. During the century it's been open, the Gladney Center for Adoption in Fort Worth, Texas, an international leader in adoption services, has placed more than 26,000 children in forever homes and has assisted more than 36,000 birth mothers. Mike McMahon, its president, told me in an interview that when a boy is considered for placement in a single-mother family, the organization always queries the prospective mother about the child's opportunity for male role models: "Among ourselves, yes, we have a fear . . . that the boy [adopted by a single woman] wind[s] up without a balance in his life and [he may] wind up very effeminate as a consequence of that." He further explained, "We ask [single mothers of sons] a lot more" about their plan for parenting.

McMahon agreed that women can and do raise sons successfully without a husband, but he claimed the need for a male figure of some sort still exists. "If we had two women living together," he said, "we would still be pushing to say, 'I know you have a plan and it's great you have somebody who can care for this child when you travel, but you still need to have a male around somewhere.' That's hard to say. It's pretty judgmental on our part, but we think it's the right thing to do."

However, when Gladney places a girl in a single-mom family, it doesn't require the same plan for having a male figure around. "We don't. We should, but we don't," McMahon admitted. "That's probably more candid than I should say, but we really don't. There's probably a bias that it's not as important [with girls], frankly, when it is."

Are such concerns—evident not just among social conservatives but among liberal-minded people at places like Gladney—truly warranted? Are the sons of these women in danger? The traditional developmental view pronounces the presence of a strong male family figure to be vital to a child's development. This view holds that the nuclear family remains the only model that doesn't by its very nature damage kids. Some social scientists have declared that children reared in homes led by women are always at a disadvantage, suffering from increased levels of poverty, greater risk of involvement in crime, higher levels of teenage pregnancy, and lower levels of educational achievement. According to these scientists, boys are especially at risk if they're fatherless.

Can parents in nonnuclear families, without both a mom and a dad in the household, successfully raise children? Even more specifically, can mothers raise boys, since young males seem more vulnerable than girls to familial discord, drugs, and social violence? In a world where the radical transformation of family and parenting has caused consternation, worry, outrage, and fear, the question of nonmarried mothers raising sons has become one of our most crucial and contentious social issues.

I became convinced that it was my job to investigate the causes of this attitude toward single mothers and two-mother couples raising sons and to find out whether this was justified, or simply a prejudice that had worked its way into our belief system.

No family configuration has stirred more controversy in recent years than that of same-sex parents. Whatever rights and status gay and lesbian people may have secured, the way gay men, lesbians, and children live as family units has generated immense curiosity, fury, and uneasiness. Most specifically, the idea of lesbian mothers raising America's sons causes many raucous debates.

The fact that researchers at least a decade ago estimated the number of lesbian mothers in the United States to be as many as 5 million—coupled with the more recent flurry of gay marriages that prompted heated national debate—underscores a growing phenomenon of lesbian couples having babies and raising families. According to the Family Pride Coalition, a national advocacy group for gay and lesbian families, some 9 million children in America have at least one gay parent, and one in five lesbian-coupled households includes a child under age 18.

"Same-sex couples and single women are 40 percent of our business, and it is the fastest-growing segment," said Marla Eby, vice president of marketing at California Cryobank in Los Angeles, which ships semen nationwide.

Despite this trend, the majority of Americans still seem to believe that it is better for a child to have two parents of the opposite sex than to be raised by two lesbian mothers. A clear majority of Americans also agree with President George W. Bush's simple position—marriage should be between a man and a woman. In a *Time*/CNN poll, 62 percent of respondents said they opposed the legalization of same-sex marriage; fewer than a third favored it.

Clearly, lesbian and gay families continue to be viewed with reproach and disdain by many in the dominant culture, who worry that the estimated 6 to 14 million children living in these types of families are bound to suffer grave harm from being raised by homosexuals. Was that so? I wondered. What was the truth about how lesbian mothers raise sons?

In addition, I wanted to find out what lesbian parenting would tell all of us about how mothers—whether they are what I call "maverick mothers" raising kids without fathers, or mothers in more traditional mother-father families—foster values, character, and assurance in their sons. Later, my study would extend to single mothers by choice as I sought to answer a vital question: Could sons prosper through the power of mothers alone?

After obtaining a master's degree at Columbia, I continued to explore the issues around raising children as a clinical social worker and a faculty member in the Department of Child and Adolescent Psychiatry at the Payne-Whitney Clinic of New York Hospital/Cornell Medical School. In 1996, during my graduate work at the California School of Professional Psychology, motivated by curiosity about the nature of a phenomenon I was witnessing firsthand—and long fascinated by how all nontraditional mothers parent their children—I decided to do my dissertation on the moral development of sons of lesbians. How, I wondered, did these boys attain the moral compass required to be ethical and balanced adults, without the presence of a father who knows best? I began my study by comparing the moral development of elementary-school-age sons of lesbian couples with that of boys from more traditional families, using both standardized psychological tests and extensive one-on-one interviews with the boys and their parents. My work grew into a larger investigation of all the issues facing the sons of lesbians in couples. It evolved further to include the sons of single mothers by choice.

In these two later stages of my work, I conducted extensive interviews as well as other research into how the boys interacted with their mothers, how they interacted with adult men in their lives, how they related to their classmates, and how they developed a sense of maleness without having an adult male in the household. Not only did the parents in my study take time from their busy schedules to talk with me—usually in person—about their feelings, motivations, and emotions; they entrusted me with their sons. Each family, parents and children alike, participated to the fullest, openly sharing their thoughts and feelings with me. I was often privy to information that mothers did not have about their sons, that sons did not have about their mothers, and even that partners did not have about each other.

In reviewing these extensive interviews, I looked for individual distinctions, as well as shared qualities among the participants. In this book I'll present the data I compiled and the patterns I observed as collective experiences. In all cases, I have honored the confidentiality I promised, by changing names and disguising identities.

Throughout this book, you will read in detail about my findings and their implications for these boys, their mothers, and all mothers who raise boys.

Beyond the specifics of how women are successfully raising sons, I came to see that good, loving, growth-encouraging parenting is what sons need. Parenting, moreover, is not anchored to gender. Parenting is either good or deficient, not male or female. A good female parent will change diapers *and* coach soccer. A good female parent will help a boy to develop his full potential as long as she values his manliness and encourages his growth, independence, and sense of adventure.

My work challenges the tide of opinion and the research arguing that boys need fathers in order to grow to manliness. My findings have incited both support and vehement opposition. That two women could raise a boy to a man without warping his manhood is an idea that challenges the preconceptions of social scientists, health care professionals, judges, politicians, pundits, and parents. The consequences of such research bear on notions of family that encode Western culture's most profoundly held convictions about gender, sexuality, and parenthood. While the implicit presumption governing the discourse is that healthy child development depends upon parenting by a heterosexual couple, I came to rely on a controversial literature that challenges the commonly accepted risks of fatherlessness.

As word of my work spread, and as America began to pay serious attention to "alternative families," I was frequently asked to speak about my study at conferences that brought together professionals from all over the country, at independent schools around the United States, and at hospitals and colleges, including Harvard Medical School and Harvard Law School. People were very interested in my study, which after extensive review by my fellow professionals was published in 2002 by *Gender and Psychoanalysis* and *Bulletin of the Menninger Clinic*. So I traveled from coast to coast, as well as to states in the middle of the country, like Missouri, and to the south, like Florida, and I spoke at all kinds of educational institutes to parents and teachers from preschools through graduate schools, and at family service agencies and community centers.

Universities also demonstrated their interest in my work. The New York University Child Study Center asked me if I would be willing to serve on its board of directors. My research on sons of two-parent lesbian families was and is innovative and groundbreaking, and in a highly unusual step, Stanford University renewed my appointment as a gender scholar for a second term. I began to be consulted as an expert on the changing American family and the lives of boys by both mainstream publications and television journalists.

I felt that my conclusions were important and significant enough to publish in book form as a "report from the field." This book seeks to be the kind of systematic study of lesbian parents and their sons that Robert Coles undertook when he studied children from Appalachian families or Black families in the rural South or in northern ghettos. My study of these children resembles in scope and, I believe, in social significance the work Judith Wallerstein has done with children of divorced parents. I believe sexual distinctions can be as significant to the well-being of children as those based on race, class, religion, and family structure. Moreover, with all the freighted meaning that America assigns to its boys, especially in an age characterized by anxiety and uncertainty about what masculinity should be and how it manifests in the world, I want to show what it has been like and continues to be like for these boys to pursue their lives.

I am well aware that scientifically definitive research on the children of lesbians and of mothers who are single by choice will take many years to complete. This book represents a cross-sectional analysis of two phases of a planned long-term engagement with these boys and their families; it is a snapshot of a moment in time in these boys' lives. Yes, it's tough to write a book when, as in life, there are no final answers. But I believe strongly that the boys I know are at a significant moment in their young lives, a moment worth noticing and understanding. Each stands on the cusp of adolescence with an intact and powerful sense of self. I plan to revisit the families I studied when the boys are well into their teens and young adulthood and report on what I've found. So stay tuned for a second and maybe even a third volume.

With this book, I invite you into my living laboratory of two-mother and single-mother-by-choice households. You will see how it is possible for mothers to raise boys on their own, the way that so many women in this culture are called to do. The stories, voices, data, and findings here will reassure, hearten, and empower you, whether you are a maverick mother or a traditional one. For women weighing their ticking biological clocks and their craving to nurture children, this book shows that you have reason to take that informed leap of faith. But the lesson for all mothers—including the ones with husbands—is that women possess the innate *mompower* that in itself is more than sufficient to raise fine sons. The mothers and sons in this book offer us the opportunity to rethink and reshape our community of caring. They are not just reshaping our family trees. They are calling on us to enlarge the possibilities of love.

One of the strongest weapons we have against violence in our neighborhoods and schools, as well as ultimately in the larger world, is our ability to communicate with our boys about what is going on in their lives. Simply put, we must talk to them, and listen to them. This book is rooted in the many, many hours I spent having these conversations.

When I speak around the country about raising boys without men, people want to know how I was able to get the information I did from the boys. Why were they so open with me? The question implies that I must have a special trick that made it possible for notoriously taciturn young males to reveal their true selves to me. I laugh and tell my questioners the truth. Although I do have special training, it's simpler than that. I was curious and eager to know these boys—and I still am. They inspire me and give me hope. In a world that sometimes disappoints, scares, and hurts them, they still want to connect.

I have written this book for the wonderful boys I drove around San Francisco in my little black VW Beetle, listening to their dreams and fears, their plans and frustrations, their jokes and homework hassles, their sense of justice and their fierce love of family. It is their story, and this book is for them.

CHAPTER ONE

THE BAD RAP
AGAINST MOTHERS

"I hope you have a father for that baby!"

*—Male bus driver to a well-dressed, single-by-choice, professional
mother in San Francisco struggling with moderate success to get her
wailing 4-year-old son, his rather large truck, and her briefcase onto
the bus after picking him up from a playdate*

"HI, MY NAME IS PEGGY, and I'm a mother." I'm also a worrier. I
always thought that was a Jewish thing, but then Catholic friends,
Episcopalian friends, and Muslim friends, Black, White, Asian, gay,
straight—you name it—friends all swore it was their thing. Now I
believe that with mothering, worry is an equal-opportunity opportunity. It comes with the job and is fanned by expert advice on
child rearing that implies that a boy's healthy development is thoroughly dependent on his mother's parenting.

Like most new mothers, when my son was born, I relied on
numerous child-rearing books, including one by T. Berry Brazelton,
M.D., that identified three different types of babies and their time
lines. My son did not fit neatly into any of Dr. Brazelton's categories, and that drove me nuts. I obviously wasn't measuring up as

a mother. So I kept reading more books by child experts, trying to follow their unending advice. And still my son never seemed to fit the mold. When he did meet the mark, I didn't bother to underline those more positive passages. Like most of us, I didn't dwell on the things that were going well. Whatever wasn't quite right stood out like a headline. And the biggest headline of them all read: YOUR SON STILL DOESN'T SPEAK.

That 13-month-old Alex wasn't walking yet also concerned me, even though 14 months (which is when he did start to walk) is average. But the fact that he still hadn't said his first word nearly drove me to distraction. I would listen and try to figure out if he was saying something, because he did make a lot of incoherent noises. Every time he opened his mouth, I'd think, "Is it this word? Is it that word?"

We lived in the pressure-cooker environment of Manhattan, where all the mothers I knew were highly educated, high-powered women like me, and just as concerned, eager, competitive, frightened, and anxious. That held true for the two other women in my mommy-baby group, both of whom had girls. Since girls tend to be developmentally quicker than boys, I had to contend with that as well.

"I have some concerns about Alex because he's not talking. And, like your daughter, he is not walking yet," I confided to one of them on our way to a Tumbling Tots class shortly before Alex started motoring around our apartment as if he'd been walking his whole life.

"Well, at least my daughter is talking," she shot back. "If my daughter wasn't talking, I'd be really upset."

I was crushed. I had already reviewed every week of my pregnancy to try to figure out what it was that I had done or not done to myself that could have caused this problem. Remembering how my baby had banged his head on the sink as

I bathed him one day, I felt sure that my clumsiness and inexperience were responsible for his seeming inability to speak. It didn't matter what the pediatrician told me. I was to blame.

Just before he turned 2, I enrolled Alex, who was still not saying an intelligible word, in a music class for kids. Its location was inconvenient, but everyone said it was "the best," and God forbid my son did not learn how to bang on a tambourine with other toddlers. After class one snowy afternoon, we headed out to catch the Third Avenue bus uptown. We reached the bus stop in minutes. Then we waited, and waited some more. Eventually we started getting cold. Since there was still not a bus in sight, I decided to hail a cab. Suddenly I couldn't find one of those, either. As the snowstorm intensified, I began to panic. We were a fair distance away from home. What if I couldn't find a cab and the bus never came? I could probably walk home on my own, but what about my 2-year-old, who was bundled in a big snowsuit? I had chronic back problems, and there was no way I could carry him.

"How the hell am I going to get us back to the apartment?" I asked myself, feeling increasingly frantic. All of a sudden, Alex put up his hand and yelled: "Taxi! Taxi!"

After all the angst, his first word!

What a relief. I was convinced that whatever went wrong with Alex, it was my fault. I was an educated New York woman who had been raised on books and movies featuring pushy, troublesome Jewish mothers, thanks to Philip Roth, among many others. I had learned the lesson of blaming mothers long before Alex's birth, and I remembered that in the early days when the pioneers in Israel were formulating the design for living in the kibbutz, they consciously tried to break the mold of the overly close family, diffusing mother-child closeness by having children sleep away from the parents and having everyone eat communally to avoid the intense family meals they remembered from the old country.

It was in the air. Mothers who were too close to their sons made them homosexual; mothers who were too distant made them autistic. Mothers were even blamed for schizophrenia. The term of blame was the "schizophrenigenic mother." (Try saying *that* five times fast.)

This is not meant to blame the experts for all the angst of being a mother. I think we naturally carry a sense of deep responsibility for the health and happiness of our offspring. Why shouldn't we? But something happened in psychology during the 1930s that made a tremendous difference to my sense of guilt—and yours.

It all started out innocently enough. A large number of infants and small children who were orphaned were not thriving in the orphanages, and too many of these babies were not surviving. These were good orphanages. The babies were fed and changed and kept clean, but many became quiet and weak, and then died. According to the wisdom of the day, infants and small children were not to be picked up and held. That was considered to be bad for their young characters. Researchers were sent out to see if they could understand what was happening to these babies in their cribs. First they looked for physical causes for this unusually high mortality rate, but they could find no specific diseases. Then they sent in a pioneering child psychologist named Lauretta Bender, M.D. She observed the babies and came back with a clear answer: They were starving for love and human attention. Infants must have contact with people. Hug them, play with them, hold them, and they will thrive and grow. Leave them alone, without attention, and they will suffer. The very distinguished psychologist John Bowlby, M.D., was one of the researchers who worked with children in hospitals in London, and he began to understand the importance of attachment in the lives of children (and, of course, in the lives of us all). But instead of calling his study "Human Contact Deprivation" or "Parental Deprivation," he called it

"Maternal Care and Mental Health." By focusing on maternal deprivation, he spawned many of the concerns that weighed so heavily on me and my generation of mothers.

Dr. Bowlby also published studies about mothers who worked in factories all day, and he found their children were perfectly normal. This research has not been widely disseminated because it is neither sexy nor sensational. And it has not influenced cultural notions about the impact of working mothers in the raising of their children. What a shame!

PUT THE BLAME ON MOM

The news of Dr. Bowlby's preliminary research and other studies like it hit the American culture after World War II, when women were no longer needed in the workplace (the fathers were returning from the war and ready to provide for their families). These women went to their new homes in the suburbs, there to become the Cleaver moms, trying to make everything perfect for their husbands and children.

The tendency to blame mothers for how their children developed persisted. Then, to make matters worse, mothers who stayed home in the 1950s were accused of *momism*—being so overprotective that they created selfish and spoiled children.

Over time, scientists have begun to discover the biological causes of schizophrenia, autism, and homosexuality. But we continued to look around for the guilty party when children weren't doing well, and we found The Mom.

That attitude has lasted down through the decades. The mother is supposed to be responsible for everything her son is and will become. It's as if she holds all the cards. If she's a good mother, her son will turn out okay. If she's a bad mother, she winds up with a bad son. And, curiously enough, the father plays a minor role in taking the blame for the problems the children may have. It's a double bind for moms because fathers seem to carry much less responsibility for the problems their sons may have, but in the political and popular culture of today, they are considered absolutely essential to raising good sons.

There's really no research to back up this notion of maternal omnipotence, but it sticks to us like glue, creating unending anxiety in mothers, who often judge themselves by how their sons do and blame themselves for their sons' deficits.

As a specialist in the study of gender, I am extremely sensitive to the bad rap against mothers. These days, deprivation is the name of the blame game. That's what is making boys more aggressive, critics say, and the mothers have to be home or else. Mothers are blamed, even though studies of children raised in the same Israeli kibbutzim that separated the kids from their parents most of the time—and where they spent many hours away from their mothers, often sleeping elsewhere—revealed sons who were quite the opposite of aggressive: They were cooperative, friendly, and well-adjusted.

And then we have custody fights. More and more when the father wants custody, he uses the successful mother's career as a strategy to get the children. Pamela McGee, who plays for the WNBA's Los Angeles Sparks, lost custody of her 4-year-old daughter while the court investigated whether McGee's work prevented her from being a good mother. In his motion for temporary sole custody, McGee's ex-husband, the Reverend Kevin E. Stafford, asserted that a career and motherhood are mutually exclusive. McGee's "level of achievement," he argued, impaired her ability to parent their child. McGee was on the road 4 weeks a year. And the father said it took away too much from the daughter. But the court did not investigate whether the father's travel schedule, which took him on the road 7 to 8 weeks a year, made him an unfit father.

"We live in a culture where we want mothers to do everything, and whenever something goes wrong, it's the mother's fault," Mary Becker, who teaches family and domestic violence law at DePaul University in Chicago, told the *New York Times*.

This perception is reinforced daily by everything from the people around us to the news. In 2002, the *New York Times* published a story about a mother named Tabitha Pollock, who was convicted of first-degree murder "by accountability" (meaning that if you have certain knowledge that a crime will be committed and you do nothing to stop it, you are as guilty as if you had committed the crime yourself) and sentenced to 36 years for having failed to anticipate the murder of her sleeping 3-year-old daughter by her then boyfriend. The Illinois Supreme Court finally overturned the conviction, finding that while Tabitha Pollock may have been guilty of poor judgment in her choice of men, there was no basis in law to judge her for someone else's crime. That decision came after she had served 7 years in prison.

Noting that there are hundreds of cases across the nation like this one, the article went on to question whether mothers are held to an unreasonably high standard of behavior and whether the resulting punishment of the mother and her surviving family was unduly harsh. According to legal experts, mothers in situations similar to Tabitha Pollock's have been repeatedly found guilty by accountability, but fathers have gotten off without penalty.

Blame intensifies when mothers defy convention. More often than not, the treatment of moms without husbands in the professional literature focuses on a mother's aloneness (translate: not with a man) or sexual preference (again, not with a man), rather than her parenting skills. Despite the relative prominence of many varieties of mothering families raising sons, both social scientists and popular opinion continue to make erroneous assumptions about the single-mothering experience and its impact on children.

Single- or two-mother families are portrayed as deficient, inadequate, broken, or flawed. And judgment is cast as a result.

When the experts look at the impact on kids' lives of having a single mom or two mothers, they see the numbers, not the people. Remember the mantra of the first Clinton campaign—it's the economy, stupid? That's what we're really talking about here. Social science data show that socioeconomic status is a stronger predictor than almost any other index of child welfare. Not marriage status. Not the number of parents in the household, or their gender, for that matter. Still, we persist in seeing single-mom families as wanting, two-mom families as unnatural, and both as threatening to a boy's masculinity. Instead of looking at those unconventional families that are succeeding, we focus on the stereotypes of the man-hating lesbian and the overburdened, stressed-out, isolated single mother who's incompetent and neglectful.

For as long as any of us can remember, parenting theory and popular culture have promoted the notion that Mommy and Daddy—the traditional family unit—produce the best sons. That message has become louder in recent years. In 1992, President George H. Bush announced that children "should have the benefit of being born into families with a mother and father," citing the number and the gender of parents and their biological bond as central to optimal family life. And his son has supported a constitutional amendment to ban gay marriage and thus protect the hallowed nuclear family. Whether conservative politicians and religious leaders like it or not, the family structure has changed—dramatically—and the Bush definition of family seems, well, less than definitive.

Across the country, a lightning bolt has split the trunk of the family tree, and it is growing in new and challenging directions.

Some have labeled this a family crisis, though as Laura Benkov, Ph.D., points out in her book *Reinventing the Family*, "A careful look at other places and other times reveals [the nuclear family] to be but one of many possible human arrangements.” Further, according to historian Stephanie Coontz, “Families have always been in flux and often in crisis; they have never lived up to the nostalgic notions about 'the way things used to be.'” We cannot roll back history, nor—once we tear away prevailing misconceptions about the American family—would we want to. So get ready for a little myth-bashing reality check.

Myth #1: Families of the past didn't have problems like families do today. The reality is that desertion, child abuse, spousal battering, and alcohol or drug addiction have always troubled a significant number of families. Many of those perky housewives from 50 years ago depended on mother's little helper (tranquilizers, mood enhancers, and alcohol) to see them through their mind-numbing days. In other words, the good old days weren't what they are cracked up to be.

Myth #2: The 1950s male-breadwinner family is and always has been the only traditional family structure in America. Families have regularly been torn apart and reassembled throughout human history. Not until the 1920s did the majority of children in this country live in a home where the husband was the breadwinner, the wife was a full-time homemaker, and the kids could go to school instead of working for their wages.

Myth #3: The sexual revolution of the 1960s caused the rise in unwed motherhood. The reality is that the sharpest increase in unwed motherhood occurred when it tripled between 1940 and 1958. During the Great Depression, abandonment rates rose, with husbands leaving their wives (and children if they had them). Out-of-wedlock sex shot up during World War II. And below the surface, the underpinnings of traditional marital stability continued to erode. After this shift, nontraditional families (including divorced families, stepfamilies, single parents, gay and lesbian families, lone householders, and unmarried cohabiting couples) would never again be such a minor part of the family terrain that we could count on marriage alone as our main institution for caring for dependents.

While women's out-of-wedlock sex and the breakdown of the nuclear family are issues for politicians who see it as the root to society's ills, women—whether in lesbian relationships, widowed, divorced, or as single mothers by choice—are transforming the way we think about unwed mothers. In my neighborhood and neighborhoods all across this country, single mothers and mothers in pairs are at the forefront of what it means to re-create the new American family. They are a galvanizing force in American society as our nation struggles to accommodate a broader and more useful—yet no less loving—definition of family.

Myth #4: Children of divorced or unwed mothers are sure to fail. The reality is that it's how a family acts, not the way it's made up, that determines whether the children succeed or fail. The number of times you eat dinner with your kids is a better guide to how well they'll turn out than the number or gender of the parents at the dinner table. Marriage is no longer the gold standard when it comes to being a good parent. Though residual condemnation still hits here and there, Dr. Benkov points out that raising children without being married has "emerged as a potentially positive decision, not an unwanted circumstance."

We all can understand the appeal of a perfect mom-and-dad family. But we have to wonder, how many children and parents in this country actually live there?

Diversity is taking over America. The U.S. Census Bureau reported that in 2000 only 23.5 percent of households in the United States contained families with a married mom and dad and their children. The percentage of all households that were unmarried in 1950 was 22 percent; in 2000 that number had reached 48 percent. Figures released from the 2000 census show that mothers raising sons (and daughters) alone or in pairs in this new world are just as prevalent as the 1950s Donna Reed mom-and-dad version. The number of families headed by single mothers increased 25 percent between 1990 and 2000, to more than 7.5 million households.

This new breed of mothers without fathers is likely to be financially secure, straight or gay, and of any age and any race. The median age for unmarried mothers is late twenties, and the fastest-growing category is White women. Whether these women are divorced or never married, mothering singly and in pairs has not only entered the popular culture and become acceptable; it also is now considered chic. High-profile moms like Angelina Jolie, Isabella Rossellini, Wendy Wasserstein, Camryn Manheim, and Diane Keaton are parenting sons and daughters without husbands, and lesbian moms such as comedian Rosie O'Donnell and singer Melissa Etheridge are coming out with their partners and are mothering together. Few of these women have men as full-time parenting partners. Yet despite their deviation from what's been deemed a "normal" family pattern, the media routinely refer to their motherhood in a positive light.

"We've finally stopped falling for the great palace lie that such a person [the normal mother] exists," writes Anne Lamott in the foreword to *Mothers Who Think*. "Somewhere along the way, we figured out that normal is a setting on the dryer."

THE TARNISHED GOLD STANDARD

Conservative critics tell us that family life is on the verge of being atomized, that our children are corrupted, that our moral codes are crushed. As we all know, there's a serious movement to define legal marriage as the union of one man and one woman, the conservative ideal for marriage—and for family making. Many in the so-called marriage movement (and, I would argue, in the clinical research field as well) take a pessimistic view of children raised by parents who are not a traditionally married couple. The mom-and-dad family may have its problems, conservative advocates of family values agree, but they pronounce the presence of a strong male family figure to be vital to a child's development.

Marriage proponents, however, ignore the dark side of matrimony. While overall both adults and children get a host of benefits from good marriages, the situation for kids in bad marriages is quite the opposite. Married couples in conflict don't always provide what's best for their children. Further, according to Philip Cowan, Ph.D., professor of psychology at the University of California at Berkeley, the way husbands and wives treat each other has as much impact on their children's academic confidence, social adjustment, and behavior problems in school as the way the parents treat the children. A high-conflict marriage or a marriage that isn't working can negatively affect children in a way that might never happen in a single-mom family.

In addition, social scientists have confused family structure with economic factors that can influence behavior and performance. Researchers who analyze the data of boys having problems, for example, see that a large percentage of these kids come from single-mother homes and assume that mothers' single status has caused their boys to fail. Think back to the days when mothers were blamed for their children's having illnesses they didn't cause. I believe the same thing is happening with single moms and two-mom households: They're blaming the mom instead of the economic situation of the family. A study by researchers at Cornell University found that single mothering did not automatically spell trouble in school for elementary-age sons. How much schooling the mother received and her abilities had the biggest influence on her children's school performance—not the fact that the boys were without fathers.

Similarly, it had been assumed that boys from divorced families had more problems than children of two-parent, mom-and-dad families, until a 2000 study reported by the New York University Child Study Center discovered that the same boys had been demonstrating behavioral problems even prior to the divorce. When the researchers controlled for earlier behavior problems, the differences between boys from intact families and from divorced families were significantly reduced. The researchers concluded that to blame the boys' difficulties after the divorce on the actual divorce or separation limited the scope of understanding. The likely turmoil that preceded the split had to be a considered a contributing factor to any problems observed in the boys after the divorce.

So now we have seen a series of bad raps against mothers. I would say that ever since Eve, women have been blamed for the evils of the world (and she gave Adam the apple even before the children were born!). The mother is labeled overprotective when she worries about her children, negligent if she doesn't worry;

smothering or bossy if she engages in her children's lives, selfish or icy if she doesn't; overly self-involved if she pursues a career or holds down a job, overly involved with her kids if she doesn't. She can't seem to get it right, and if anything goes wrong with the children, it's her fault.

SNAP JUDGMENTS

If you think that's a problem, consider how much more severe the judgment is on single or lesbian mothers. Because the economics have not been factored into the difficulties single mothers face, many people assume that single mothers are bound to have trouble raising their sons. And the prejudice against lesbians carries over into the expectation that they can't raise healthy sons. These are the biggest myths of all.

In my research, which I describe in the next chapter, I have found there is absolutely no reason to expect that single or gay moms cannot raise sons on their own. These maverick moms and their families are living their lives with an everyday consciousness of the problems they and their sons face. They are not ideologues working out a theory about different ways to parent in our culture. They are real mothers raising real boys, boys who should not be marginalized in the least. These boys may not live with biological fathers, but they are in no way illegitimate. The families their moms have created are as real and as legitimate as any other, and have much to teach everybody who cares about children.

We simply need to be ready to learn. Nicole Sands mothered her partner Michelle's sons Connor, then 15, and Adam, 18, ever since they became a family 13 years before. She remembered a time when Connor, then in first grade, came home in tears but wasn't able to tell Nicole what the problem was. Later in the evening, when Connor had apparently forgotten his distress, Nicole received a phone call from another parent in the class who explained the mystery.

"Connor had been asked to draw a picture," Nicole recalled. "They were making number books, with a drawing on each page representing a number. For page three, the teacher asked them to draw their family, their two parents and themselves. Three. So Connor drew me, his mom Michelle, and himself. When he showed it to his teacher, she said, 'That's not what I mean. Everybody has one mother and one father. Give me that picture. Do it again.' The other children in the class protested that the picture really did represent Connor's family, but the teacher wouldn't listen. So Connor cried."

The children understood what so many do not, that Connor's family was every bit as valid as a mother-father family. "We had a judge in family court tell us that the boys have a right to spend time with a real family, meaning their biological father and his wife, even though they had moved out of the country and lived abroad," Nicole told me. But *their* real family—Nicole, her partner, and their two sons—was already firmly established. "We're the ones who are there. I think the time you spend with the boys is hugely important in being a good parent. Just being around. Those drives to and from school are great opportunities for talking about stuff."

That these two women are doing a fine job raising their sons to be thoughtful, responsible adults is not in doubt. "We were on the streetcar, going downtown to look at something at the Museum of Modern Art," Nicole recalled. "It was a little crowded. Michelle and I were in one of those front rows right by the little booth where the driver sits. The glass in front of us was reflective enough so we could see our teenage sons a couple of seats behind us. She and I were talking. We came to a stop, the door opened, and two older women got on. I saw the boys in the glass, and without saying a word to each other or looking to us for guidance or anything, they just both got up and immediately gave their seats to these two older women. I looked at Michelle, and we could tell that we were both thinking how proud we were of those two boys."

WHEN RAISING BOYS, MAVERICK MOMS:

- Reject social judgments about their family structure, and in the process model strength, character, and conviction to their sons.

- Recognize that how much time they spend—and how they interact—with their kids matters much more than whether they're single, married, straight, or gay.

- Realize that their sons' family priorities include eating dinner together, spending more time together, and having their parents watch them play sports.

- Know that their personal achievements—from schooling to the workplace—will help rather than hinder their sons.

- Take an active, considered stance when it comes to mothering their sons. Mothers who have thought ahead about being a mother, and who line up one or several other mothers as a support system, are way ahead of the game.

CHAPTER TWO

GOOD NEWS FROM THE NEW HOME FRONT

"I'm gonna make a club, and my friends can be in my club no matter what they wear."

—*4½-year-old Quentin*

TWO-AND-A-HALF-YEAR-OLD QUENTIN was kicked in the shins by another little boy on the playground. Crying, he ran over to the yard monitor for comfort, then, of his own volition, approached the little boy who had kicked him. "I do not like what you did, Martin," he told him in a voice full of emotion. "I would not kick you—you should never kick, and that's the truth!" Rather than impulsively kicking back, as many boys his age might have done, Quentin was using his words effectively at an exceptionally young age. A couple of years later, when Quentin found himself excluded from a group of other boys because he was wearing the wrong shoelaces, he announced, "I'm gonna make a club, and my friends can be in my club no matter what they wear."

Eight-year-old Mac was already a talented cartoonist who was into music, sports, math, and language arts. He developed an especially close friendship with his buddy Alec. The two would sit with their arms around each other in the car when one of their parents drove them to soccer games or the playground. Later, after playing rough and tough together, they would read a book side by side and just talk to each other. Then Alec transferred to another school. "It was lonely, like cloud rain," Mac recalled. "You know how a rainy day makes you feel bad? It was like that."

Quentin and Mac are both being raised in households led by women. Quentin is the son of two lesbians; Mac's mother gave birth to him as a single woman, using an anonymous donor, and is parenting him on her own. Like nearly all of the boys I interviewed for my study of sons parented solely by women, both Quentin and Mac exhibited striking levels of stability, independence, creativity, and caring. As I will show in this chapter, these mom-raised sons are avatars of a new social moment, one that is producing boys who promise to become good, even exceptional, men.

Focusing on how these children view themselves, the studies that became this book were the first to investigate lesbian couples and their sons in their own homes and as they lived their lives. To my knowledge, no researchers had previously introduced themselves so intimately into the lives of gay and lesbian families to perform what child psychoanalyst Anna Freud called "direct observation"—establishing a sustained involvement with a person or family that is maintained long enough so that the observer has some basis in experience, in words heard and actions witnessed, for coming to more general conclusions. My similar research of single mothers raising sons (of women who were widowed, divorced, or separated and their sons whose fathers were otherwise not on the scene) is unique in this very new field of study.

I began my work by examining the elementary- and junior-high-school-age sons of lesbians in planned, intact, stable, two-parent relationships in the San Francisco Bay Area—first comparing their moral development with that of boys from two-parent heterosexual families. I also explored how these boys grow up with a sense of their own masculinity with no father around. How do they react to not having a father—indeed, in many cases, having only an anonymous *seed daddy*? Coming from America's newest and fastest-growing sector of minority families, how did they deal with teasing and harassment from other children? Were they developing the kind of moral spine that our culture believes it is up to fathers to provide?

Just to give you a taste of some of those findings: The two groups of boys showed no significant differences in their moral reasoning, and both sets of parents showed no significant difference in their basic beliefs regarding moral behavior. However, when I subjected the parental attitudes data to a sophisticated measure of statistical analysis, I found that lesbian mothers scored higher on the moral attitude scale than their heterosexual counterparts and were more likely to create opportunities for their sons to examine moral and values issues. They were also more likely to talk about morality in terms of broader social implications. The Rasch analysis also suggested that there was a positive correlation between the lesbian-led families' parental attitudes about moral issues and the rate of moral development in their sons.

It turned out, however, that the nonbiological mothers (I call them *social mothers* throughout this book) and the fathers in the heterosexual couples were more likely to teach their sons by talking about principles and what ought to be. The biological mothers, in both groups, tended to teach their sons ethical behavior using emotional and empathic language. The heterosexual fathers and social mothers more readily praised their sons. The biological mothers in both samples were more worried about their sons than the social mothers and heterosexual fathers. But by and large the similarities between the couples outweighed the differences, with a couple of notable exceptions.

My findings revealed that the sons of two-mother families spent less time with an outside caregiver than those of two-parent families. "We don't like the concept of having our children in the care of other people, however lovely, for long periods of time," a lesbian social mom told me. My study showed that not only did these mothers spend more time with their children; they shared parenting responsibilities fairly equally. That didn't go unnoticed by other mothers around them. "In some ways I'm jealous of your relationship," Christine Carson, a 41-year-old married professor and mother of two, told the lesbian mother of one of her son's friends, "because you two tackle this thing [raising children] 50-50."

I did not use questionnaires, but for the first phase of my study, I did rely on objective or standardized measures to ascertain if there were any differences in the moral development of boys from two-mother homes and their counterparts being raised by a mother and father.

A vast majority of studies have concluded that the sons and daughters of gays and lesbians are no more anxious, depressed, insecure, or prone to emotional troubles than the children of heterosexuals.

Michael Lamb, Ph.D., chief of the section on Social and Emotional Development of the National Institute of Child Health and Human Development, has also asserted that being raised by gay parents would not have negative consequences for children. "It's become clear that the absence of a male figure is really not important," Dr. Lamb said. Louise Silverstein, Ph.D., and Carl Auerbach, Ph.D., have agreed with that assessment, concluding that children don't necessarily require an adult male as one of their caregivers.

Still, in the present climate of bias, any differences found in the children of homosexual parents have been equated with deficit.

Charting the moral development of the boys was complicated because it required me to analyze the verbal responses of these children, taking into account developmental-stage issues and levels of sophistication, as well as beliefs about morality. Children share two worlds, one with parents and other adult authorities, and another with peers and friends. The relationships in each world contribute equally, but differently, to children's development. To function successfully in the world, children need to discover why and under what circumstances they have to obey authority figures and how to handle conflict with their peers—including issues of sharing and fairness, such as who gets what when, why, and under what circumstances. By examining how boys from two-parent lesbian families thought about and made use of moral principles with both adults and peers, I was able to ascertain whether these boys were the same as or different from those reared in more conventional families. In addition, in both groups I evaluated the families' parental teaching methods about morality, parental time spent with the boys, and important figures in their lives from birth to their present age.

My original query (and the subject of my dissertation) was intended to establish whether and how the sons of lesbians developed moral character without the presence of a moralizing father figure. Hearing of my proposed work, some of the faculty and my fellow students laughed at me, wondering how I would actually find enough planned, two-parent lesbian families raising sons between the ages of 5 and 9 to perform a direct observation. I admit that I shared their concern. But even as early as 1996, it turned out that these families were everywhere. Word of my study spread, and I ended up with a waiting list of two-mother lesbian families from all over the San Francisco Bay Area, and a few more from across the country, who were raising sons. In a nation still preoccupied with issues of single mothers, lesbian and gay parents were flying under the cultural radar.

Like many straight people of my generation, I had very little firsthand knowledge of gay and lesbian lives. Having lived first in New York and then in San Francisco for 18 years, I knew many gay and lesbian people, but I had never explored their issues and circumstances in any systematic way. I worried about how I would be received by the lesbian-headed families I planned to study. Would they wonder if I was a lesbian, and if they found out I was not, would they accept me? Would they perceive me as violating their hard-won turf, or think me primed to be judgmental of their parenting? But only 1 out of the 32 lesbian mothers I interviewed asked me if I was a lesbian. Most of the lesbian mothers I inter-viewed—as well as the single mothers by choice that I went on to study—said they felt like pioneers in uncharted territory. They em-braced any psychological exploration that would help them raise their sons well. All the lesbian mothers I interviewed welcomed me into their homes, proved extremely cooperative and eager to talk with me, and trusted me. The frank, wide-ranging conversations we shared readily normalized our differences. I learned that I did not have to be concerned about asking honest questions. In fact, the mothers were asking themselves the same questions about their sons' development.

This study centered on two-mother lesbian couples who had given birth to sons they were raising in intact, two-parent house-holds. None of these 16 boys had a father on the premises. Many of them did not even know the names of their fathers—nor did their mothers. Thanks to the technological revolution of anonymous-donor insemination, the identity of a founding father may not even be part of the basic proposition of a two-mother family or a single-mother family.

Once a technology that served mostly married couples, donor insemination is now a practice that assists unmarried women, both straight and gay, and thereby yields many different sorts of families. The fathers of sons I studied were unknown donors, only some of whom wanted their identities to be revealed to their offspring; known donors; or donors who were family friends or relatives of nonbiological mothers. In one situation, a child shared a known donor with a classmate, and in another the father of a classmate was the donor. Whether or not a donor has a social father relationship with his child, he usually has surrendered his legal paternal rights. The relationships vary. In Thomas's case, "I see Chris, like, once every month. I guess he's my dad, but he's mostly my uncle. I don't think he's a parent, exactly, but we have a lot of fun going to the zoo and stuff." Nathan, another boy in the study, saw his own donor father infrequently at best. However, his sister's donor father actively participated in family activities on a weekly and sometimes daily basis.

Because lesbians are constructing families that do not fit standard legal definitions, they cannot usually adopt as couples but must instead undertake single-parent adoptions. Lesbian couples have generated the revolutionary concept of the social mother—the parent who has no genetic connection with the son she helps to raise, who may or may not have a legal relationship with him, but who possesses a vital emotional bond. Talking about his social mother, Nathan said, "It was Stephanie who taught me to play basketball. So when I get to play in the NBA, I'll invite her to the games."

It takes strong women to build a family from scratch. The lesbians I studied were mostly white-collar workers who had succeeded as businesspeople or in their professions. These lesbian moms were "social saboteurs," women who were living and raising children outside the dominant culture in conscious, courageous ways. From coming out as lesbians to deciding to have children, they exhibited the will and temperament to buck prevailing notions and create their own family structures, with very few models from which to work. Moreover, they were very conscious that they were on the cutting edge of a social movement. "Mostly we just have a normal home with Nathan and Beth," said Stephanie Goldman, 10-year-old Nathan's social and adoptive mother and 8-year-old Beth's biological mother. "We go to work, take the kids to ballet lessons and soccer games. But you can't help but realize that beyond your own domestic sphere, you're doing something really new and significant."

I have come to think that this sense of significance informed the parenting style of the mothers I studied. But other factors contributed to their mindfulness. We all know that it's better to be wanted than not, and adoptive parents often repeat that being chosen makes for a very special child. The very nature of parenthood through donor insemination means that children are thought about and brought into the world with care and preparation. Women who are inseminated—and who adopt—must think hard and long before making a family. The children brought into families in these ways are not accidents, and they are not surprises because so much planning has gone into their births. Since many of these women were older, the testing they had undergone had provided information about the sex of the baby (or babies) early, and so they had had more time to begin the mental preparation for having sons or daughters.

In addition to being older, these lesbian mothers tended to be better educated and more financially secure than average moms. They had the wherewithal to develop a parenting style that was both intense and considered. The developmental advantages this offered may help to explain why their sons were so remarkable.

The families who participated in my study turned out to be an extremely stable group. The couples had been together from 8 to 22 years and had lived at the same address for an average of 5½ years. They were predominantly White, middle- to upper-middle-class, and highly educated. I have been asked why there were almost no people of color in my study. Like mine, most research in this area has concerned a primarily White and privileged population. Lesbian identity among socioeconomically subordinate groups is generally less visible or less affirmed than it is among more prosperous, White, educated, urban populations. Ethnographic evidence suggests that closeted lesbian and gay people of color often value racial solidarity over sexual adhesiveness. Racial/ethnic allegiances may deter disproportionate numbers of people of color from coming out.

After my research was completed and analyzed, and my dissertation written, defended, and accepted, I found myself continuing to think about the sons of the two-mother families I had come to know. The boys stayed in my mind, and I wanted to learn more about them. So I went back to the families I had interviewed and did further research on them, using the same methods I had for my initial study. I wanted to explore the larger issues of the parenting these boys received and how they were forming their identities as boys at home and in the world. Throughout my studies, I was known to these children as a psychologist who came into their homes, talked with them, played games with them, drew with them, and was very interested in what it felt like to be a boy growing up and to come from an alternative family. I also had plenty of questions to ask these boys' mothers.

This time my questions were even more far-reaching. What kind of parents did lesbians make, anyway? What kind of values did they hold up and try to see their sons live out? What were the children of these families like as they grew up? Were the gay and lesbian families representative of families in our society?

I also wanted to look at the major problems and challenges these families faced. Was one mommy more real than the other? In the absence of the standard mom-dad dynamic to divide up the tasks of parenting, which roles did lesbian mothers take on, and how did their sons relate to two female authority figures? What were the fears, worries, and desires of children of gay and lesbian families? Did they look at other, more "normal" families with envy, fear, or even contempt? Was it possible that they felt special having two moms? Might they even have seen benefits accrued as the result of having the extra mom that other children lacked?

My work took me into these families' homes over the course of several years. Spending hour after hour with the boys and their mothers, I encouraged them to talk about the specifics of their lives growing up with two mothers and no "everyday father." When conversation lagged, I played games or had the boys talk about the drawings they made for me. I gathered information through notes, tape-recorded conversations, and summaries of observations.

When I first began visiting the boys, I was on an intellectual journey, seeking to explore a specific psychological and moral issue. But like many journeys, mine was full of twists and turns, and my destination turned out to be different from what I had expected. It became a journey of the heart as well as the mind. It led me beyond the basic questions of my research into the broader and even more compelling issues of maverick mothers of all sorts, women who were raising sons on their own.

After I finished the second stage of research with the sons of lesbians, I happened to be talking to Kamala, a heterosexual single mother by choice who had two sons in their early teens enrolled in my daughter's school. She told me that when she asked one of her sons to define the most important part of being a boy, he replied, "Taking care of others." She was proud of him for that because caregiving is not usually associated with teenage boys. Kamala's comment spurred me to see whether what I had witnessed in the sons of lesbians was also true of boys raised by single mothers. I set out to intensively interview 30 single mothers by choice who were raising sons all across the country, in places like Arkansas, California, Louisiana, New York, North Carolina, and Texas. I also interviewed 30 mothers who were single by circumstance—such as the death of a partner, separation, divorce, or the complete abrogation of a partner's parental responsibilities—who were raising sons without a father present in the home.

Like the lesbian couples who had chosen to have children, the single mothers by choice were highly motivated, successful, self-supporting career women. Though geographic considerations prevented me from meeting many of their sons, their views about raising boys turned out to be very similar to those of the lesbian mothers I interviewed. They were dedicated to their beliefs in non-sexist parenting and said they accepted who their sons were rather than consciously molding them into what they thought their boys should be. They believed in open communication and respect for differences, but they enforced firm limits and sought to instill a high sense of personal, intrafamilial, and social responsibility in their sons. "You are my emissaries," single mom Anna Malicki, 43, would tell her sons. She kept Matthew, 12, and Eddie, 14, in line by making it clear that they represented her best self out in the world.

At home, the sons of both single- and two-mother families were expected to be participatory members of the household, doing chores and fulfilling other age-appropriate responsibilities. By the time he was 6, Quentin was already earning his allowance by pulling the sheets off the beds, helping with the washing on Saturdays, bagging the newspapers for recycling, setting the table at night, and even washing the salad for dinner. "What we say to him is 'Everybody works in this family. We all work. Nobody gets to sit and be waited on,'" his co-mom, Sarah, told me. "He likes having a role in the family and having jobs that are his. I think it's important to a kid to feel like he's got a role and he's part of the team."

These mothers' high expectations stretched past action to interaction. "The guidelines we set up for behavior—treat each other with respect and kindness—extend outward from our family to our neighbors and friends," one social mom told me.

Single mothers and co-moms fostered independence in their sons, encouraging them to do whatever they could by themselves, from sounding out letters and writing their names to closing the car door and carrying their dishes to the sink. They facilitated this process by providing the tools their sons needed. Single mom Deborah Iverson, for example, made cleanup easier for her three sons by storing little dustpans and whisk brooms under each sink and in the playroom. These mothers also worked to keep their boys connected with their parents and siblings, encouraging free expression of a broad range of feelings. Those sons that I did meet—both grown men and younger boys—reminded me of the sons of lesbians I had come to know so well.

During the time I spent as a gender scholar at Stanford University, I evaluated my clinical data and the sons' and mothers' narratives. Patterns and categories began to jump out at me. To interpret my research, I also drew on my personal experience as both a biological mother and an adoptive mother happily married to a very busy man and a good father. My own experience would serve as a one-woman control group representing married mothers, and as a useful example of a mother who found her maternal role and her relation to fatherhood to be continually evolving.

My study determined, essentially, that boys will be boys. I found sons raised in woman-headed homes to be astonishingly deft at answering questions about—or simply figuring out for themselves—how to be boys. Their mothers were also very good at instilling male confidence in their sons. These boys readily engaged in the task of relating to their parents, siblings, and the men in their lives. Whether they grew up in single-mother families or lesbian-led nuclear families, these boys had an innate and astonishing ability to get what they needed in order to establish a strong and resilient sense of their own masculinity. In chapter 3, "Tapping into Boy Power," I tell of my experiences and show how these maverick mothers worked to nurture their sons' development and the various ways in which the boys exhibited their masculinity. You will see that they were acutely aware of the very process of becoming manly and that their mothers fostered this awareness.

The boys in my study were not sissies or mama's boys. Nor did they compensate for the lack of a father figure by becoming overly aggressive. Other studies have shown that sons raised in lesbian households are no more likely to become homosexual than they would if raised in heterosexual families.

But how could they be so boyish without fathers as role models? In the first phase of my study of lesbian and heterosexual families, I found that lesbian mothers reported that their sons had fewer male role models than their heterosexual counterparts did. Yet when I began to meet with the boys biweekly over a 2-year period, I saw that those boys actually had more male figures in their lives than did boys from heterosexual families, where the father was often the sole male in their lives.

Boys raised in mother-only families were remarkably resourceful in securing role models for their masculinity. They searched out teachers, friends of the family, coaches, and neighbors. If the boys were having trouble finding these men, their mothers stepped in to help. Most of the boys were fascinated by sports figures, and they had precocious knowledge of the details of the lives of their heroes. They were especially intrigued by the lives of two-generation athletes, taking special pleasure in following those father-son duos. Since the boys themselves had a big say in the choice of males they admired, they were able to select men whose interests and personalities were in harmony with their own. They gave short shrift to those who were unkind or authoritarian, whether blood relatives or not. The range of choices, the ways in which the mothers helped, and the ingenuity of these boys can be found in chapter 4, "Finding Their Own Role Models."

Still, I assumed that the boys I studied must have suffered from the stigma of being raised in unconventional families. Not necessarily. I found that their mothers made serious efforts to help their sons deal constructively with the prejudice they faced, thereby helping them develop significant strengths. Perhaps as a result, maverick mothers' sons seemed to have an easy time thinking independently and standing up for what they believed. They had an advantage when it came to acquiring moral standards and courage.

These boys were remarkably sophisticated about the world and about themselves. They were unusually able to articulate their concerns and their joys. Over the years I spent with them, I learned to expect—and to appreciate—the high degree of emotional savvy they exhibited. I call them *head-and-heart boys*, and in the chapter by the same name, you will see how they dealt with the vicissitudes of their lives, navigated the shoals of complex family situations, and grew into strong and sensitive young men.

Throughout my work with the boys, it seemed clear to me that their essential boyishness was hardwired (and most biological research into gender substantiates my observations). But I needed to understand the dynamics of the nurturing environment. I listened to many single, widowed, divorced, and lesbian mothers tell me about their ups and downs and their boy-rearing strategies, which are described in chapter 6, "The Mental Work of Mothering." Almost universally, I found a commitment on their part to talk and talk and talk with their sons. The communication imperative proved to be another big lesson of my research.

We have been raised in a society where mother-son closeness is approached with suspicion. I wanted to find out if this trepidation—especially of maverick mother families and their sons—was warranted. Simply put, it isn't. I found that the combination of closeness and conversation led to a natural intimacy between mother and son that continued throughout their lives. A major factor in this connectedness was the mother's ability to acknowledge mistakes to her son, to let him know what she was feeling, and her determination to treat her son's feelings with respect. By admitting to being only human, these mothers encouraged their sons' humanity. And by taking their sons seriously, they imbued them with self-respect. This clearly constituted a healthy version of mother-son closeness, a point set forth in chapter 7, "Staying Connected."

I also wanted to know how these single or lesbian mothers went about creating a family setting for their sons. Chapter 8, "Collected Families," tells stories of moms who carved out rich and varied environments for their children from all the parts of their lives: blood relations, friends, colleagues, community organizations, and special groups for single moms. These families reminded me of the Advent calendar, on which each day until Christmas you open another window and see a different scene. It could be soccer with Mom, piano in the afternoon with Grandma, and a tutoring session with a donor dad across town, or perhaps dinner with him, his wife, and their teenage son. A complex summons to adulthood looms for these boys. The challenges they face are also the ones that most preoccupy America's moral arbiters—namely, are sons (even more than daughters) from alternative families equipped to come to terms with their own sexuality? Can they reconcile their sexuality with that of their parents without undue confusion? And most important, can they navigate the larger world without protection from their parents or the communities in which they were raised?

"I admit, sometimes I wonder if Evan would be better equipped for the world if he had an everyday dad around," Vivian told me. "And sure, I worry about what Evan is going to face when he's on his own. When they hear he was raised by two mothers, will they ever vote for him for president?" Vivian shrugged and rolled her eyes. For his part, Evan was pretty sure he'd still get to play first base for the San Francisco Giants.

From the evidence offered by their childhoods, I believe these boys will have the social and psychological equipment they need to become steady, inquisitive, well-balanced teenagers able to reconcile the conflicting demands they will face. All of these boys will be strongly supported by their mothers as they venture toward their independent sexuality. "As a young boy and then as a teenager, I did all the same things every normal son does: play sports, have girlfriends, break curfew, have parties when my parents were away," 34-year-old Gene Leighton, son of a lesbian mom and a straight dad, told me. Gene's mom divorced his dad when Gene was 8 and formed a life partnership with another woman. "Like most teenagers, I was confused about a lot of things, but my sexual preference was not one of them," Gene added. "In that sense my growing up was perfectly normal."

Certainly, sons of gay parents will have to establish the terms of their sexuality with more self-consciousness than most other teenage boys will. If my experience with sons in lesbian-led families is any indication about how these boys feel about women, they will probably be able to relate to other females with great respect and openness. In fact, they may grow up to be the strong yet openhearted men women are purported to want to marry. As lesbian co-mom Sarah confided to me with amused pride about her 12-year-old son, "Quentin is going to make some woman a great husband someday. He'll be a great catch."

WHEN RAISING BOYS, MAVERICK MOMS:

- Accept who their sons are rather than consciously mold them into their own vision of what they think they should be, thereby widening the gamut of identities their sons can adopt. By allowing their sons their own space to move beyond their mothers and establish their own sense of identity, mothers give their boys the chance to live up to their potential.

- Expand—rather than constrict—their sons' lives by not imposing their own fears or limitations on their offspring.

- Instill responsibility in their sons by making them participatory members of the household and expecting them to do their share of the chores and other age-appropriate duties.

- Encourage responsibility to self by having their sons set—and then live up to—their own goals and expectations.

- Establish clear guidelines regarding behavior and expectations vis-à-vis how family members and others are treated. Raising reflective, conscious, centered sons who have developed a sense of identity and moral fiber means helping boys to relate in families, with peers, and to themselves. It also means helping them negotiate complex family relations, which more and more children have to do in the face of divorce and remarriage.

- Enforce firm limits at home. Sticking to these clear boundaries without harshness sets the groundwork for growing confident, self-assured boys.

- Rely less on babysitters, compared with heterosexual couples.

CHAPTER THREE

TAPPING INTO BOY

POWER

"Nobody's gotta tell me I'm a boy. I know it inside. Always did, ever since I was little."

—*6-year-old Sean Hill*

THE VERY IDEA OF ONE—let alone two—women raising sons without the presumed benefits of having a dad on the premises stirs primal trepidation. Can these boys grow up without even an absent father to long for and react to? Who will teach them how to throw a ball, to be moral, to act like men? Growing up in gay households, are these boys somehow predetermined to be gay? At the very least, will the boys of lesbians be confused about their gender identity and unable to take on their proper social role?

Current research suggests that many of these fears about boys' not being sufficiently masculine when raised without a father in the home are groundless. The roots of gender difference are located in our genes, and those genes come into the world with us. Thus, the engendering of what I call *boy power*—a generous, confident sense not of masculine entitlement but of natural male possibility—is not merely the patented practice of dads. Boyishness is a quality that can be nurtured by moms as well.

But if boys' brains are wired from birth to work the way they do, how do we ensure that our sons develop into men we can be proud of? The paradox between the "father knows best" gold standard and the reality of the violence committed by boys from traditional families raised questions for me about what exactly our sons need in order to become decent men. Books about how American culture silences and scares our boys have drawn attention to the idea that boys are depressed, angry, and cut off from connection with others. As mothers, my friends and I worried about the influence of just about everything our sons encountered, from violent movies and video games, to divorce, to gangs, drugs, and alcohol. How can our boys learn to be masculine without being destructive? How can they learn to be caring without being faint of heart? What kind of men do we want our boys to grow into? These were among the questions in my mind (and heart) as I met with my young research participants.

At the beginning of my study, I was trying to assess the differences in moral development between boys raised by lesbian couples and boys raised in conventional families. I was fascinated to find that there were virtually no differences between the two groups of boys. In addition, I found that the boys from less conventional families were "all-boy"; being raised in a predominantly female environment appeared to have no effect on their sense of themselves as male. I also discovered that the boys raised by lesbian mothers exhibited a wider range of comfort with a variety of styles of being a boy than did the boys of more mainstream families. This was one of the many surprises of my research: There were real advantages for a boy raised in this new style of family.

A BOY'S LIFE

When I first met Henry, he was almost 7 and had just started the first grade. Slight for his age and wiry, he showed exceptional talent in baseball. The baseball cap he wore seemed to be permanently attached to his sleek, brown-haired head. "People don't recognize it's him if he's not wearing his hat," one of his mothers told me. "That and a shirt tucked out, never in. That's just Henry."

Henry and his sister, Hillary, along with their beloved golden retriever, Maddie, lived with their moms, Mary Grazziani and Laurie Edwards, ages 42 and 51. Mary, a magazine copy editor, was Henry's biological mother; Laurie, who had a degree in economics and worked for a brokerage firm, was Mary's partner and Henry's adoptive mother. They lived in a quiet suburb of San Francisco in a neighborhood of mostly White, straight families, where they and the two other gay families in the area felt safe and accepted.

When I next saw Henry, he was almost 9 and in the third grade. Aside from his sporting a different baseball cap and being slightly taller, he seemed not to have changed much. I met twice a month with him, picking him up from his guitar lessons or his after-school sports activities, until he had almost completed fourth grade in the nearby public school. Over those 2 years, we talked about whatever was uppermost in his mind—on the drive home, at a local grocery store where we shopped for a snack of his favorite granola, or later, in the kitchen at his home, over his daily treat of milk and cookies.

During those chats, Henry openly shared the details of the discord between his moms. Laurie was suffering at the time from an undiagnosed complaint that made her tired, forgetful, and irritable, which put considerable strain on the family. Her fatigue made her impatient with the children in a way that she hadn't been before, and it increased conflict between the mothers. Henry confided that he felt relaxed around Laurie only while outside playing catch or while watching sports together.

Once Laurie was diagnosed with fibromyalgia and successfully treated, things in the family began to improve. Finally safe to vent his feelings about the ways his mother's condition had affected him, Henry went through an angry period, which his mothers allowed and even encouraged.

Then the obviously bright little boy began having trouble in school, despite the fact that he could memorize something he'd heard only once. Though math remained as easy and fluid as riding a bicycle, he wasn't reading up to his grade level. Told that he would catch up without remediation, his mothers worried nonetheless. "Henry tends to be self-critical and has a perfectionist streak," said Laurie, concerned that Henry's failing to do well in school would sink his self-esteem for good. "He wants to achieve instant mastery, and when he doesn't, he gets very frustrated. He yells at me about that a lot. I figure he yells because I'm his mom and I'm supposed to make everything okay."

While Henry's mothers couldn't (and didn't try) to fix everything, they did make a point of catering to Henry's need to control his environment. "He makes mental maps of what he needs to do and what will happen," Mary said, noting that to facilitate that, she and her partner made a point of informing him daily of everything that would be happening in their lives. "He really needs to anticipate, almost to the point of forgetting about the present. He has a lot of nervous energy, and he's not what you'd call methodical. We had him make his own checklist of everything that he is supposed to do, either around the house or outside it, that he can refer to and make sure everything is getting done. I think it makes him feel better, gives him a little more control. I told him if he did his checklist for 2 weeks, he would earn a prize. So now he makes his own lunch, packs his own backpack. It's great. The checklist helps."

They also encouraged activities that might help loosen up their stressed-out little perfectionist. "I want him to relax more, to be able to take what life dishes out without flipping out over it," Laurie told me. Enrolling the natural athlete in sports activities was an obvious decision. "He's a total sports fanatic," Mary explained. "He was hitting a pitched ball when he was 2. It's great, really, because organized sports is one of those places where he can feel totally comfortable. It's like you can see the worries just fall off him when he's playing ball." Guitar lessons also helped. That time "became a space where someone was paying attention to him one-on-one and listening to him express himself creatively," Laurie recalled. "It was like therapy."

As the fourth grade progressed, Henry blossomed. His reading improved, and he was placed in the advanced program. A team player—whether in junior choir or Little League—he amassed a diverse group of male and female friends who widely ranged in age, nationality, and ability. He even ran for class office, winning with the slogan "I'm the kind of guy your mothers can be proud of." When it came time to give him his own room, which he'd requested for months, Henry insisted on being allowed to stay upstairs in order to be close to his moms, instead of moving downstairs "all by himself." Though obviously still a little boy in some ways, he would also "walk around the house naked like he's Mr. Man," Laurie told me. "I love that." She treasured Henry's pride in his body and his sense of his own physicality.

By the end of that summer, which had included a happy sleep-away summer camp experience, Henry was clearly different. Although the baseball cap was still in place, he had grown up, demonstrating an independence and confidence that I had not seen in earlier meetings. Upon our arrival at his home, Henry had asked in the past that I open the front door for him and enter first into the empty house. After that summer, he took charge of opening the door himself and invited me inside, neatly taking on the role of host in his home.

Just in case his posture, words, and overall demeanor weren't enough to clue me in, Henry escorted me into his sanctum. In the room that had belonged to both Henry and his sister, Hillary, and that now sported a large, colorful KEEP OUT sign on the door, twin beds had been replaced by a sturdy bunk. A hoop for Nerf basketball stood center stage. There were no more dolls strewn across the floor, and although one battered bear remained on Henry's bed, Hillary's pile of stuffed animals was gone.

That day, we sat together in the corner of the playroom that was dominated by the Ping-Pong table.

"Yeah, well, I'm good at anything with a ball," he said, matter-of-factly describing his physical skills when I asked about his interests. "I'm good at basketball, I'm good at soccer, I'm good at baseball, I'm good at bowling."

When I asked if he liked biking, something I enjoyed for its speed and endurance, he answered easily, "Well, to be honest with you, I really haven't learned yet. Don't know why. But I Rollerblade, and my favorite sport is skateboarding," he continued spiritedly as he warmed to the topic. "I do it down our hill. I always make it to the end."

Getting up from the table, he demonstrated, angling his body as if the board had magically appeared and he had started cruising down the incline. His speech became breathless, as though he were really gathering speed.

"What you have to do is turn this way, and then immediately you have to turn back because the street curves. Once, I made it past the corner where the hill makes a sharp turn way down there.

And it's like once I make that turn around there, I quickly just lean back as hard as I can. The first time I made it all the way down, I didn't know what to expect and I fell into the bushes. I'm like: 'Wheeee . . . whoosh . . . oh.' But I wear a helmet and wrist guards. Sometimes I also wear elbow and knee pads."

By then I felt as though I had made the trip down the hill with him. "So the first time you didn't know what to expect?" I asked. "Was it fun or scary or both?"

"Well, it's both. It's really neat. It feels like flying! I like skateboards and Rollerblades and that kind of stuff because you don't always have to use just your power. You can use its power."

"And that makes you feel more powerful?"

As if he felt himself cruising down those hills with "extra power," he nodded his head vigorously. "Yeah! Anything with wheels is cool. And it's fun because you go faster and so you get the wind in your face, and it's just good to be alive. It's like, vroom! Alive! It's cool."

Whether Henry was riding down his hill on a skateboard, pumping under his own power on his Rollerblades, or playing just about anything with a ball, he projected a joyful boyishness. Though raised in a two-mother household, he refuted the notion that boys raised by women will be sissies, shrink from challenge, or be unable to identify or connect with their own power.

POWER PLAY

For years, psychologists hypothesized that only fathers could instill their boys with a sense of masculinity. From my first encounters with mothers and their sons, however, I saw boys exhibiting their boyishness in ways that seemed to be inborn, and constructing a boyhood by using not just social cues but what appeared to be innate male-identity-building talents. "I knew it was definitely nature over nurture . . . [when] my son's first words at 11 months were 'big truck,'" said a single mother by choice, admitting that the phrase actually sounded more like "dig dow." "Though he had a kitchen that was a favorite of all kids, boys and girls, and has turned into an excellent cook, when he was little, he wanted nothing to do with dolls, nothing to do with stuffed animals. At 2½ years old, I caught him drinking milk out of the carton. Now, he's never seen me do that, so it's obviously somewhere in the chromosomes. I've already apologized to several men in my life for yelling at them about things that are somehow ingrained in them."

The mothers I interviewed often recalled years of rambunctious behavior that they had rarely experienced in their own childhoods. Jane Snyder, a TV executive and divorced mother of two sons, reminisced about how as a 6-month-old, her son would crawl over to the houseplants and eat mud, which he'd have all down his face. In later years, he would push his tricycle (which had no pedals) to the top of the steep lawn in front of the house, then launch himself toward the street below. "Andrew was an interesting challenge," Jane told me. "He wasn't ever really bad, but [most of the time I wanted to] wring his neck. . . . I worried about [him] because he wouldn't listen. His first day of kindergarten, I was very worried about him organizing around other kids. I didn't know how he'd do in a larger group. The teacher called me in soon after school started. She began telling me what a wonderful boy I have, and how well he got along, and how he listened, and how much of a joy he was. I actually replied, 'I'm Jane Snyder? My son is Andrew?'"

Boy-associated qualities often came out in the selection and enjoyment of playthings and pastimes despite their mothers' best efforts.

Three-year-old Ian loved to take his mother Leslie Jenkinson's hairbrush and blow-dryer—unplugged, of course—and pretend that he was doing her hair. Happy to encourage this gentle pastime, Leslie, a single mother by choice who worked as a bond trader, bought him a little plastic blow-dryer for Christmas. "It came with little curlers and stuff like that, and I put it in his stocking," she recalled. "The first thing he did when he pulled this baby blue hair dryer out was to hold it up like a gun and point it at me and go, 'Ooh!' He didn't say 'bang bang,' thank God, but he was like 'I'm going to get you!' and I thought 'Oh, nooo. Where did this come from?'"

Though Mac's single-by-choice mother, Susan, a food and beverage manager at a major hotel chain, tried to shield him from aggression by keeping him away from TV and videos until the age of 2, Mac picked up sticks from the time he could walk and used them to poke whatever was in his path. By age 7, despite his mother's ban on plastic toy guns, Mac and his younger brother chewed their morning toast into a pattern to make pistols and shoot each other. Boys will create what they need to express themselves, and if gun-shaped toast is on the menu, it's on the menu with or without a man at the table.

As most scientists now believe (and as we saw earlier in this chapter), boys are hardwired from birth to be boys, no matter what kind of environment they're raised in. Their boyhood has a way of expressing itself willy-nilly; witness this story told to me by single mother by choice Theresa Pressman. Though her son Dirk was surrounded by women—including his mother and his nanny and their female friends—during the entire first part of his life, "your stereotypical gender distinctions came out loud and clear," she told me. "He had a different way of approaching toys. The way things work fascinated him: Levers and dials interested him for hours and hours. He was a little budding engineer [who] wanted to send his LEGO constructions to the LEGO Company and was sure he'd win a prize."

This kind of male confidence and sense of self comes in many flavors, since not all boys are cast from the same mold. Single mom Jane Snyder described the differences between her two boys, who were 7 and 3 when her divorce was finalized and are now adults. "It's amazing to see it play out. Nicholas is the kind of person who will work hard and do well. Whereas Andrew . . . Let me give you an example. When Andrew was 4—Nicholas was maybe almost 8—we walked into the garage of the home I'd rented, and I couldn't believe it—the washing machine was overflowing! I turned to Nicholas.

"'Call someone,' [he urged].

"I agreed. [Before I could move,] Andrew went over to the machine.

"'Wait a minute,' he said. [Then] he kicked the washing machine, and it stopped! Unbelievable."

Andrew has translated that can-do attitude into his adult life. "He speaks from the heart," his mom told me. "He's very sensitive. Incredibly empathetic. I had surgery last summer. When we got to the entrance of my house, the two women friends who had brought me home from the hospital could clearly not help me up our stairs. Though Andrew was initially very anxious and worried when he heard about the operation, he quickly was able to contain his own feelings and be supportive. Upon my return from the hospital, he immediately became aware of the three of us stuck at the bottom of the steps. Racing outside in a flash, he gently picked me up and carried me into the house."

At first Jane wasn't convinced that she could properly raise her boys without a live-in male presence. "I was very concerned about them because of some of the research that's been done—the Wallerstein stuff about boys being the most adversely affected [by divorce], especially those between the ages of 7 and 9. But actually they turned out to be absolutely wonderful boys."

HAVING YOUR SWAY

A boy's solid sense of himself doesn't evolve independently. The mothers I got to know so well showed me how they helped their sons tap into their boy power. What is boy power? It's loving to mess around in the playground mud and then running home to help Mom fix dinner. It's the ability to be all-boy and then something more. It's an artful combination of physicality and sensitivity. It's the pairing of healthy aggression with empathy in a way that the sons in mom-and-dad families often don't manage. "You know, I like seeing him wrestle with his friends," one maverick mother told me. "But I also like that he's not a thug out to humiliate anybody. I just don't see an oppressive power struggle going on when he's roughhousing."

The maverick mothers I met played an important role in the flowering of boyishness and the ability to develop a healthy sense of self despite the constraints of the outside world. Caleb, the 10-year-old son of single mom Ursula Hardy, a dedicated environmentalist who runs a large nonprofit agency, was struggling with being small for his age, and his classmates were starting to tease him about it. Ursula said she "talked with him about all the great things about being small. We brainstormed about things you can do. When playing hide-and-seek, you can find a really good place to hide. People underestimate you, and he's an incredible athlete, so he's sometimes a secret weapon. The funniest thing is I overheard him playing with his cousin who is 6. He's 10. She said, 'Caleb, you're really small for your age, aren't you?' He said, 'Yeah, I am. There's a lot of good things about being small,' and proceeded to enumerate them."

This boyishness and boyish confidence can be nurtured by moms as much as by dads. Fathers, indeed men, hold no patent on encouraging boys to use the power of the male body and to build the confidence that goes with it.

The sons of the single- and two-mother families I studied and interviewed were clearly very boyish boys. They were secure in that boyishness and as physically assertive as the boys from traditional families. "Nobody's gotta tell me I'm a boy," said Sean Hill, who at almost 7 had a well-developed affinity both for judo and for baking chocolate chip cookies. "I know it inside. Always did, ever since I was little." Or as Corey McClintock, an 8-year-old whirl-wind, told me, "Sure, I'm a boy. I do boy things like play ball and stuff. I look like a boy. What else would I be?"

Of course, a little confusion does arise here and there with boys, whatever kind of family they call their own. "I wish I had a penis like you," one young boy announced to Harrison, son of two moms, admiring his friend's uncircumcised appendage. "Well, maybe you could ask your parents for your birthday," the 5-year-old responded.

Being masculine doesn't exclude boys' interest in female activities. The boys in my study, like boys across the nation, cooked, cleaned, gardened, and primped, all in their own ways and with their own goals in mind. By engaging in these activities without undue parental pressure, they made them their own.

Ursula Hardy told me that when her son Ethan had a choice of electives for his seventh-grade year, he chose cooking and sewing. "He really likes it," his proud mother reported to me. "I'm sure in some circles that wouldn't be a very popular choice for a seventh grader to make. When he told me, I didn't say, 'You're what?' I said, 'That sounds great. What are you learning to cook?' When I think about growing up, my peers were everything. Ethan just doesn't seem to be affected very much by what people around him might think."

Children are keen observers of the adults around them. These boys were no exception. Not only did they know how to be boys, but given the opportunity to expand their repertoire of acceptable behaviors and activities, they often proved surprisingly creative in their expression of themselves and their boyishness. I found that many of the boys I got to know participated in an unusually wide range of activities. Why was this so? Probably because their mothers encouraged them, giving them the freedom to enjoy a greater variety, thereby enriching their young lives.

TJ discovered that he was hip and cool in an unusual way. Fiona Dansinger, a divorced mother of two rambunctious boys, has always painted her kids' nails. "It started out as a bribe to get them to let me cut their nails, and it turned into a big treat," she told me. "At one point, both boys had toenails in every color of nail polish I own. I work full-time freelancing as a writer and a chef, and I still consider myself a full-time mom. I spend a lot of time with my kids. The nail polish thing was like our little in-joke."

When TJ, her eldest, started kindergarten, he struggled in school, even though he was a cute, bright, articulate kid who taught himself to read at age 4. The social pressures of school had him reeling. He adopted a strategy of hanging out at the edges of a group until called on to participate, and whenever it was all too much, he would whip out a book and read.

In an effort to fit in, he decided against having his fingernails painted because the other boys thought it was strange. Fiona told him that painting or not painting his nails was his own choice. Loving his colorful nails, TJ compromised. "Paint my toes because that way the boys won't know," he told her. So she painted his toenails.

In first grade, TJ suddenly decided that fingernail polish was cool again, so they went through purple, gold, fire engine red, and green (Godzilla nails).

In second grade, a fellow parent came up to Fiona and asked, "Does your son paint his nails?"

"Yes, why?"

"Oh, it's no big deal. It's just that my daughter came home and told me she's sitting next to a boy who paints his nails," the mother answered. "We talked about why it was okay for him to do that if his mommy thought it was okay."

By third grade, it was no longer okay to even have the toes done, so nail painting went by the wayside. "Then one day when TJ was 8, he suddenly wanted them all blue," Fiona remembered. "Fine." Though he took some ribbing for it on the playground, this time around he didn't care.

His personal choice and refusal to bow to peer pressure was validated a few days later while the family was shopping at the local organic market. "Nice nails," remarked the guy at the checkout counter, who sported a nose ring and a black leather jacket and who happened to be wearing black fingernail polish. Putting on his best tough-guy look, TJ ducked his chin in a nod of acknowledgment. "Thanks," he replied, obviously feeling oh-so-hip. "That really made his day," said Fiona. "He walked taller, spoke in a deeper voice, and acted cool for the rest of the afternoon. I had to hide my smiles and give him the kudos he deserved. He had figured something out about identity and belonging, and it wasn't about conforming to the playground. He didn't have to talk about it—I could see it in his eyes."

This mature boy was still the same kid who sometimes seemed as if he'd never stop hitting, and to whom Fiona had to explain that no, he could not take sharpened sticks to school (he wanted to tape them to his fingers so he'd have claws like the X-Men's Wolverine). He was also a boy who liked things that were sparkly and delicate, and would even spend his own pocket money on trinkets that caught his eye.

"He stood forever in front of a street vendor in Chinatown who was selling tiny animals made out of beads and wire, debating with himself whether or not he wanted to buy one," said Fiona.

"He would pick one up, then notice a different one, and change his mind over and over again. He finally narrowed it down to a cat and a camel. Then he spied a 3-inch sinuous Chinese dragon with tiny claws and funny little antennae tipped with glittery beads. His eyes got all huge: He had to have the dragon. I think it cost $2. He wore it hanging outside his backpack for years. As far as I know, no one ever commented on his special toy, but he cherished it. He would show it to me periodically and remind me of how delicate and tiny and perfect it was. No one ever used the word 'feminine' about it or about TJ, either."

BUSTING THE GAY SPECTER

While the sons of single and gay mothers may feel increasingly comfortable bending gender roles and rules, our culture continues to express discomfort with boys' showing traditional feminine characteristics. One of the worst insults one boy can hurl at another is to call him a girl. It's much less common for girls to put each other down by saying, "You're a boy." The main reason boys reject girls and scorn anything that seems like girlish behavior in a boy is that they come to see males and masculine behavior as having higher status. Even though we have made many strides in equality, we still live in a paternalistic society, and the fear of being a "sissy" remains important in boys' lives.

Anything not deemed masculine must be feminine and therefore wrong (i.e., gay) for a man. That's why "fag" is such a common slur. Even teachers and coaches have been heard to use that kind of language as potent epithets to whip "the men" into tough-guy shape.

While many believe homosexuality to be a lifestyle choice, recent studies indicate that homosexuality is, like gender, innate. In addition, research and clinical experience have found no specific family configuration to be associated with either heterosexual or homosexual development. The development of sexual orientation is not completely understood today, and no study has conclusively shown a correlation between upbringing and sexual identity. But the idea that boys of mother-led families grow up to be gay is still prevalent. Surprisingly, most of the lesbian moms I interviewed expressed a strong preference for their boys not to be gay. Although they were quick to affirm that they would support their son's sexuality no matter what, they were fully aware that being heterosexual is the easier life path. But they didn't for a second feel that it was necessarily the better path. These lesbian moms had come to understand through their own experiences in life that their sexual orientation was a part of who they were, and it hadn't been altered by family, culture, or the difficulties they faced. That hard-earned understanding was passed on to their boys, who didn't share their mothers' anxiety about this issue.

The boys were comfortable with their mothers' sexuality and even took pride in their mothers' lifestyle choices. Andy, an adaptable, happy 8-year-old boy with a talent for Creole cooking, found out that he would be marching with only one mother in the Gay Pride parade, since the other one was participating in the AIDS bike ride from San Francisco to Los Angeles that same weekend. "If it's only the two of us, how are people going to know you're a lesbian?" he asked.

Although the fantasies, play, drawings, and references to their own lives and the culture were all heterosexual in both groups of boys in my study, when I asked the boys from lesbian families to consider their future, I found that they were more willing than the boys from conventional families to entertain discussion about a broader range of sexual orientations. They were willing to consider a wider range of possibilities of sexual orientation for themselves and were able to think more creatively about structuring a family.

A few worried about whether homosexuality could be hereditary, concerned that they would be gay because their mothers were. But most were more matter-of-fact. "I'm too young to think about that," one boy told me. "I'll know if I'm gay or straight when I'm older."

The boys from the lesbian group were also more fluid in their definitions of masculine behavior. The fluidity that I observed in the boys from two-mom families can best be explicated by a recent personal experience. Not long ago, I was rushing up the street, carrying groceries and my briefcase, barely closed from all I had stuffed inside it, trying to not to be late to pick up my daughter from basketball practice. One of her classmates, 11-year-old Damien, was walking from school toward me.

"Can I help you with that?" he asked in a concerned voice.

Although the bag was tearing from the weight of its contents and the awkward way I was holding it, his question almost made me drop everything completely. People were meandering in both directions, and no one else noticed that I was struggling, but Damien saw in one glance that I needed help and immediately offered it. He took my grocery bag and walked back up to school with me. I not only thanked Damien profusely for his help but insisted on high-fiving him (much to my daughter's embarrassment). Cool as a cucumber despite my frenzy, he just smiled politely, said it wasn't a problem, waved, and continued off down the street. When I thought about it later, it clicked in my head: This is a boy being raised by two moms.

I'd known Damien for years. Until fifth grade, he wore his hair short and dressed in nothing but jeans and T-shirts. Even after he let his hair grow long in sixth grade and wore red bandannas like the Hells Angels, he didn't let anybody's idea of what was "girlish" affect his behavior. In the school's annual musical, Damien stole the show with his theatrical poise and warm response to the loud applause from the audience. His onstage theatrics, a very liberating experience for boys, did nothing to prevent him from being the first out on the play yard at recess for kickball, running successfully for class representative to the student council, or being a sometimes goofy but articulate class participant.

If, as current research seems to indicate, sexual orientation is genetically determined, then the attitude of these mothers makes perfect sense for these sons. "[Homosexuality] would be one of those things where I've said to myself that it isn't something I control; he is what he is," a lesbian mother told me.

The experience of being gay is itself a lesson in human development and is potentially a factor in making the mothers more relaxed about their sons' sexuality. All the boys in my study were strongly supported by their mothers as they ventured toward establishing their independent sexuality. Results from other studies indicate there is no evidence that children raised in gay households are more likely to be gay or lesbian themselves. Children of gay parents were found to be more sexually tolerant than their peers, and they had more open-ended ideas about sexuality and same-sex experimentation, but statistically the same percentage of children of gay parents identify as homosexual adults as the children of straight parents.

Most sons of lesbians will ultimately grow up to be straight, if only because most boys grow up to be straight. If we believe that homosexuality is neither a choice nor an unlucky orientation, then we can relax and trust that these young men will find out what possibility comes naturally to them. Unquestionably, they will have to establish the terms of their sexuality with more self-consciousness than most other young adults will. I did find that they related to other females (me included) with great respect and openness, which augurs well for heterosexual romantic relations as adults.

MO' BETTER BOYS

Most of the mothers I interviewed had an accepting attitude toward the choices their boys made as they grew up. Perhaps the difficulties they had faced in their own lives made them more tolerant of variation. In addition, these women were dedicated to supporting their sons' self-made identity. It was for them an extremely important family value. Many parents want their kids to turn out just like them: If they like piano, they want their kids to be pianists, only better—and the same with sports, choice of career, and lifestyle. But maverick moms didn't seem to hold those narrow expectations for their sons. Having chosen their own individualistic paths, they appreciated freedom of choice in others.

Rather than see their boys as entities to shape at will, the mothers I interviewed unequivocally believed that their sons were individuals, entitled to be the people they were. "He's just who he is," asserted Lydia Farnham, a heterosexual single mother who describes herself as more on the masculine end of the continuum than her ex-partner and Charles's father, Neil. Lydia said of her son Charles, "I can't categorize him. I don't see him as a heavy-duty male. He likes to create things; he's not much into sports. Sometimes we'll watch a game on TV, just to expose him to it. But it's not him, so if he picks up on it, it's great, and if he doesn't, it's great, too."

Leslie, the single mom who bought a plastic hair dryer for her toddler for Christmas, is there for her son Ian at every step, making sure he is becoming the person that he is meant to become—not the person she wants him to be. "I want him to be strong in his convictions, strong in his beliefs whatever they happen to be. I want him to be happy, and I want him to be compassionate, caring, thoughtful, and smart. I want him to be with a significant other, whether it's a man or a woman. And I want him to be successful in terms of how he defines success, whether that's just having a wonderful, happy marriage and doing a job that he likes, or climbing the corporate ladder to be CFO or CEO of some big corporation—that's fine, too. I want him to consider himself successful in whatever he does."

How these moms define success differs from traditional parents as well. "I'm not as interested in him being a leader as I am in him judging," Henry's biological mom, Mary, told me. "What does he want? What makes him feel like he's doing the right thing? What makes him happy? I don't want to define his happiness for him."

Could it be that today's single moms and two-mother families are creating a new norm? Maverick mothers saw their sons' acquisition of this kind of healthy masculinity—however their sons choose to define it—as a naturally occurring process they only needed to aid. By giving their sons wider options of behaviors, these moms not only challenged gender and stereotyped roles but also provided their sons with a greater repertoire of potential identities. The boys who are a result of this progressive method of mothering are still all-boy. And who knows? They may even make better men. The maverick mothers' ability to celebrate the boyishness of their sons was essential to the process because it was on that firm foundation of natural assertiveness, enjoyment of physicality, respect for their own territoriality, and sense of independence that these boys might build a better future for themselves. When boys are given the opportunity to experience parental acceptance of who they really are, it's a recipe for success.

Gene Leighton, whom we heard from earlier, is a remarkably self-assured 34-year-old with two advanced degrees and a job that involves supervising many employees. As we learned, he was raised by his mom (who came out when he was 8 and divorced his father) and her lesbian partner. Gene realized early on that despite a childhood and an adolescence that in many ways was "perfectly normal and a lot like everyone else's"—with curfews, homework, and girlfriends—his experience was not like that of his friends or the families he saw on television. The upshot? "Having been exposed to all that, it's a lot more difficult to faze me than it is someone else," he told me. "I'm surprised by a lot less. I'm a lot more willing to accept people on their own terms and not bat an eye, and that has stood me in good stead. I think I'm less willing to jump to conclusions; slower to come to judgments about people or the world."

When Gene entered the Peace Corps as a young man, he found that he was better at dealing with the stresses inherent in the job than the other volunteers. "I found that when I was there, I had a greater ability to roll with the punches and be more adaptable. Quite honestly, a lot of the other male volunteers were—I'm thinking of a handful in particular—'What the hell?' 'Why are they doing this?' So willing to condemn right off the bat. They were much less willing to accept the fact that these people lived differently from the way they did and, initially, much less willing to accept that there were reasons for the ways they lived. They were more unbending in the sense that they weren't really willing to compromise and a lot more willing to criticize these people, the locals, or the country for the way that they lived, or their customs, and so forth.

"There are more or less useful ways for going about living, and it doesn't serve you very well to be [closed-minded]. It makes for unhappiness. Accepting people for what they are is a lot better and easier way to live because you're not in constant conflict.

"It almost seems impossible to draw conclusions about what it means to be a 'man' because there are so many different ways of living," Gene concluded.

THE PUZZLE OF GENDER

In our society, we give a complex significance to gender that, juxtaposed with gender's elusive nature, creates a real puzzle. As humans, we prefer simplicity, and the simple explanation is that the male gender has some traits and the female gender has others, and that they are different and distinct. Not so. Simple explanations may be comforting, but they don't even begin to address shared characteristics, or the varieties of combinations and overlap that constitute our true everyday experience of gender. Gender is simply not a tidy way of organizing what we know about human beings. Witness Tasha and Hannah's daughter Paige, who, at age 5, routinely wore a tool belt over her pink tutu. In fact, children who are not bound by gender conformity seem to be better adjusted than ones who are rigidly identified on one end of the gender spectrum or the other.

"I think of my two sons as guy's guys, but if I defined their qualities, they'd come out on what the world considers the feminine side," said 61-year-old Dr. Mimi Silbert, divorced mother to grown twin boys, and founder and president of the Delancey Street Foundation, the nation's leading self-help residential education center for former substance abusers and ex-convicts. "They're nurturing, they're warm, they're incredibly giving and kind. They love other strong people. They like to be around intelligence and strength. They like risks and challenges. They also have all those 'boy' skills that I don't: They can fix clocks, make puzzles. They have enormously logical brains." Laughing, she noted that she liked to tease them about how disgustingly emotionally healthy they both were.

For decades, a body of evidence has been growing that describes the psychological damage done by strict enforcement of gender roles. For adolescent girls, overidentification with rigidly defined gender roles is a major causal factor in low self-esteem—and therefore negative health and educational outcomes. In the case of boys, overidentification with gender roles is thought to account in part for violent behavior. Because psychology has told us for centuries that each person is a mixture of male and female attributes, this strict delineation of acceptable and unacceptable gender-determined behavior is quite unrealistic. Think of the pain it brings girls who want to be plumbers and boys who love art.

In addition, this gender typing exacts a toll on emotional development. As Terrence Real says, "Traditional socialization takes aim at girls' voices. It takes aim at boys' hearts." Yet too many parents continue to treat boys and girls in gender-specific ways. Using extensive cross-cultural data, Jeanne Block, Ph.D., found that both mothers and fathers stressed achievement and competition in their sons, encouraged boys to control their emotions, emphasized self-sufficiency, and developed a tendency to punish boys. Fathers in particular were stricter with boys, and mothers were concerned that their sons conform to external standards. Both parents characterized their relationship to their daughters as warmer and typically closer than with their sons.

Boys who are not trapped by these standard gender roles may in fact be more independent and more open-minded than the mainstream of American boys. "Eeewww! Gross!" exclaimed the youngsters in one boy's sex-ed class when presented with the basics of sexual intercourse. "Well, just think kids. It's not so bad," announced the teacher, grasping for a better reception. "It got us all here." At 11 years old, Ned Warner-Collin was already in the know about his own sperm bank conception and was not inhibited or ashamed about it. He raised his hand. "Well, not all of us!" Ned—who was the spitting image of his social mom, Suzanne Warner, perhaps because Suzanne's brother is also his donor father—was blond and blue-eyed and, because of his good looks, was sure to stand out in a crowd. He also had a ready smile, and a sense of humor we often wish for in adults.

As "special" kids, these boys had to learn at an early age how to deal with a potentially hostile outside environment. What seemed to matter more than the stigmatization that comes from difference was the kind of support the boys got, particularly from their families. Children who are taught to deal constructively with discrimination are likely to develop significant strengths; they learn to think independently and to stand up for what they believe in.

"I had both [my sons] Oscar and Zane dance ballet," said single mom Maria Black, a hospital administrator with vast responsibilities and a hip, no-nonsense way of speaking her mind. "I just thought it was a good cultural experience for them and that they should have a range of cultural experiences. I was giving them piano and everything else. I did it with both of them before they were old enough to say no, when they were 3 or 4." As the boys grew older, the prejudices against ballet for boys began to come up, and teasing ensued. "That's one of those myths about ballet, that all the men are gay. It depends on the company, but mostly they're not. They both loved dancing until they realized it might touch them and turn them into gay boys. Oh, God, no, so then they didn't like it anymore." Oscar, the older son, decided he didn't like ballet and quit. Zane kept on dancing, until at age 8 his friends saw him in what they deemed to be an effeminate costume and taunted him mercilessly. So he quit, too, only to find that he missed ballet.

"You can handle this teasing thing," Maria told him. "Tell your friends to shut up and get over it."

Deciding that he wasn't going to let his friends influence his decisions or actions, Zane made his friends apologize. Then he returned to ballet class.

"He's a great kid," Maria said proudly. "He didn't let the teasing stop him from doing what he liked."

Unfettered by the gender straitjacket that oppresses so many American men, sons of two-mother and single-mother families may find themselves to be more accepting of variation in their own lives and therefore able to take more pleasure in the vast array of possibilities available to us all. A wise teacher of mine once told me that you can gauge a person's psychological health by the range of things they love to do. The maverick moms I studied took great pride in their sons' wide and sometimes unusual gamut of interests and hobbies. The boys themselves were original in their choices of activities and were thoroughly engaged in them. Let's hope these boys—and the mothers who raised them—create a groundswell of enthusiasm about life and its endless possibilities, so that the rest of us can catch this joy.

WHEN RAISING BOYS, MAVERICK MOMS:

- Value their sons' manliness while encouraging growth, independence, and a sense of adventure.

- Respect their sons' differences and display a wide range of comfort with a variety of styles of being a boy. By not insisting that their sons acquiesce to standard gender roles or play with "gender-correct" toys, they just may be creating boys who are more independent, open-minded, and sensitive than their mainstream counterparts.

- Balance their sons' physicality with sensitivity that these moms make a point of promoting. The end result of this balance is the sons' remarkable ability to reach out to others.

- Encourage their sons to participate in a wide variety of activities, thereby enlarging their scope of interests and enriching their lives.

- Teach their sons how to be assertive and stand up for themselves while discouraging pathological forms of aggression and encouraging empathy.

- Help their sons to deal constructively with prejudice, thereby encouraging their ability to think independently while increasing their capacity for empathy.

- Help them develop a sense of justice by recognizing and challenging social inequity.

CHAPTER FOUR

FINDING THEIR OWN ROLE MODELS

"After I read Grant Hill's biography, I felt, like, 'Wow, he's really a good player and a cool guy. He thinks kids should be good sports and put their all into things but first and foremost treat other kids with respect. So I'm gonna go on with him.'"

—*Kenny about his newest role model*

DOES A BOY NEED A MAN around to become a man?

Surprising as it may be to some, my research revealed that maverick mothers are raising boys who are confident about the terms of their own maleness. In fact, I found that sons raised in two-mother families are deft about figuring out how to be boys. Whether from the stuff of his own life or from more remote figures, each boy I studied found his own role model, having sought out male figures to admire and emulate among his teachers and coaches, his parents' friends, and relatives—and among the sports heroes and fictional characters of the culture at large. In short, what a boy lacks in the home, he will find in the society around him, often with the help of his mother(s). In the initial phase of my study, I found that lesbian moms were more willing and more active in their efforts to recruit male figures like babysitters, coaches, and tutors than were heterosexual, mom-and-dad parents.

What do their strategies tell us about what these boys need and how they get it? From the internal urge to have admirable men in their lives, the boys created external heroes, projecting onto them the qualitative elements they admired. Under their own steam, they learned what they needed to know about how men should behave.

WHAT A BOY WANTS, WHAT A BOY NEEDS

Early for one of my bimonthly visits to talk with 8-year-old Brad, I caught a glimpse of him unawares. He sat in front of the television, wearing a brown plaid flannel shirt over his team's basketball shirt, sneakers with laces untied, and gray sweatpants with an elastic waist over his shorts. His black bangs hung just above his eyebrows, as usual threatening to block one of his beautiful, bright hazel eyes. He was every inch the picture of the all-American boy, laughing uproariously at the antics of the characters in the silly video he was watching. When he noticed that I was there watching him, he broke into a huge grin, jumped up from his chair with so much energy he knocked it over, and galloped into his room, beckoning me to follow.

The interior of Brad's house was sleek and modern. It reminded me of a favorite aunt and uncle's home I loved to visit in my childhood. Every room was inviting, hinting that the festivities were just about to begin. When I entered Brad's house, my first impulse was always to momentarily regret that I had not brought a novel along so I could snuggle up in one of the many comfortable chairs and read. Both houses—my relatives' and Brad's—had the air of places well loved and well looked after, both lively in their use of color and form. Correspondingly, my response to Brad's home was to feel I was in familiar territory.

An impish-looking boy who loved riddles and would immediately relate the latest joke he had heard, Brad was the only child of Margaret and Andrea, both in their early forties and successful in their careers as a landscape architect and a preschool director, respectively. His mothers had good senses of humor and were efficient, strong-minded, and bright. They were also thoughtful and gracious. Invariably a hot drink was offered during my visits, served in a steaming mug. Brad's snack was also beautifully prepared and showed a thoughtfulness not often associated with the word "snack." Homemade muffins accompanied by freshly brewed cider topped with cinnamon made up only one of the many "snacks" we shared.

I started meeting with Brad when he was 6 and continued on and off over 2 years. Our meetings took place at his home. Mostly we talked, drew, and played with sturdy wooden blocks of all sizes and shapes. Occasionally we played board games. When he beat me, Brad took great pleasure in victory, but he was always a gracious winner, never lording it over me that he was the better player. But of all our shared activities, Brad liked drawing best. Side by side, we would sit on the carpeted beige floor in his room and draw supersonic jets, futuristic trains, and maps of outer space. The drawings themselves, while not intricate or sophisticated, were products of his careful and painstaking efforts to get them just the way he wanted. A very bright boy, Brad was able to express extremely complicated ideas in these drawings. As we drew, we talked.

From time to time, Brad would be concerned that I might be uncomfortable sitting on the floor and, without fanfare, would offer me a three-legged stool to sit on. Other times, he would clear away an oversize, brightly colored beanbag housing all his stuffed animals and offer it to me as an alternative to the floor. I was always touched by his thoughtfulness but would assure him that I preferred sitting on the floor next to him. Brad would look down knowingly and nod his head respectfully at my decision. It was as if any choice I made would work for him.

Brad's room was roomy and well equipped. All the books and toys he enjoyed were placed in open cabinets around the room. The size of the room was well suited to Brad's favorite activity, building wooden blocks into complicated trains surrounded by delightfully intricate villages. On guard were carefully constructed LEGO blocks, engineers, spacemen, soldiers, pilots, and race car and truck drivers. All his creations were purposely ordered according to which fantasy he had chosen to elaborate. He was so proud of his creations that he was planning to photograph his designs and send them to the company that made his blocks to use for their advertisements. "I bet they've never seen one like this," he said to me, and I agreed. To my amateur eye, his creations were truly spectacular. To my professional eye, this was a boy who, either despite or because of his family situation, was both happy and well adjusted.

Brad was clear about whom he wanted in his life, even at an early age. At 6, when I first met him, Brad had picked out a special guy to emulate, a young man named Ron who worked in his after-school program. When his mother picked him up at the end of her long and often tiring day at work, she would find herself grinning. Why? Because for the nth time that week, she would spot her son happily hanging on to Ron's leg, exhausted but in high spirits, after having played his last game of tag for the evening. She knew she didn't need to worry about Brad's lack of an everyday father in his life.

Brad, an affectionate boy who even as a baby responded to the tenor of male voices, glommed on to his mother's male friends from an early age. Ron, however, he claimed as his own. In ensuing years, Brad even took on some of Ron's characteristics, including the way Ron wore his baseball cap and how he waved his arms when he was excited.

A favorite with other moms, in part due to the fact that he rarely had a need to crush or humiliate his peers in competitive sports or rough-and-tumble play, Brad was an outstanding athlete with a special skill in baseball. Still, as a guy's guy who liked to mix it up with the other guys, he was troubled by the teasing he got from other boys, who taunted him—not because he came from a sexual-minority family but because he was physically immature. Perhaps as a result, he looked to culture to provide him with an example of a small hero who vanquished his foes. He found the story of David and Goliath.

"Some other religion sends out this big guy, Goliath," he told me, launching into the play-by-play during one of our meetings. "He comes along, and then the Jewish religion sends out David. He's a little guy. David shoots his slingshot, and it hits Goliath right in the face and he falls over and dies.

"I like David's strategy," he told me. "I mean, Goliath is one of those guys that just goes out there and hits. David thinks about it. He uses his mind—and brute force."

"Are you like David in some ways?" I asked.

"Most of the time, I think before I act."

Brad applied David's approach to the politics of his own playground when another boy threatened to "knock him upside the head." While Brad wouldn't shoot from the hip, he didn't wimp out, either.

"Like you're really going to do that," he announced in response to the attempted intimidation. He then proceeded to "explain why [the boy was] not going to do it, and he doesn't do it. And I say because if he does, 'I'm gonna go to the principal, and you're gonna get in big trouble.' He listened; then he just walked away."

Brad, who regularly asked about what happened to the women in the passages he read at temple, also loved the story of Hanukkah. "There were seven brothers who, like, knew the land, and they fought the Roman soldiers. They knew the holes and the ditches. They didn't exactly fight physically. They made traps and made the Romans fall in. They used their brains," he concluded. "They used strategy rather than force."

Though Brad's mothers made a point of drawing similarly admirable male role models into their social circle, Margaret told me, "We don't have enough men in our lives anymore. So I'm very grateful for my father and for our rabbi, who Brad likes quite a lot and who we see about once a month. Brad's temple teacher is a man this year, which I love. And these are all such sweet men. They're just wonderful men for our son to be close to."

I asked Brad if he had ever wanted to have two dads, rather than two mothers. He gave it some thought and answered, "That'd be cool—as long as I can keep my two moms also." Without reticence, he added that he had just asked his mothers to introduce more men into the family's daily life. Uncertain as to how receptive his mothers would be to his request, I gingerly asked if it had been scary to tell them that he needed more men in his life.

Brad quickly assured me no, it hadn't been. But I persisted in my questioning, trying to understand how Brad saw this entreaty to his exceptionally sensitive and loving mothers—a request I thought might have been explosive or, at the very least, guilt inducing. After all, they had created an everyday family without a man.

"You weren't afraid that you would hurt their feelings?" I asked.

Brad shook his head. "I had told them, and they just said, 'Okay, we'll work on it.'"

Having more men in his life had clearly become a priority. I asked him why he thought this had happened. He thought hard for a few seconds. "Because it's the age before you're too old to not want to do anything with your parents, and the age where you're old enough to do stuff with your parents," he told me. "And . . . it's just to be with your own sex, I think."

Sons of lesbians go to great effort to define the terms of the bonds and relationships in their lives that other kids might take for granted. Brad, for example, strove to figure out how he was related to his sister, his mothers, and his donor father and his donor father's family. All terms in his life were complex, from who his dad was to the names, roles, and attitudes he assigned to his mothers. At an early age, he possessed a sophisticated comprehension of the dynamics of family making and of relating to others and the verbal dexterity to articulate his feelings. And his mothers, who had encouraged these traits, responded positively rather than defensively to their son's perceived need for more male role models.

I was impressed with Brad's perception that he needed to connect with adult men now, at a time in his life when it was still okay for kids to hang out with adults. He wisely wanted to avail himself of some time with adult men before he entered the adolescent phase of relating only to peers, and was willing to keep asking his moms to help him make those connections.

Another boy, 10-year-old Nathan, evaluating aspects of men he knew, thought his soccer coach was very smart, even though he wouldn't want to be a coach himself. He'd rather be an engineer, like his cerebral but playful neighbor Bob, who took him to the library when he needed to research a paper for a school report. Steve, who had recently turned 10, had developed an interest in the guitar and loved to jam with his teenage babysitter, Julian. Despite the fact that Steve and his moms had decided that some of Julian's songs were off-limits for the time being, the two guys thoroughly enjoyed their practice sessions (and from what I've been told, so did the neighbors). These socially adept and directed boys were able to find the male identity figures they needed.

Though the idea of raising boys without men alarms a significant segment of the population, boys in mainstream families don't always have as much access to their fathers as they'd like. It has been reported that the typical American father spends, on average, only 11 minutes each day with his children. Most children claim that the parent in short supply is the father, whether their parents are married or single and whether or not their mothers work. The research of demographer Cheryl Russell has revealed that the majority of children feel good about how much they see their mothers because the latter spend most, if not all, of their free time with their children and religiously attend sporting and other important kid events. (Single moms compensate for any time shortfall by shortchanging themselves.) What's lacking is time with their fathers. For teenagers, according to a study done by the National Center on Addiction and Substance Abuse, bad relationships with fathers are much more common than bad relationships with mothers, who are much more rarely absent or distant.

No wonder our society is growing ever more anxious about the nature of its boys and young men! But are maverick mothers to blame? Read the newspapers about the epidemic of school violence, the rash of school shootings, and the rising crime rate. They report that the boys involved (and they are primarily, if not exclusively, boys) often come from the families with a mother and father at home—not boys raised by mothers alone or by mothers in pairs.

CAN MOTHERS MAKE MEN?

Kenny and I had been getting together for some time to talk about how his life was shaping up as a boy growing up with two mothers and no everyday father to turn to at home. As you know, I had originally begun my investigation into Kenny and 15 other boys like him to explore how boys could develop a strong sense of right and wrong and a strong sense of self, if they—in some cases—didn't even know the identity of their fathers.

I discovered that in contrast to the previously ascribed notion that a boy developed confidence about his masculinity through interactions with his father, the sons of mother-only families may have more self-assurance and have less to prove or live up to because they are not faced every day with an idealized or devalued masculine model. Like other boys in my study, Kenny did not seem desperate to have just any ol' man around. As his mother told me, "He doesn't give people a lot of energy if he doesn't like them. There was a guy down the street who really took an interest in our son and wanted to play ball with him. It was interesting because it was during a time that our son was wishing for a man to play sports with him, and this guy coincidentally took him on. The man told Kenny, 'I want to play with you once, twice, three times a week, and we're going to have a goal: When that ball is thrown at you, you're going to catch it every time.' You know, just like what a dad would do. Only this guy was rigid and militaristic, and our son hated it! Kenny knew this was not what he wanted and just sort of pushed this guy away as soon as he understood what this guy was about and that it wasn't for him."

Sometimes male role models turn out to be disappointments. But the community at large—the neighborhood, the school, the extended family, the moms' friends—can also offer connections with men who have something positive and sustaining to share with the boys.

Henry's mother Mary had a longtime male best friend, a science teacher named Corey. "They [Henry and Corey] have this world," his other mother, Laurie, said. She laughed affectionately as she described their adventures to me. "They go out and collect bugs, they analyze mud, they look through the microscope, and they make up stories. They have a very nice friendship."

WHERE'S DADDY?

Who among us do not have holes to fill? Most of us long to fill those we can't and try to fill in those we can. Did the boys from lesbian-led families feel they were missing out on not having a father? Well, yes and no. I found that most of the sons of two-mother families had a heightened fascination with sports and sports heroes. Ned spent many hours showing me each baseball card in his book and describing each player's special characteristics, how valuable each card was and would be in the future, and whether it was rare or not. This 8-year-old had chosen a special baseball hero, Boston Red Sox shortstop and 1997 American League Rookie of the Year Nomar Garciaparra. Part of this player's appeal—aside from the fact that "he's just as good as Barry Bonds and Ken Griffey"—is that "not as many kids [in my school] know about him." Ned felt that among his friends, Garciaparra belonged to him alone.

Nathan wished for a brother if he couldn't have an in-house father. He definitely would have preferred to have had another male in the house.

When I asked Nathan how he had understood when he was younger that he had two moms and that his dad did not live with him, he said sadly, "I felt a mom and a mom did not like boys." That made Nathan scared sometimes, "but sometimes I thought that I was just wrong. Now I know that's usually because a girl loves another girl or a boy loves another boy. And I like that. I like that [families are] all different. And now my opinion is I like having two moms, but I wish I could see my dad more. And I also wish he was a little young. Like more young. 'Cause he's old and he's used to these old-fashioned things, and he's not very excitable."

Nathan told me that his sister's donor/dad is a lot younger, and "he's excitable. He likes doing things with us, like bike riding and swimming and walking and shopping. He loves to shop."

Five-year-old Justin fashioned himself into the fathers he lacked. "The other day I found Justin in his room just before he left for school, fishing pennies out of his desk and looking for more," his mother Cheryl told me.

"What do you need pennies for?" Cheryl asked her son.

"I have to give them to Maryanne and Tyler [both young friends]," Justin replied.

"What's that about?"

"I have to give them their allowances," Justin answered.

Apparently his role-playing had an impact because for a time Maryanne started calling Justin "Daddy" and his 39-year-old mother "Grandma," which I'm sure pleased Justin as much as it filled his mother with pride-tinged dismay.

This is not to dismiss the fact that there is a very powerful pull for boys to identify with their fathers, even for boys like Kenny, who rarely saw his donor/father. After several years of not being terribly interested in seeing his father, Kenny, then almost 12, began lobbying his moms to visit with his dad, who lived in another state with his wife and their two children. Why, I asked Kenny, was it so important for him to see his donor/dad at this juncture of his life? Kenny thought for a moment and said, "I know he's smart. My moms have told me that. But I have to make sure he's not a nerd." With the usual anxieties of preteens wanting to be cool, Kenny was trying to figure out what male he might look like now that his interest in girls had started to blossom. His moms agreed it was a good idea, and Kenny reestablished contact with his father. Interestingly, after this contact, when his biological father wanted to continue their connection through e-mail, Kenny did not respond.

I was puzzled by Kenny's lack of interest and said, "I would have jumped at the chance to get to know my father better," explaining that my dad died when I was 3½. Kenny's insight and emotional sophistication surprised me when he replied, "Your father raised and took care of you, or he would've if he could. Mine never did."

After I left Kenny's house that day, I found myself thinking about the nature and necessity of social fatherhood. Is it necessary for a son to have a father in his life? What did fatherhood mean for these lesbian couples and their sons, and what do their experiences tell us about fatherhood in America today? Fatherhood is a wonderful thing, just like motherhood. But good fathering, like good mothering, may be no more important than simply good parenting. And perhaps most central to the challenge the lesbian family presents is its very basic revision of the idea of "father." Lesbian parents are defining a new category of "sperm donor" as a natural participant in the organization of family.

As one mother, Millie, told me about her 6-year-old son, "Jed understands that we got the seed and that we put the seed in me and that he grew in my tummy. We have volunteered information when it seems appropriate. And he really loves referring to the guy as 'the chemist who is my father.' We tell him, 'You know, Grandpa was good in math and we got the seed from a chemist, so of course you're good at math.' He's very aware of the where-I-came-from thing. It's very important to him. But I think it's not so much a male thing as a where-I-came-from thing."

In our society, often we idealize and elevate the role of father in a boy's life without giving credence to the fact that actual fathers can be destructive and a boy may be better off without his father. Sometimes a father can be an aggressor who berates the mother, is hypercritical of his children, or—in less dire circumstances—is simply not a good model. Brad saw his donor/father regularly, but I found that he was able to be picky about which of his father's qualities he wanted to admit into his life and able to step back from characteristics that did not suit him.

When Brad told me that he thought "men scream more. They get angry faster," I asked if his own donor/father, whom he sees for a month in the summer and 2 weeks during the year, gets angry easily.

"Yeah, that's true. When he gets really angry, he may make the house shake if he screams really hard."

Hesitating a bit, Brad told a story about an incident when his father hit his younger half brother for having accidentally broken a pool table. Brad could hear the slap from outdoors where he was playing in the yard.

"What did you think?" I asked him.

"That I wouldn't like to mess with him," Brad admitted. "I feel good when he's happy, but when he's angry, I stay away from him. But if he talks to me or something, I won't just walk away. I'll try to hear him."

"So it sounds like you're more careful with him than with either of your moms," I observed.

"Yeah," Brad replied.

Cultural myth teaches us that to become a man, a boy must toughen up, turn away from his mother, and identify with his more aggressive father. This notion not only separates boys from their mothers; it can also propel them toward destructive men and destructive tendencies.

DYNAMIC FAMILY DYNAMICS

Nathan, at age 8, wanted to be a basketball player when he grew up and was concerned that when he applied, he would be required to fill out a form that had room for only one mom's and one dad's name. He mused about his worry to me: "Then I could write my dad's name, but whichever mom I did not write might feel kind of bad I could not write them." His solution was to fess up after he completed the form and say to the form givers, "'I did not write all of my parents,' and if they say, 'Why—is there another guardian who takes care of you?' [I'd] say, 'No, I have another mom,' but they might think that's kind of weird." Nathan was then stumped, thought some more, and ultimately decided, "I would probably put down one mom and my dad, and the other mom would not care so much because they would know it was for a good cause." In response to my question about which mom would go on the dotted line, he was perplexed because "I look like Nessa, I act like Nessa, and she's my birth mom, but Stephanie [his social and adoptive mom] taught me how to play basketball. Nessa had barely anything to do with basketball except she helped me a little bit with what my attitude should be like in basketball."

Kenny's social and adoptive mom, Tasha, told me, "Kenny says he likes having two moms, but he wishes he had a dad, too. Mostly [wanting a father has] come up very interestingly around sports because he is very into sports, so he's wishing he had a man to play sports with. But what's so ironic is that Hannah [Kenny's biological mom] plays sports more than most of the men I know. So I think he actually has a lot of what he needs in us. I'm not really athletic in terms of competitive sports, but I jog with him and bike with him, things like that. But he has some concerns about not having an everyday father, and sometimes it's painful to hear. On the other hand, I feel like we give him a lot—a lot of what I understand to be the functions of both mother and father. So some of my initial worries have been calmed."

SUPERHEROES

I found that most of the sons of two-mother families were even more fascinated by sports and sports heroes than their mom-and-dad family counterparts. Nathan was intrigued by sports figures' salaries and could recite many of them. But he told me that was only part of the reason he wanted to play basketball when he grew up.

"I want to be able to play 'cause I love playing," Nathan told me. "But, like, $100,000 a season . . . Actually, that is a lot because my aunt gets $100,000 a year, except a year is a lot longer than a season. And that's for *bad* players. For good players they can get, like, a lot more. Dennis Rodman, before he stopped, he was paid $9 million."

"So these guys play a lot of games, work hard, and make a lot of points, and that's worth a heck of a lot of money?" I asked.

"Yeah, they have to play more than 80 games, and the really good ones get usually more than 20 points in each game they play. They entertain people with dunks and really long shots and stuff, and it is kind of fair to get paid so much. If you do all that, it's kind of fair."

"So they must be amazingly special guys," I observed.

"Uh-huh," Nathan said.

I also observed that the boys regarded these figures in a balanced, rather than a worshipful, way. They enlisted these well-known figures from the world of professional sports to help them understand aspects of how men behave.

Nathan was fascinated with the basketball star Kobe Bryant, who had been recruited straight out of high school to the L.A. Lakers and was at that time the youngest player in the National Basketball Association. Kobe was big news—young, dynamic, and enormously highly paid. At the time, in his early twenties, Kobe was engaged to be married and about to start his own family. Nathan admired Kobe not only because he was good at the game but because he saw in Kobe some ineffable quality of sportsmanship.

When I first spoke with Nathan, he was longing for sports prowess but a little bit nervous about trying out for his school's basketball team. Watching Kobe Bryant helped him take on the courage to do it.

"I like the fact that Kobe doesn't get mad at himself, 'cause that's what I need to learn, 'cause even the times that he'll be playing basketball and he'll accidentally make the ball go out or make a bad pass or misses the pretty easy shot, he's still usually smiling. I like that," Nathan told me one afternoon as he lounged on his living room couch after an active day at school.

Nathan observed and extracted excellent qualities from his hero. Kobe Bryant also had exhibited some less admirable traits, but Nathan knew how to respond to the star's misbehavior.

"It was a Lakers–Knicks game. I was watching it, and Kobe Bryant got in a fight with Chris Childs and he got expelled from the game. That was disappointing for me because he's my favorite basketball player."

He thought about it for a little longer but was truly troubled.

"It was disappointing," he said again.

Kobe's fight led Nathan to make a complex moral judgment about someone he admired and sought to emulate. Like the other boys from two-mother families, he displayed the inner sturdiness required to make distinctions about the people he esteemed. Someone he looked up to had exhibited violent behavior. But despite Nathan's admiration, even idealization, of Kobe Bryant, his reaction to the player's outburst on the court was unambivalent; his standards of decent behavior remained very clear. Nathan was disturbed by his hero's behavior and did not think it would be cool to try that kind of thing himself. But his response was also not to categorize Kobe one way or the other. Nathan was able to voice his more complex feelings about the impossibility of anyone (the Kobe Bryants of the world included) living up to an ideal image and about the disappointment that inevitably follows the tarnishing of one's hero. The accusations of sexual assault against Bryant occurred after my study was completed. Nathan was then 13, and he presumably confronted disconcerting allegations regarding a man he admired—which is an unfortunate part of growing up for any child.

Nine-year-old Ned was very aware of players like Barry Bonds, the "King of Swing," who at the time of my study aimed at baseball's all-time home run record and was a three-time National League Most Valuable Player. The son of Bobby Bonds, himself a onetime Giants All-Star, Barry grew up playing with Willie Mays, his god-father, in San Francisco's Candlestick Park. Today Barry's son Nikolai continues the family tradition as a Giants batboy. However, many of the boys from two-parent lesbian families were also aware that Bonds had been tagged a league leader in lousy attitude and someone who harbored considerable bitterness toward his first wife, with whom he shared custody of his two older children.

Able to observe character and discriminate among players according to not only their abilities but also their personal quali-ties, many of these same boys, including Ned, expressed particular interest in the generational relationships between sports figures and their fathers.

On one of my biweekly visits to Ned, I arrived just in time to see him pull up with his mother Amanda in their bright blue station wagon. Before he was even out of the car, Ned had rolled down his window to urgently shout at me from across the street, "Peggy, we have your red glasses. I'll give them to you as soon as we get inside." (I am constantly losing or misplacing my glasses.) Once I crossed into his house and was given back my glasses, Ned was contagious in his excitement. "And guess what!"

"What?" I asked, eager to hear his news.

"I have Ken Griffey's father's baseball card!"

Ned already admired the Cincinnati Reds center fielder and was thrilled to make this two-generation connection.

"It's interesting that the father and son both would play baseball," I said.

"Yeah, and they're both really good. And you know what else? I think of Ken Griffey Jr. and Barry Bonds as the same. You know why? Because they kinda play the same position, both their dads were good players, they both had fathers that played, and they're both one of the stars of today and they're just really good."

"Do you think if I asked the sons who they looked up to, they would say their fathers?" I asked Ned.

"Maybe. Yeah, probably."

"Is your father somebody you look up to?" I asked.

"Well, no. He's not . . . We don't get to see him that much, so I don't look up to him that much."

"So you don't know him enough to look up to him?"

"Yeah," Ned said. But he was more interested in getting back to his baseball heroes, who were more easily accessible than his donor. "Here's a Barry Bonds baseball card that's really special," he said, handing it to me.

Although Ned's donor was his uncle Rich, they did not have a close relationship and saw each other only sporadically. Ned's mothers, Suzanne and Amanda, tried to foster a close relationship, but Rich lived out of the country. They described him as a cold, emotionally shut-down type of man who had trouble nurturing his own two children conceived with his wife, Marcy.

Kenny, another one of the boys you've met and one I visited regularly, told me which sports figures particularly appealed to him. Detroit Piston basketball player Grant Hill was "the man" for Kenny, and he, too, spontaneously brought out his vast collection of cards depicting the ballplayer. "I've read his biography and autobiography," Kenny said. "It seems like he's a really cool guy. He's respectful. He thinks kids should be good sports and put their all into things but first and foremost treat other kids with respect."

Kenny's moms, Tasha and Hannah, consciously steered his interest in sports figures toward Grant Hill. "For my birthday 3 or 4 years ago, I asked for a sports book, and I got a Grant Hill book because my moms had read somewhere that he was a good player. After I read it, I felt, like, 'Wow, he's *really* a good player. I'm gonna go on with him.'"

FINDING MR. RIGHT

Paternal experiences need not be with a live-in father. Grandfathers, godfathers (or their equivalent), uncles, family friends, coaches, teachers, and caretakers can provide figures for horsing around, mentoring, loving, sharing childhood fantasies, and imparting the business of being a man. The boys who find substitute fathers in the sports world often profit from not having someone who insists that they tough something out. "Not having a dad has let Henry off the hook, since he doesn't do well if he's pushed into things," his mother Mary told me. "He's blossomed because of the type of coaching he's had."

These male role models can also serve to balance a mother's single-mindedness. "I like people to share; I don't like people to grab," lesbian mom Tara admitted to me. "Actually, it's kinda funny. After watching [Sammy and Todd play basketball], the coaches had to take them aside, tell them about rebounding and [that] it's okay to be rude—if the ball comes down, you can grab, and you don't have to wait for the other person."

Eventually, Sammy's ball-playing skills escalated to the point that he was awarded a medal. Sammy was so pleased and proud of his accomplishment that he had a hard time even showing it to his younger brother, Todd. Tara reminded Sammy, "You did it; you earned it. But how do you think your brother feels? He doesn't have one. He'd just like to touch it, to feel it around his neck, and he'll give it back when he's done." So they worked out a compromise. Little brother Todd could have it for 2 minutes, and the timer was pressed into service. "It worked out very well," Tara concluded with an unmistakable note of satisfaction.

Sports is not the only arena in which boys can find men to learn from or emulate. The sons of two-mother families were able to summon up other worthy men from the community, as well as fictional characters and subjects of biographies from books. I remember as a girl reading every book I could find about Eleanor Roosevelt and Marie Curie; my favorite novels were about strong girls. Similarly, these boys found some of their heroes in books—and they sometimes even came to admire the creators.

Quentin, a two-mother son with a very large vocabulary and definite opinions that he freely shared, told me that he'd like to grow up to be like Jim Davis, the inventor and illustrator of the cartoon *Garfield*. "Because, you see, *Garfield*'s hilarious," he announced, proceeding to tell me a joke from his latest *Garfield* book about Odie's "drool fuel." Quentin's identification with Jim Davis was evident in his room. One day a ceramic dog on his bookshelf, painted in a wild array of colors, caught my eye. Quentin noticed my gaze and explained.

"I mixed up a lot of colors to make bad breath coming out of the dog's mouth," he told me.

"Do all dogs have bad breath, or just this particular one?" I asked.

"This one," Quentin said emphatically. "It's Garfield's enemy, Odie. When Garfield smells it, he calls him 'bone breath.' You know, Peggy, dogs chew bones, don't you?"

Quentin had real reasons—good reasons, by a kid's standards—for his devotion to Jim Davis. Quentin loved to laugh, and Garfield and Odie were very funny.

Because of the lack of a live-in father, the sons of lesbians can pick and choose their role models. They can admire brawn, and brains. They are free to evaluate a variety of males, taking on or discarding their characteristics, rather than being stuck with a single male role model, bad or good.

Some may say that the reliance of these boys on cartoon, fantasy, and media figures is pitiful, inadequate, lacking in any opportunity for real male-model interaction, growth, and learning. But my observations suggest that these boys are forging healthy, well-integrated masculine identities whether they actually meet their role models or not. Confident in the love and acceptance nurtured in their two-mother families, they can find their own roles in a variety of places.

The maverick mothers I studied often deliberately introduced selected male role models into the family circle for their sons' benefit. When writer-chef Fiona Dansinger's older son, TJ, was having trouble at school relating to kids his own age, she "consciously went out to find a role model—a suitable teenager—for him to spend time with, a Big Brother kind of thing. I found Miles, a sweet, athletic, absolute peach of a 16-year-old, who spent a couple hours a week with TJ, shooting hoops and talking boy talk."

The result? A win-win. "TJ felt like someone other than me understood, and I got some reflected glory for having provided Miles. TJ became much more mature, willing to cooperate, and be the 'older brother,' as if he had to live up to Miles's opinion of him. It looked to me like respectful imitation. His voice seemed to deepen. He acted kind of tough-guy cool, which is more how he thinks teenagers act than how Miles actually acts. I think it helped Miles, too. For a while TJ gets to have an older brother, and Miles, an only child, gets a younger brother that he doesn't have to live with."

"I want to make sure there are as many positive role models in my son's life as possible," Elaine Fields, the unflappable first-time single mother by choice of 9-month-old Blake, told me. Since his real uncles live out of town, she recruited some of her male friends as honorary uncles. "I have one friend in particular who comes by just about every week and hangs out and plays with him. He's looking forward to playing catch with [Blake], and those kinds of guy things, when Blake gets older. This particular friend isn't into sports, which is fine with me. It's not like all boys have to like sports. If Blake likes sports, I'll find people who like sports to play with him." Elaine also planned to look into the Big Brothers program for him once he was a little older. Until that time, she had chosen a day care run by a couple. "So that's another male role model for him."

Pam Ingalls made sure her adoptive 5-year-old son, Cody, interacted with males whenever she could. "When I'm with my brothers-in-law or nephews, [I say], 'You guys, take him to the bathroom' [or] 'You guys, go do guy things,'" she told me. "The same way at church—I try to pick things where he has male influences: teachers, sporting events, interactions with neighbors, playing with the next-door neighbor's grandchildren. So he doesn't feel like he lives only in a female world."

With their mothers acting as their guides, the sons in the nonconventional families I studied actually ended up with a wider selection of male role models than the boys from the more traditional families, where the father was often the sole adult male in his son's life.

Not only can strong mothers provide their sons with a range of models for manhood; they themselves also can model what we traditionally consider "masculine" attributes, as well as the heroism and coolheadedness our culture traditionally associates with dads. Henry told me about an incident that occurred when he was 3. He, Mary, his biological mom, and Laurie, his social mom, were playing with a beach ball beside a pool.

"The beach ball slipped out of my hands and rolled away, and the first thing my brain thought was 'Go get the ball,' so I slid in [Henry could not swim at this point in his life], and there I was in the water. And then Mary just panicked. But Laurie came into the pool to save me."

The modeling can transcend biology as well as gender. Remember Nathan, who loved playing basketball? He believed that his ability at sports derived from one of his mothers and gave that credit to his social mom, Stephanie, not his birth mom, Nessa. "My dad [a scientist in his sixties who is no athlete] and Nessa— their whole family are not good in sports. But Stephanie, she's good at sports, and that's something I think I got from her."

In the years I spent with these families, I saw that the mothers allowed boys to be themselves with whatever masculine and feminine attributes were available to them. They nurtured in their sons the courage to make their own choices. While mom-and-dad families took their sons' gender identities for granted and so didn't focus on them, maverick moms made it clear that the boys could choose qualities they wished to emulate from both women and men.

In short, it seems that the kinds of boys I studied promise to offer us the best characteristics of men, as well as the ones we most value in women. These kids are growing up without ingrained and preordained ideas of gender roles. They look for and find traditionally masculine attributes in their mothers, in a concrete way. As a result, they can participate in a range of social identities, and by engaging in them without undue conflict, they can make these identities their own. For example, when they pitch in with cooking, it becomes a masculine activity. Nothing is forbidden to them.

I myself turned out to be someone whom one of the boys wanted to emulate. At our last meeting, Henry told me he that was on the school newspaper and showed me a cartoon he had drawn. He also had a tape recorder on his desk, which he had requested from his grandmother as a holiday gift. Henry said he wanted to interview people.

"I want to find out what people are like and then report on them," he said.

I pointed out that although I was not a newspaper reporter, it was kind of like what I had done with him.

"Yeah," he said. "Your asking me questions made me think about what I want to know about other kids."

When I heard this and saw the tape recorder, something I had brought to and used at all our meetings, I realized that Henry had formed a strong attachment to me and wanted to be like me. I was gratified that we shared a mutual interest in each other. As Henry and the other boys I had come to know so well demonstrated, if two people are alone together, as we were over many months, an emotional bond develops, and they will learn from each other, no matter what their gender.

WHAT ABOUT DADDY?

Even though the boys I studied ended up with a wider selection of male role models than the boys from the more traditional families, many boys reared exclusively by mothers still longed for a live-in father. Taylor, the son of entrepreneur Tyra Miller, started asking about his biological father when he was just 2½. Feeling that she and her partner, Bari, had to explain, even though he was so young and they couldn't believe they were already having to talk about this, his mothers told him that "there was a nice man who knew we wanted to have a baby and he gave us his seed." Years later, the house next door sold to a gay couple.

"Two nice men are moving next door," Tyra told her son, then 6.

"The one from the seed?" he asked, assuming with typical

little-boy logic that his new male neighbors had just as much of a chance of being his biological father as any other "nice" men.

Remember Leslie Jenkinson, the single mother by choice who gave her son a hair dryer, which he morphed into an imaginary gun? Leslie, whose own, married mother was an early feminist, told me about dealing with similar reactions from Ian when he was 3: "We'll be watching television, and he'll point to a man and say, 'There's my daddy.' And I'll say, 'No, we don't have a daddy in our family.' But it kind of just goes right over his head—whoosh—he doesn't get it. And I'm sure he gets that from day care because there's plenty of children there who have daddies who come and pick them up, so he knows what a daddy is, so I know it's just a matter of time—it's coming up soon—where he'll ask, 'Where's Daddy?'"

Is this a sign of "father hunger," commonly assumed to be inevitable among boys raised without at-home dads? No.

As any parent will tell you, children are not born asking for Daddy, nor do they have any idea what "daddyness" means to their mother except through her own expressions. If the lack of an everyday live-in father is not an issue for a loving and attentive maverick mom or two, so-called father hunger might not be an issue for her son. Will he evince curiosity, whether occasional or prolonged, or longings and fantasies about men? Sure, some boys do more than others and to different degrees, depending on the boy. But humans are complex, multifaceted beings no matter in what family situation they are raised. Will some little boys trail after men they don't even know, perk up at those lower-decibel voices, or hang on to the pant legs of the men who cross their paths? Maybe. Do they need a male to take them into the bathroom? Okay. But is that pathological father hunger? I don't think so.

Boys with secure attachments to their female caretakers are no more at risk of experiencing "father hunger" than boys in the general population. We all know a lot of boys who feel a longing for their in-house dads who are off working 14-hour days or racking up millions of miles as they travel for their companies and are rarely home. In fact, the theory of "father hunger" was originally developed because these boys from heterosexual, mom-and-dad families were being seen in psychotherapy.

Many of the maverick moms I interviewed were very sensitive to daddy longings in whatever form and were increasingly learning how to help their sons with "daddy" requests. In the process of being open, they began to understand more about their child's wishes and fantasies. In Julia Shaw's case, by the time her son said, "I want a daddy," she had learned enough from other single moms not to freak out. "Instead of going, 'Oh, my God! He wants a dad!' I let him talk it out. He said, 'That way, you'd go to work and he'd play with me.'

"'Actually, probably I'd be at home, and Dad would be working. Or we'd both be working, but I can understand you wanting a daddy. Daddies can be wonderful.'

"He thought about that," Julia recalled, "then said, 'Well, he would take me to that movie even if you wouldn't.' So to him a dad is loving and somebody else who would do what he wanted, as opposed to me not doing what he wanted."

It's only natural to long for what you don't have. When high-tech database manager Darlene Michaels asked her affectionate and rambunctious son, Isaac, if he ever wished he had a dad, the 5-year-old, whose notion of treasures included the rocks and old cat food he had found in the park, answered in the affirmative. Why? Because that way he would have "someone to stay at home and play with him so that when I went to the store, he didn't have to go with me!" Darlene reported to me. "Just recently Isaac said we could find a daddy and he could move in with us."

These days, there are plenty of boys from traditional family structures who experience father hunger because their dads have literally disappeared from their lives after a divorce. "It is estimated that 25 percent of the children in the United States have little to no contact with their fathers," wrote Olga Silverstein and Beth Rashbaum in *The Courage to Raise Good Men.*

"I have no father," Martha Lester's son, Riley, now almost 8, recently announced.

"Sure you do," she replied. "You have your dad [who lives 250 miles away], and you have Michael [her very warm, loving brother, who's a terrific father figure]."

"No I don't," Riley insisted. "I don't know my dad at all, and Michael's not my real father."

Evan and his mothers have to contend not with an absent father but with a critical father. "Evan is so excited about his father [sperm donor Paul Thompson] seeing his schoolwork," his biological mom, Joyce Gould, recalled. "So he showed Paul his writing journal, told him how well he does in spelling, and pointed out how much he'd written."

His father's reaction?

"You misspelled this and this and this."

His father doesn't pick up on what Evan says even when they talk about sports. The problem? Paul rarely hears what his son tells him, let alone the subtext, according to Joyce. When Paul mentioned that he was going on a cruise, Evan, wistfully seeking some connection with his father, said, "Will you take me?"

"Maybe when you graduate from high school," his father replied, completely missing that his son was really asking to spend more time with his dad. Maybe Paul just has a tin ear, or he doesn't spend enough time with Evan to develop the kind of easygoing relationship his son needs. But Paul's responses are a far cry from what Evan gets from the other men in his life.

Clinicians working with men in therapy know how difficult it is for the men from mom-and-dad families to psychologically reject those aspects of their fathers that cause them conflict. Sons have a hard time accepting those characteristics in their fathers that cannot be changed, and even into adult life spend enormous amounts of energy wishing, hoping, fantasizing, and trying to transform their fathers into the loving models they never were and most likely can't be. As a result, sons from two-parent, heterosexual families will often unconsciously hold on to these hated qualities and unknowingly act them out with their own children. Of course, this is a potential problem for both men and women. Having the opportunity to select role models from a myriad of sources—like the boys from lesbian-led families who take on or discard their characteristics at will—might offer psychological benefits and even serve as an antidote to the intensity of the often strained, distant, or hostile relationships that some boys from heterosexual families have with their fathers.

The popular media have reflected just how widespread dysfunctional father-son relationships have become. In a *New York Times* article, "Generations Divided," Anita Gates wrote: "Everywhere you look this summer, there are fathers and sons working out their relationship on the big screen. [In them] boys and men bicker, mourn, manipulate, and reach out for the closeness they never had." The article goes on to provide a lamentable rundown of celluloid father-son disconnection and the inevitable lifelong hurt, anger, and attempts at reparation with dads by sons. One example of the yearning for recognition by dad was portrayed in the movie *Goldmember*, where Austin Powers's distant dad did not show up when Austin won an important award at school or when he was knighted. Austin's things-to-do-before-I-die list included "Earn Daddy's respect."

In movies, as in real life, we see examples of boys raised in traditional, mom-and-dad families unfortunately longing for the closeness they never shared with their fathers. This father hunger is more than just a phenomenon on the movie screen. It has been observed in boys and men in psychotherapy who were pathologically disappointed by the poignant search for the perfect, ultimately unattainable daddy. This population of men—deemed problematic by its very nature—came from traditional, mom-and-dad families where secure paternal attachments were lacking despite the presence of an everyday father.

Studies about father hunger, which stipulate that boys from mom-and-dad families yearn for the attention of fathers who are emotionally absent, have not differentiated between boys who were literally or figuratively rejected or abandoned by their fathers—and who have pathologies as a result—and those whose fathers simply weren't present, as in the cases of the sons of the two-mother families that I studied. The theory of father hunger just doesn't apply to such a different group of sons.

Of course, many fathers show their sons plenty of loving consideration. On the days that Colton's father, Mitchell Thornton—a veterinarian formerly married to one of the single moms in my study—had custody, his 7-year-old son sat on his lap during breakfast. Forty-five minutes before school started, he reminded his young son of the time, helped him into his clothes, and gathered his belongings. In the evening, he picked him up from the after-school program, helped him with his homework, and made dinner. Once the basics were covered, the two huddled around their latest project. "Colton and I have a lively interest in things," he told me. "We both open up pens to see what makes them work."

Mitchell didn't care for his son's penchant for wrestling or for the fact that Colton would occasionally strike his father when angry. Still, "I try to respect Colton's personhood and not dominate him overly just because he's a child, but to have him learn fairness by being on the receiving end of it," says Mitchell, who admitted to being less of a disciplinarian than his former wife, art historian Isabelle. "And by showing him that it's important to me, I believe he does the same." When I asked for an example, he told me about the time that Colton, denied a video that he desperately wanted, pitched a not-so-small fit during the drive home. Midscream, he asked for a pack of gum as compensation.

"After the way you've been acting, no, you certainly can't [have any gum]," his father snapped.

Suddenly Colton stopped screaming. Turning to his dad in the most serious way, he said, "Can't you forgive me? I forgive you when you do things that hurt me."

Mitchell was "so astonished by the seriousness and some sense of the validity of what he was saying that he said, 'All right, I do forgive you. Let's go down to the store and buy some gum.' And we did. The obnoxious part hadn't been any fun, but the overall process of him saying what he said, and my responding to it not by ignoring it but by respecting it, was satisfying."

A MODEL FOR ALL FAMILIES

The fact that the sons of lesbian moms I studied were constructing an internal father image has significance for all mothers raising sons alone. It seemed to me that boys from single-mother households were also commonly extracting male models from the culture to compensate for a lack of a father in their lives. I saw that even boys with dads around developed heroes from other sources. What I observed over the years of my research runs counter to the emphasis that mental-health professionals, social scientists, and our culture at large place on the deprivations that boys are assumed to face if they have no everyday father in the home.

Knowing that boys can find their own role models in the absence of an active father is good news for all parents, whether they are in mom-only households or are in the increasing minority of the mom-dad-and-kids configuration. What I observed among two-mother boys should make single moms feel more confident about their boys' identity and should allow dads the leeway to interact with their sons without the heavy baggage of old-fashioned notions about a man's having to be all things at all times to their sons. It lets dads off the proverbial hook.

The boys I worked with evinced curiosity about their friends' fathers, but when I asked them to speculate on what it would be like to have a dad in the house, most of them told me almost immediately that they thought a dad would be "strict" with them. As Kenny explained, the father of his best friend, Bart, had always wanted to be a pro golfer. That father pushed Bart, making him practice golf all the time. Although Kenny at age 11 did not have the words to articulate his feelings more specifically, it was clear to me he was trying to communicate that Bart felt he *had* to turn out well to validate his dad as a father.

"I wouldn't want a dad like that," Kenny told me. "He doesn't give Bart a chance to be a kid. I have more choices than Bart. I can play soccer, baseball, and football. All Bart can do is practice his golf swing." Kenny's perception of fathers, prevalent among boys from all sorts of families, suggested that there is a limitation to the exclusive paternal relationship that is so highly valued in our society. "Among themselves, men compete for dominance, status, and power, often just for fun," wrote Dan Kindlon, Ph.D., and Michael Thompson, Ph.D. "In adolescence a boy's competition with his father reaches a fever pitch, with predictably volatile results."

Perhaps because competition, dominance, and control are not the mainstays in the homes of many of the boys that I studied, the boys can and do develop what is thought of as more the "womanly traits" of self-expression, access to feelings, compromise, and stronger attachments to those in their everyday lives. For instance, at Kenny's house, rather than discuss his ability to beat his peers at sports or how he aced a test, we would sit at his kitchen table and talk about everything: his life as the son of two mothers; how he managed some of the tough kids at school; the movies he liked; the disparity among the income levels of some of his friends; and his parakeet, Mikey, the only other male in the house. Kenny was at the age when he had become slightly embarrassed to be accompanied by an older adult, and he did not introduce me to the neighbors, who gave us a wave or a smile. But once when I was trying to find a parking space, Kenny pointed one out and said, "Over there—it's closer to our house." He quickly caught himself, realizing he had mistakenly included me as a member of his family.

At my last meeting with Quentin, as my study concluded, I gave him a present, a videotape called *Yankee Sluggers*, about Babe Ruth and Lou Gehrig, a gift I gave to all the boys I had come to know. I enjoyed witnessing how each boy unwrapped this unexpected boon, expressing as he did so the particular personality style I had come to know so well.

Quentin, who usually wore a lumberjack shirt he had inherited from his older male cousin, had a very large vocabulary and was not without definite opinions, which he freely shared. His style was not to rip into the paper (as another, more impetuous boy, Steven, had done) but to try to guess the contents in an analytic fashion by shaking it, measuring it, and putting forth some educated guesses about its contents.

For me the gift symbolized my journey with him and the other boys I had come to know. It stood as an answer to the questions I had been asking since the inception of our voyage together. It refuted the notion that these boys were suffering. It spoke directly to the boyish boys I had come to know so well.

As he opened it, Quentin began talking, as if to himself, making it clear that he was going to extract information from the video and pass it on. "I'm going to really find out some information from this that I can take to school for my daily 1-minute quiz to Jake, Noah, and Alan. I give a 1-minute quiz to my friends every morning, and now Babe Ruth is going to be in that 1-minute quiz. I'm going to know more about Babe Ruth than them, and I'm going to teach them about Babe Ruth."

This is a boy finding his own role model.

WHEN RAISING BOYS, MAVERICK MOMS:

- Actively recruit male figures from their families and the community—including babysitters, tutors, coaches, and Big Brother–type pals—to be in their sons' lives. As a result, their sons wind up with more, rather than fewer, men upon which to model themselves.

- Guide their sons toward noteworthy male role models who exhibit the kinds of human qualities they deem important. Whether a sports superstar or a fictional character like Harry Potter, these heroes provide the sons of maverick moms with a range of males to respond to and emulate.

- Learn and then actively pass on the savvy, skills, and strategies their sons need to meet developmental challenges, academic hurdles, and social challenges at school, at play, at work.

- Personally model the kind of strength and heroism commonly associated with men, thereby setting examples for their sons that are up close and personal.

◉ Stress that their sons can find qualities they wish to emulate in women as well as in men, which not only helps erase culturally ingrained gender stereotypes but allows boys to participate in a wider variety of social identities and activities and make them their own.

CHAPTER FIVE

HEAD-AND-HEART BOYS

"He'll read my eyes or a twitch in my cheek. He'll register bemusement, even when you're not really smiling yet. He'll talk about it. It's not as surprising with me because he sees me all the time, but he'll also pick it up in other people. He'll take cues from a facial expression or a way of sitting and read them accurately."

—*Theresa Pressman on her 6-year-old son, Dirk*

AS A SOCIETY, WE AUTOMATICALLY WORRY that unorthodox family arrangements will at best confuse or alienate kids and at worst cause irreversible psychological damage. When we look to the kids themselves, however, we have to rethink those assumptions. In fact, I found that the boys from two-parent lesbian families and the boys from single-mom families exhibited an unusually high degree of emotional savvy. Some call that emotional intelligence. You might also call it *sachel*, the Yiddish word describing an intuitive grasp of people and situations. But I call the maverick sons with these qualities head-and-heart boys.

Back in the 1990s, psychologists began to formulate the notion that the strongest marker for a secure self in adulthood is the ability to reflect on one's own experience. Mary Main, Ph.D., and her colleagues demonstrated that the capacity for consistent reflection determined a solid sense of self, along with a high level of emotional security. The term *reflection*, as I am using it here, is a genuine understanding that other people have minds of their own, that people are different, that there are varied realities and options. Reflection in this sense also means the ability to take aspects from that diversity to form one's own identity. Of course, there are variations among people in the quality of reflective thinking and in their sense of "objectivity."

Using Dr. Main's work as a marker to understand the boys in both groups I observed, I found that the sons in two-mother families were conscious, even self-conscious, about the content of their lives in a way that boys from traditional families were not. Sons of lesbians went to great efforts to define the terms of the bonds and relationships in their lives that the boys from straight families seemed to take for granted. All terms in their lives were complex— from who their dads were to the names, roles, and attitudes they assigned to their mothers. However, the sons of the lesbians seemed up to the task. At early ages, they possessed a sophisticated comprehension of the dynamics of family making; they readily engaged in the task of figuring out how they related to their parents, their siblings, and the men in their lives in a way that the sons in more mainstream families did not.

As self-aware, "special" kids, the sons of lesbian couples learned to negotiate the outside environment, developing keen skills that helped them gauge other people's motives and how open they could be in specific situations. Repeatedly I discerned how the sons of two-mother families were more sensitive to the slings and arrows of other children and were keenly aware of others' feelings, perhaps as a result of their being raised by two women, who conventionally are considered to be more in tune with their and others' feelings than men. Exhibiting a heightened capacity for empathy, these boys also tended to be thoughtful in how they exerted themselves in the world—encouraged by openness and the sense conveyed by their parents that their situation was not a secret or a shameful thing.

SAVVY, STRONG, SENSITIVE

As I did every second Tuesday afternoon, I pulled up in front of 11-year-old Kenny's run-down redbrick city school. I was there to pick him up for one of our regular meetings. At 3:30, a bell rang loudly, signaling the end of classes. Kenny's bright, smiling face and dark, wavy hair came into focus as he ran across the blacktop play-ground through a sea of kids of every color and size—White kids, Black kids, Asian kids, Hispanic kids. Fearful of being late, I had as usual arrived 10 minutes early. As was my practice, I had parked as close to the school as possible. At first Kenny—the boy we met earlier who could discern his need for contact with his father but who could also limit it—did not locate me among the mass of cars and kids. He scanned the area until he caught me waving from my little black VW Beetle with a large, bright orange, synthetic flower perched in a holder on the dashboard. I had made sure I couldn't be missed.

Once he spotted me, Kenny threaded his way through the crowd, his stride determined, a self-conscious half grin on his face. He swung open my car door and energetically maneuvered his way into the backseat. "Hi, Peggy," he said as he jumped into the car. Losing his adolescent awkwardness, he gave my arm a friendly thump as I turned the car toward the home he shared with his 7-year-old sister, Paige, and his two moms, Tasha and Hannah.

Before I started up my car, I looked at him in the rearview mirror. Backpack slung over his shoulder, glasses glinting in the sun, Kenny was a little small for his age but was agile and athletic. Just another American schoolboy at the end of the school day.

Kenny, an articulate, self-possessed boy who planned to become a professional basketball (or soccer) player when he grew up, seemed the epitome of a well-adjusted child with an astonishingly positive attitude. Despite Kenny's obvious stability, his biological father, George—an old friend of his mothers, who lived out of state with his wife and two children—remained concerned. So when Kenny came for one of his annual visits, George—like any good, concerned father—tried to make it clear that he was ready to listen if Kenny felt conflicted about his alternative family. "You know we have this special relationship," he told his young son as they watched a girls' soccer match at the park. "If you ever want to talk about it or ask me anything, you should feel free to." After a lengthy silence, Kenny piped up with "Do you think they're wearing cleats?" nodding toward the female soccer players. So much for the moment of intimacy George had hoped for. Kenny used a smart and sensitive tactic to tell his biological father that he didn't feel like confiding in him just then.

The youngster I'd gotten to know so well over the years of my study almost always took the time to think things through and make a heartfelt decision based on what he deemed right. At age 9, spotting a dog running loose during the drive to school, he asked that his mother pull over. When she refused because they were running late, he insisted. "Mom, that dog is hurt. Please stop the car." A closer examination revealed that the dog wasn't injured, just lost. With his mother's coaching, Kenny secured the dog, wrote down the information on its collar, went to the administrative office upon arriving at school, and called the owner. "Are you missing a dog?" he asked before directing the owner to where the dog had been left. That afternoon, he called back to make sure the dog had been picked up. Though the owner had promised Kenny a reward that never materialized, it didn't matter. The dog was back home.

An affectionate kid who made friends easily and wished for a healthy family instead of the latest Game Boy when he blew out his birthday candles, Kenny also revealed remarkable social savvy during our conversations. I remember Kenny at 12 telling me about his friend having a short all-boys party. "At a short party, it's not good to invite girls because everyone is shy at first," he explained. "So with a girl-boy party, you need a longer time to warm up, so you only invite girls to long parties."

But his generous nature was what really stood out. Even at age 2, when most kids are rabidly possessive of their toys, he established the habit of offering a departing guest the opportunity to borrow something to take home. "He did this on his own," his co-mom Tasha told me with a little shake of her head, as though she didn't quite believe it herself. "I think it was a way for him to share and to instill some continuity into their relationship, but I also always felt that it was a part of his understanding about fairness."

By the time he had turned 8, Kenny would take that respect for fairness out into the world. While dining at a restaurant one Mother's Day brunch, he pulled Tasha aside and whispered, "How come there's no Black waiters? It's weird." After a pause, he continued. "I think it's racism 'cause I see there's a Black guy who's a busboy and a Black guy who's the parking valet, but none of them are waiters. That's racism, that they only let the White guys be waiters. It's not fair.'"

Kenny's words and actions testify to a remarkable sensitivity, as well as an ability to reach out to others at an age when many boys are self-centered. As the impact of single and lesbian moms spreads, with luck these kinds of boys will increasingly become the norm. It's starting to happen already.

BOYS DO TOO TALK

It was the Fourth of July. At the picnic supper after the day's festivities, Cooper, almost 8, filled his plate with corn on the cob, potato salad, and the rest of the traditional spread—everything minus the hot dogs. Aware of his bottomless appetite and his prior fondness for franks, his family tried to press a hot dog on the freckle-nosed boy, who had spent the day dribbling a soccer ball, hitting balls on the public tennis court by the house, romping in the playground, and watching a funky Independence Day parade in Sausalito. Surely he should be starved! Quietly but insistently, and for the first time in his life, Cooper repeatedly turned down the hot dogs. That evening, the reason for his refusal finally surfaced. He wasn't sick. He hadn't suddenly evolved into a picky eater or a vegetarian. He wasn't trying to be ornery. Having seen two costumed dachshunds dressed in rubber buns—complete with plastic squiggles of ketchup and mustard the length of their long, skinny backs—in the parade that morning, he had put two and two together and, observant boy that he was, decided that eating dog just wasn't for him.

What was most striking was that after tactful prodding, he eventually discussed what was bothering him. Had he kept quiet, he would have just been considered stubborn, as most boys are considered to be. His words not only solved the mystery but also revealed that he could analyze and share his feelings.

Most boys his age and older don't do that, in large measure because we often accept their silence as inevitable, not bothering to do the hard work required to get to the essence of what they are really going through. Society doesn't encourage this kind of emotional follow-through with boys. We have bought into the myth of the uncommunicative boy (and the subsequently quiet man). If we don't pursue the reasons for our sons' behavior, we'll never encourage them to trust that we will accept and understand what's going on inside them. And if they don't trust us to be sympathetic, they certainly aren't going to open up to us or anyone else. It's a never-ending circle of silence.

I've observed this firsthand. While I waited in my pediatrician's office—my daughter Katherine was in with another ear infection—I witnessed the following exchange between the doctor and another little patient's mother. The pediatrician entered the exam room and greeted mother and son. The mother replied with a "hello," but the little boy turned away from the doctor and said nothing. In fact, he didn't even look up from his book. Instead of using the opportunity to investigate the boy's lack of acknowledgment or to gently teach some basic manners, the doctor laughed and said, "He's all-boy. He'll be like that when he's in his twenties." His poor mother!

"I'm lucky if I get a sentence out of him," she said with what I perceived to be a note of desperation in her voice. "He comes home from school, and he doesn't talk. I ask him how school is, and 'Fine' is a big answer from him."

The pediatrician was too busy with his own notion of How Boys Are to hear that this was something the mother was unhappy about. For the doctor, a boy doing his own thing and not engaging in appropriate social contact is not only to be expected; it is to be accepted. The truth is that the mother was right to be concerned.

There are so many ways that doctor could have helped change the this-is-how-boys-are status quo. He could have said something like, "Perhaps you don't feel like talking now, but I am really interested in getting to know you," or he could have taken the initiative and offered to show the boy some interesting gizmo in the examining room. He might have helped the mother by suggesting ways to better engage her son, by advising her to get more involved in activities that he enjoys, as so many of the mothers I studied did.

In order to encourage communication, those maverick mothers would take advantage of opportunities to talk during the potentially mundane tasks of everyday living. They found that their boys often needed to be doing something and to have the opportunity to look at anything but the person with whom they were speaking.

One mother tried everything to get her son to share his feelings when he got a low score on an astronomy test for which he had refused to study. Though the preadolescent was clearly upset, he consistently refused to discuss the matter, insisting that he had received the grade he wanted. Though his mother was struggling with her own feelings of dismay about the lower-than-usual grade and, worse, the fact that her boy hadn't tried, she realized she couldn't push. Eventually her son did open up—during a mother-son bike ride.

Single mother Denise Tauber, a 49-year-old former business owner whose success enabled her to retire early and raise her son, told me, "I've learned if I want to have a conversation with my son, I don't just sit at a table and look him in the eye and have a conversation. It doesn't work. We have to be doing something if I want to have a really successful conversation with him."

Denise, like so many of the maverick moms I interviewed, found out through trial and error about a common tactic among professionals who work with children in the research and psychotherapy arena. Sitting her son down for a chat wouldn't elicit more than a few grunts. So Denise learned to initiate conversation while shuttling her son to and from practice or music lessons and while cooking, playing catch, building toy models, or gardening. In effect, she and the other mothers I studied had figured out for themselves exactly the advice that the professionals would have provided.

A few of the maverick mothers I interviewed used toys to prompt conversation with their sons. One mother had a pair of puppets that she and her son used to dramatize and discuss the events in their lives. "These puppets are very dear to him," she told me. "He can talk to them if he has any problems. The other day he decided that they should be married, so he married them. He had a little ceremony, and when we got back to our house, he wanted to make a cake for them. That's how he let me know that he was thinking about marriage and divorce, and we could talk about love and relationships in a respectful, affectionate way through the puppets."

A message that I heard loud and clear from these mothers is that the long-held assumption that it's not boys' nature to discuss feelings is simply wrong. As I talked to the boys over many years, I provided a venue for them in which they could think about and articulate their experiences both of boy culture and as sons of maverick mothers. This wasn't therapy, though I do feel our meetings were therapeutic. What really counted was that they could tell I was genuinely interested in what they had to say, and that translated into an outpouring of their thoughts and emotions.

Time and time again, I found that the boys didn't shut down if they were encouraged to open up. Almost anyone will respond to an ardent listener. As one grown male colleague put it, "I wish I had had someone who had come to my house to talk with me when I was that age."

Communicating with boys can sometimes require a little excavation. "I just try to listen for the times when my son TJ is telling me more than usual," single mother Fiona Dansinger told me. "It's hard to drop everything and listen on his schedule, but that's what I have to do."

Difficult as it sometimes was, the moms I interviewed were willing to engage in a real conversation, rather than just react. That helped to set both an example and a precedent for their sons to do the same.

"Just recently, I had several days in a row where I spent almost no time with TJ," Fiona told me. "Rare, but it does happen. The next time I had both boys, TJ got screaming mad that I was reading a book to Mike. This is not usual behavior. I stayed calm for a bit; then I got a little fed up with what looked like pretty immature jealousy from the big brother, but as he got madder, he finally let it out that he was angry because I had been absent and that he wanted to spend time with me and he didn't want to listen to Michael's book. Oh. So we had hugs and reassurances that I would play catch at a particular time—no ifs, ands, or buts—and that I was sorry I'd been gone and that I appreciated him letting me know how he felt but could he please tell me without screaming, et cetera. It was pretty intense. But thinking about it afterward, I'm glad he found any way to tell me."

The rewards of this drive toward intimacy are immense, laying the groundwork for emotional responsiveness and sensitivity, something we usually expect from girls but not from boys. Perhaps boys growing up in households where they are encouraged to express their feelings will exhibit some of the connectivity we prize in our daughters. And perhaps the interpersonal skills of maverick mothers can help explain why they had such close, communicative relationships with their sons.

Lorraine Monroe, Ph.D., founder of the Lorraine Monroe Leadership Institute in New York for the education of educators, teaches her teachers to listen for clues dropped when boys aren't necessarily aware that anyone is really listening: "Kids will often open their hearts and speak about their special problem or pain while in the midst of doing things with their hands. For many kids, that's easier than opening up to a counselor in an office." Still, the direct approach can work, too. When Cameron's mom Kelli asked her son whether there was anything bothering him, "it's funny, but usually he'll say, 'No. Nothing. I don't know. No,'" she told me.

"I'll say, 'Well, what do you think it could be? Could it be this? Could it be that?' 'No, no, no.' 'Well, what do you think it could be, then? There's only one person who knows: It's you.' And then usually it just comes out."

Even so, getting Cameron to loosen up and talk could be like pulling teeth. "Two weeks ago, he seemed upset. I said, 'Tell me what's going on.'" As usual, Cameron said he didn't want to talk about it. After a few of these fruitless exchanges, Kelli kicked it up a notch. "You don't wanna talk about it? That's your favorite answer right now? Am I gonna get that all the time?" Her gentle teasing succeeded where a direct question hadn't. "He kind of laughed," she remembered, "and then he relaxed a bit" and told her what was on his mind.

When Cameron was unperturbed, his mother was amazed at his ability to "express what he needs and what he wants or find a solution to a problem. He says to me, 'You know, I'm pretty good at finding solutions. I think maybe I got that gene from you because I think you find good solutions, too.' So I say, 'But I don't find a solution for everything. The genes are sometimes things you create by yourself. Maybe you're the first of the line to find the solution; then you'll be creating the gene yourself.'" Cameron walked away from that conversation feeling about 10 feet tall.

SAVING THE WORST FOR YOU

As we all know, those mothering highs are almost always countered with lows, especially during the early through preadolescent years, when our sons seem to lose it for no discernible reason at all. "Our boys work so hard to be good in the outside world," the mother of Nigel, 6, told me. "They save all that emotion for you. They need to let it loose at home, where they feel safe."

How to handle a boy's issues can be a delicate dance between wanting to elicit a response and pushing too hard for a resolution. As late as the first grade, Lily Jacobs's son, Zack, continued to struggle with articulation problems. Because Lily and Zack had just moved to Florida from New York, his first-grade classmates (who understood him as well as his mother did) figured he had a New York accent and that was why he talked funny. But it wasn't an accent, and it was causing increasing anxiety for her and increasing frustration for Zack.

Lily remembered sitting, along with a number of other mothers, in a kindergarten class during circle time. When Zack raised his hand to answer a question, it was clear that the teacher, like most grown-ups, didn't understand a word that he was saying. Now that she'd gotten a taste of the huge aggravation her son experienced on a daily basis, Lily's heart went out to him.

Shortly thereafter, Zack started speech therapy. Every time they would get into the car to go, the boy would explode at his mother for no apparent reason, yelling and crying. She couldn't imagine what had set him off. All that anger seemed to evaporate after speech therapy. Each time, Zack would come out in a good mood and feeling great. Unfortunately, having just been put through the emotional wringer by Zack's incomprehensible rage, his mother didn't bounce back quite as readily.

The outbursts continued. Lily tried to talk with her son both mid-rant and after the fact, but he wasn't able to tell her what it was that had him so upset. Stymied, she finally had to conclude that his eruptions were triggered by two related factors. Even though he adored his therapist, a terrific woman who made speech therapy fun, stimulating, and exciting without any pressure to "get it right," he was feeling irritation at having to go to a speech therapist at all. That at school he was expected to contain his energy contributed in no small measure to his letting it all out as soon as school was over.

Boys don't always have the language they need to convey the mix of squashed-down anger and pent-up feelings they experience during the day. That was certainly true of Zack. Over the next few months, Lily continued to try to talk to her son about what was going on, with Zack blowing up and his mother calming him down. Finally, he announced, "Mom, I'm frusterated [sic]." As he got older, it became a private joke between them. It was a signpost, a cue that he was feeling overwhelmed and ready to explode and that he was letting her know that he was in control of it, just by using the word "frusterated." It became their signal to sit down and talk about what was going on in his life.

I call this lexicon they created to help identify and connect with each other *mothertongue*. Years later, Lily and Zack continue to use it. Just recently, Lily received an e-mail message from her son that said, "Ignore my previous e-mail. I wrote it in a moment of frusteration." Their code word, started at a very young age, continued to help Zack (then 21 years old and a senior in college) identify his feelings and act in the interest of good social relationships.

Some of the maverick mothers found that in order to handle outbursts in a positive way, they had to give their sons space after they had lost it. They would disengage but still leave an opening for the boys to reconnect. This took patience and practice. "My son Kenneth became much more cranky in adolescence," Frances Lee, an extremely independent 62-year-old divorced mother of four, said in our interview. "I think that was his way of pushing me away. The funny thing would be, he'd come home from school, I'd open the door, he'd look at me, and immediately I knew it was a bad day. I'd say, 'I'm going to be in the kitchen, honey. You know where to find me.' But then I'd find I'd be doing my schoolwork [Frances was in law school at the time] or reading on a Saturday, and every Saturday he'd come in and sit down, I'd stop everything

I was doing, and he'd start to talk about his week." Frances kept herself open and accessible to Kenneth, despite the crankiness.

Flash back to Cooper, a year before the hot dog incident.

"What happened at school today?" his mother asked after collecting him from school, part of their daily ritual.

"We had chocolate at recess, I got a star in reading, and it's not true that I pushed those two boys in the school yard."

Yes, the sensitive little boy who wouldn't eat a hot dog because he thought they were made from dachshund had gotten into a fight at school. Cleverly trying to avoid trouble at home by preemptive and thoroughly self-protective conversation, Cooper, then 6, did the best he could to tell the story his way. If he had just been a little older, he probably could have come up with a less transparent version—but what a communicator he will grow up to be!

That's not to say that dealing with these sensitive sons doesn't tax even the most patient parents. Sometimes kids are so hard to understand, and every mom can remember being ready to pull out her hair. When Bailey asked his mother, a financial manager who described herself as a moderate Democrat, about the different political parties during the presidential debates, she told him that "the Democrats were real humanitarians and that they cared about people more." Bailey promptly burst into tears.

"Son, what's wrong?" his bewildered mother asked.

"I'm afraid," the boy replied. "What if I become a Republican?"

"Bailey's fear I think was, what if I don't care about people?" his mother explained to me during our interview.

That concern for others translated to Bailey's personal relationships—most of the time. His mother said, "He sits down with people and talks with them and is open. Anytime a friend is crying or lonely, he always tries to sidle up to people in that situation and help them out. [But] he alternates between being extremely generous and extremely selfish with his sister, with seemingly no middle ground. One minute he's doing something that just takes my breath away, he's being so generous, and the next minute they're fighting over a nickel as though their lives depend on it." I think it is terrifically important to remember that however hard we work to keep in touch with our boys, and whatever success we may have, they have to be themselves, and they sometimes need to be angry and selfish and infuriating. It's how we deal with these natural aspects of our children that makes all the difference to them—and to us.

SPEAKING YOUR TRUTH

In my work with these boys, I was impressed to find that new family values of self-determination and open-mindedness were taking hold. I noticed with delight that these mothers regularly involved their sons in decision making. They tended to care about what their sons thought, and so they gave them chances to speak their mind. Henry's mothers, for example, consciously resolved to be less structured and more spontaneous so they could hear more from their son about what he wanted and accommodate his wishes, even encouraging him to plan and take charge of family outings. We know from academic research that kids who are valued for their individuality and who are listened to are better able to reason about moral issues. The ability to involve our sons in decisions and to appreciate what they have to say is what creates boys—and, later, men—who not only are able to think for themselves but also can tackle sophisticated and complex issues.

Self-expression is better encouraged than suppressed, the maverick mothers told me. It's even better when both mother and son give full voice to their own thoughts and feelings. From what I could see, their sons benefited from being surrounded by open ears and open hearts. The same is true when boys got into trouble.

Beverly Noonan, the mother of three whose husband left her abruptly when the children were very little, told me about her son's first—and to her knowledge only—foray into drug use when he was 14. "I was away at the shop when Laura [his younger sister] called me and said, 'I've just come home and I smell marijuana; you have to talk to Jason,' who was at home with his friends after school. I told her I would talk to him. I wanted to get him on his own, even though I didn't quite know how I was going to approach this. I had no idea because he was young, kids try things, and I know that, and it didn't really bother me that much, but I thought in the interest of justice and fairness, I had to say something."

Later that day, Beverly sat with her son and chatted a little about his homework and about school. Then she told him, "I understand that you had some friends over, and that's okay because this is your home; you're entitled to have friends over. I understand that you were smoking pot here. That's okay because it's your choice. I've raised you, I think, to think very freely, and if you want to try pot, that's fine. Trying it is one thing; smoking it continuously is another thing. But again, it's your choice to do that. I understand that one drug leads to another drug, and I understand also that a number of men are in prison because they form these habits and then they don't have the money, they've dropped out of school, they didn't go to college, and so they commit crimes in order to keep this habit going, and they really don't have productive lives. But you know, again, that's your choice. I brought you in the world, and I've loved you. What you do with your life is entirely up to you, but I want you to know that if anything like that should happen, you'd break your mother's heart."

Her son just sat there silently, with great big tears running down his face, and he said, "'I'm sorry, Mom. I'm sorry. I'll never do it again.' And he didn't. In his forties today, he stays in close touch with Beverly over the phone. "When I told him I would be talking about him [for this book]," she told me, "he said, 'Are you going to tell her about the time you caught me masturbating?' I thought it was so funny because I don't remember that! He said, 'Well, that's good; you've got a selective memory.'"

Even now, they still connect on an emotional level. Beverly's moving account of the close bond she shares with her son is testament to how tenaciously mothers can love their sons and create men in the process. This unusual depth of intimacy enables their boys to establish deep ties with other people in their lives, which surely will help them as they grow up.

WARM FUZZIES

I don't want to present these maverick moms as saints in the making. But from what I've seen, the way they really listen to their sons, combined with the way they try to keep an instantly judgmental voice at bay, is a tremendously effective parenting strategy. Once this comfortable level of communication is established, productive discussion tends to happen more easily in times of stress. And so their early efforts to hear what their sons have to say and to respond thoughtfully pay off through the years.

Some mothers start young. Leslie Jenkinson, who believed that "the mother is the one who teaches compassion," didn't just rely on positive reinforcement to encourage these traits. She made a conscious effort to raise her son's antennae, even though he was only 3 at the time. "I'm trying to teach him to be sensitive to me and what hurts me because he often accidentally will hurt me—he'll throw something that will hit me in the arm, or he'll step on my foot with his shoes on and what have you. What I do is I say, "Ooh, ow, that hurt, owie, that hurt," because I want him to be empathetic, and he'll look at me and say, 'I'm sorry, Mommy.' When I know he's angry, I'll say, 'You're very angry, aren't you? You're mad because the doggy ran away,' or whatever. I try to get him to recognize his emotions when he feels them. He knows 'sad' because when we see someone crying on the television, whatever program it is, he'll say, 'Oh, he's sad.' Sometimes I'll engage him in conversation. I'll say, 'Why do you think he's sad?' so he'll talk about it that way.

"Because I'm a single mother, I believe that Ian is going to grow up to be a more sensitive, caring man," Leslie added. "He already shows signs of being very empathetic and very nurturing. I bought him a Caillou doll, which is a cloth little boy doll, and he loves to put it to bed, and he'll pat it, and he tries to feed it and he puts it in the high chair. He's very nurturing, and I love that; I think that's wonderful."

I expect such mothering explains why the sons of the maverick mothers I studied tended to be so generous and loving. Leslie expressed some nervousness that this very sweetness might be a sign of weakness, and she was ready to blame herself for that.

Judging by my research, I would answer emphatically that yes, she had helped make him that way, and no, he was not being weak by being kind. Rather, he was demonstrating an inspiring new take on being a head-and-heart boy. This new breed of boy can indulge his creative and caring sides, as well as his more boisterous side, without losing his ability to be a kind and helpful citizen of his community.

By allowing our sons to tap into their emotions, to connect with their mothers and others, we wind up with caring, sensitive men in the making. When divorced mom Mimi Silbert's teenage twin boys, David and Greg, now both lawyers, wrote autobiographical essays as a school assignment, "I snuck in to read them," Silbert confessed to me. "They both started out almost identically. 'I had a very odd upbringing. My mom runs . . . .' followed by a little description of Delancey Street [a residential treatment center for ex-convicts and drug addicts]. Then one talked about risk and failure. He said, 'I learned the most wonderful thing. Some of the people here that I've come to admire most—that I've seen be successful, smart, funny, have integrity—failed and failed and failed again. I feel going into my life that I want to take a lot of risks. I don't feel as afraid of failure because I know if you go all the way down to the bottom, you can totally rebuild everything all over again. I think that was the greatest gift that I got.'

"The other wrote about this one guy who is a graduate. He said, 'He and I came in at the same time. He was a big huge guy, 40 years old, Black, with 12 brothers and sisters. Some of them are on death row. He couldn't read or write at all. My brother and I tutored him and taught him to read and write, and he taught us to lift weights. This year I'm graduating from high school. Both sets of grandparents are flying in from the East Coast and L.A. We're going out to big dinners; it's a big thing. My friend at Delancey Street is finally getting his GED. No one is flying in from anywhere. The world thinks nothing of the fact that this 48-year-old man can read and write, but I know that this is the greater achievement. I've learned to live with people, to understand that achievement has nothing to do with where you end up but with how far you've come and how hard you had to fight to get there.'"

Silbert's reaction to their insightful and remarkably mature essays? "Of course I sobbed."

DIFFERENT STROKES

The flip side for these boys was that they felt a burden of responsibility to address the intolerance that the world hurled their way. They had to decide for themselves how much they needed to respond to the slurs they heard about their mothers' marital status or sexuality. One mother talked about her son's experience at football camp, where every other word out of the other boys' mouths was "fag." She was troubled that her son would feel he had to fight her battle among his friends. Would he feel guilty if he didn't defend his mother to his junior high school buddies, and would he estrange himself from his buddies if he did? "I worry that my orientation puts inadvertent pressure on my son," Irene Wallace told me.

Even in San Francisco, one of the most gay-friendly places on this earth, lesbians live in an environment that at best is tolerant and at worst may be hostile. Many experience the negative pressure placed on them by society's biases. For a mother, the stress is multiplied by worry about the safety of her children. In our great society, adults often react to stress with all kinds of addictive behaviors. I saw many of the moms in my study, both lesbian and straight single mothers, become overly ambitious to be model parents. I sometimes thought of them as parentaholics. They volunteered for everything at their sons' schools: They were homeroom parents, athletic coaches, PTA members; they sat on boards; and they contributed money.

During one of our monthly interviews, I sat in Quentin's kitchen, talking to Sarah, one of his moms, about the school they'd chosen for him. She said to me: "We've seen to it that we are raising him in a supportive environment in terms of the school he is in now. Roberta and I have made sure to have a pretty high profile as supporters of the school wherever Quentin has been. We're out, and we're very helpful."

"Do you feel you have to be helpful?" I asked.

"I don't feel that I have to," she responded, "but I feel more like it's a preemptive strike. By being out there and being helpful, if not indispensable, you start off strongly so that people have to respect you. Then they get used to having lesbians around, and it gets easier for everybody."

What is motivating Sarah and Roberta? They are trying to inoculate Quentin against prejudice by being as present as possible to make the spaces he inhabits safe. Many of these maverick moms I talked with joined all kinds of organizations and marched in all the politically correct parades in an attempt to prepare their boys for a prejudicial slam they knew was coming. When their sons started school, it was a strenuous time for many of these mothers because their supportive networks of child-care workers, friends, and collected families were being replaced by an unknown and potentially intolerant school environment.

Some of the particular strengths and sensitivities of the boys in the two-mother families I studied—a greater capacity to express feelings or more empathy for social diversity—may have resulted from the marginality the boys and their mothers felt in their day-to-day lives.

Many of the boys I met spoke of their family structure with great ease and naturalness. Callie Howard and her partner, Nell Cummings, both 39, are parents of Jullian, who was 4 when I first met him. Jullian was born to Nell from an unknown sperm donor. During a family vacation on Hawaii's Big Island while they had breakfast around the pool, a woman asked then-2-year-old Jullian, "Oh, is Daddy still in bed?" Jullian nonchalantly replied, "We don't have a daddy. We have two mommies and a Ruffin." (Ruffin is their dog.)

As the boys got older and more self-conscious, this alternative family arrangement proved tougher to acknowledge. One boy confessed to me that he felt guilty about hiding the fact he had two moms from some of the rougher kids at his school. Upon meeting anyone for the first time, he explained, he would calculate "how easy they would be" with the fact that his parents were lesbians. Only then would he decide whether to reveal that or not.

With the help of their mothers, many of the sons of two-mother families that I studied were acutely, sometimes painfully, aware of how to present themselves effectively and securely to a not-always-sympathetic outside world. "I think I've prepared them, subconsciously, since they were young," one lesbian mother told me. "We always talked about how boring life would be if everyone drove a blue Chevy and lived in a white house. They always knew it's okay to be different."

That doesn't mean the boys necessarily got it right the first time out. Over the years of my relationship with Kenny and his mothers, I witnessed Kenny's strong, vital bond with social mom Tasha, who had adopted him as a toddler. Then the 12-year-old met his first girlfriend, a Southern Baptist whose mother was a church minister, during a cruise with his family. Afraid of being rejected and worried that his new friend wouldn't approve of his family, Kenny told the girl that Tasha was simply his mom's casual friend.

The incident caused the family to redefine itself. When his mothers heard what Kenny had said, they made it clear to him that he had two equally important mothers, co-parents, and that one could not be discarded at whim. "We needed to teach Kenny the value of teaching others who are not familiar with families like ours that his is quite a normal, well-functioning family, thank you," Tasha told me. Ultimately Kenny approached Tasha, unprovoked by either mother, and apologized. "I am really, really sorry I said that about you the other night," he told her. "I was upset because I didn't know how to tell Jane about my family, and I took it out on you."

"We both cried," Tasha remembered. "Then, some months later, we got a call from Jane's grandmother, telling us they were coming to San Francisco. And there wasn't even a question in Kenny's mind that he was going to have to come out to his new friend about his moms. But the question was, how to do it and when to do it and in what words and who should say it? He was scared that if he wrote her and told her, she wouldn't come. He decided to wait until she came, and then we were going to be very gracious to them and then tell them.

"We told the grandmother when Jane was out of the room. We didn't use the word lesbian—we just said we were both moms, and she got it. She said, 'What a lovely setup.' Basically, Jane never asked Kenny. She asked her grandma, 'He has two moms?' And the grandma said, 'Yes, honey.' And that was it. The grandmother said to us, 'I think her mother needs to explain this to her.'"

"We were great tour guides," Tasha told me with a grin. "This was for Kenny, and we really felt we knocked ourselves out. But Hannah and I also had our own agenda," she added with a twinkle in her eye. "You know, the 'change the world one person at a time' theory."

Many of the mothers I spoke with used the fact that their sons were not from traditional families to inspire them to be more thoughtful to other people with differences. Others were more concerned about shoring up their boys in anticipation of difficulties they would likely encounter because of their unconventional families. Nancy Zeitz, an art therapist with an adopted African-American 3-year-old named Lionel, realized that "our family is not society's standard by virtue of being a transracial family as well as being a single-parent family living with my mom. So I'm aware that there are some risk factors for him down the road as he develops that he could have struggles with," she confided to me. "I try now to do preparatory work for him, like in talking about how to talk about race, how to talk about our family with other people. I even have mentioned sometimes that some people may not understand why your family doesn't have a daddy or why your mom is a different color or whatever."

Two-mother families must think about the values that will predominate in their children's world. They know that eventually they will have to help their children face and deal with bigotry, homophobia, racism, and sexism. So they actively teach their sons about prejudice before they encounter it, giving them a framework for recognizing it as a problem rather than letting them internalize destructive messages. "The plan is by the time he gets to be a teenager, he'll have enough of a solid foundation and working relationship with Mary and me that we can help him deal with what's hard, and he'll have enough of a perspective not to internalize what comes at him around the boy code stuff," says one mother. Since this boy code—which emphasizes macho coolness and one-upsmanship at the expense of expressing or demonstrating feelings—is so pervasive, I wondered if these boys from single- and two-mother families were damaged by being stigmatized. As I discovered during my research, the existence of stigmatization may matter less than how children react to it and the kind of support they get from their families. Children who are helped to deal constructively with discrimination are likely to develop significant strengths: They can think independently and stand up for what they believe in. They may even have an advantage when it comes to acquiring moral standards and courage.

If they are loved well enough, there is no reason these boys will be unable to manage whatever anxieties may flow from the community's disapproval of their mothers. Perhaps because of outside intolerance, these boys may have to bear themselves with greater than ordinary fortitude. But this does not necessarily portend that their moral welfare or safety will be jeopardized

In the lesbian-led families I studied, I found that each boy's parents fostered in their son feelings of forbearance and protectiveness, not shame, toward their mothers. By their actions, words, and example, however causally conveyed, lesbian mothers cultivated courage, instilling in their kids the precept that people of integrity do not shrink from bigots. They disdained the easy option of avoiding difficult problems and following the course of expedience.

These maverick mothers encouraged regard for a fundamental rule of human behavior: that we do not forsake those to whom we are indebted for love merely because they are held in low esteem by others. As a result, these sons may be better able to perceive that the majority is not always correct in its moral judgments. They may be more capable of understanding the importance of constructing beliefs based on reason and knowledge, rather than going along with the constraints of popular sentiment or prejudice.

CHALLENGING STEREOTYPES

The maverick mothers I met made a conscious effort to challenge stereotypes, imparting values to their sons and teaching them to be better men. "I point out gender stereotyping whenever I can," Fiona said. "TJ told me once that he thought girls were bad at chess. I asked him why he thought that, and he said, with careful consideration, that he could beat any girl he'd ever played (including me) and that there were no girls in any of his chess books and that there were no girls in the world of international chess. I had to admit that he had a point, but that this did not mean that no girls were good at chess, nor did it mean that girls couldn't be good at chess. We talked that day about what a stereotype is, and how it may have a basis in apparent fact. (Note to self: Find a girl who can beat him at chess.)"

The common denominator with these moms? They didn't hesitate to share their own values, even when it seemed that their sons had tuned them out. "Did my son listen to any of what I had to say?" divorced mom Maria Black, a hospital administrator with a keen intelligence and sharp wit, asked me rhetorically. "No, but I always feel I have to say it in case he listens, in case later it means something. It's important for me to have values and try to tell them what they are."

I'm reminded of those antismoking commercials, during which the kids roll their eyes as their parents discuss why they shouldn't smoke, but then turn down the cigarette offered to them by a peer. It may not look like it, but messages that convey our values do get through. "Mark is real clear about what my views are and what upsets me," Helen, a hospice social worker who divorced Mark's father when Mark was 2, announced. She was especially vocal about the movies or television shows they saw together. "I tell him, 'Well, look, this is once again showing a completely unrealistic woman character. It's all just a form of entertainment; this is not a real female.' And so, yeah, he hears that all the time," she said, laughing. "There have been a couple of times when he would watch a movie, and then he'll be talking about it and I'll get upset and say, 'But look! Here!' And he'll roll his eyes and go, 'Okay, yeah, I see your point.'"

Subtlety is definitely not the name of this game when it comes to creating a more desirable norm for male attitudes. "What I do now is try to decode society's messages about women," Martha, a talented and well-respected publisher, editor, and author whose husband left her for another woman when their son was 5, told me. "Like 'Mommy, why are two women wrestling in a vat of gua-camole?' Riley asked me. We walked past the eyeglass store the other day. Riley says, 'Mommy, why is there a naked woman modeling glasses?' There was this picture in the window. I said, 'Well, they think you'll stop because you're a guy and you'll want to buy the glasses because it'll get you closer to a naked girl. And when you're older, that will be a very exciting thing.'

"Riley thought about it. 'Well, that's kind of stupid.'

"'Actually, it does talk down to you,' I said. 'To tell you the truth, it doesn't appeal to anything other than a certain part of you.'

"So I'm pretty candid about that, and he's getting what we call The Lecture. For instance, I told him I would let him see *Dude,*

Where's My Car? but only if he endures The Lecture. And he laughs, he goes, 'Okay, what's The Lecture?' At one point the girl's breasts enlarge; that's the fantasy at the end. And I said, 'You know, Riley, this is a very shallow approach, and it is funny, but please know that it puts girls down, and it also puts boys down because it says that's all they care about, and if that's all you care about, you're going to have a very shallow life.' So it may not mean anything to him now, but he'll have the vocabulary."

Ursula Hardy's work as an environmentalist provided plenty of opportunities to demonstrate to her boys how she felt about the way we live in the world. "Caleb is especially interested in my cases. He identifies with the fight. There's this great book, called *Hoots*, that in a way is about ecoterrorism. It's about saving the endangered burrowing owl and the environmental impact of building without proper consideration. I told Caleb that those are the kinds of documents I read all the time. I share my work with him. 'See, this is the piece of property they were going to build 200 homes on that we now have purchased, and it's going to be protected forever.' They know a lot about that. They know it's a moral stand because they know there are many people out there who do not care a whit about the environment."

These maverick moms imparted their principles though consistent dialogue in terms their sons could relate to. That's the key. "We spend an awful lot of time discussing differences," Denise Tauber, a single mom who devoted herself full-time to raising her son, told me. "How being different isn't better or worse, and how ridiculous racism is, and things like that, and then we equate this with just any other way of being different. You know, some families have just a mom, and some have just this, and some have that, and some people have blond hair and some people have brown hair; we're all just different, and if we were all the same, how boring life would be. We even joke about that sometimes. 'My

God,' I tell him, 'if everyone looked like you, I wouldn't know which kid was mine!'"

Unlike traditional parents, the single and lesbian mothers I studied celebrated that which set their sons apart. "We want to capitalize on the sensitivity that comes from him being different. I think that because he's different, he will have a kind of vulnerability that will make him more sensitive to other people who are different," one social mom said to me. "I am bound and determined to raise different kinds of men than I'm surrounded by and grew up with." In the next breath, she admitted to worrying about what her son would face because he was not like all the rest. A friend of hers helped put that to rest. "You're acting as if kids don't come out of families that are limited," the friend countered. "They do. No matter how normal they look, there's always something they're not getting or that they're getting too much of. [In your son's case] it's on the surface more explicit."

Just how does a boy acquire or not acquire a moral identity? Psychological theory has stipulated that it takes an at-home male role model to develop a boy's character, morality, and masculinity. Freud saw morality as stemming from a boy's identifying with a paternal authority, while Jean Piaget, another great theorist of human development, related morality to the child's early respect for both parents, but especially the father. This respect for the father—a mixture of fear and affection—defined the young boy's moral attitude toward others.

The maverick mothers' sons I studied, however, clearly showed that a boy's morality and masculinity could be cultivated without a live-in father. I found there were no differences in the boys in terms of their conceptions about what they considered fair, or their reasoning about moral issues. Boys scoring at higher levels of moral reasoning were simply older than those at lower levels. I found the boys were by and large viewed by their parents and teachers to be "good kids." Temperamentally they might have been regarded as "typical American boys," no matter how atypical their family structure.

LEAD ON

The boys in my study not only forged a moral code for themselves; they also offered new models of maleness to younger boys.

Describing himself in relation to his male friends one day, Evan declared, "I am the oldest. I am the strongest. I am the tallest."

Not sure where this assessment of himself was going to lead, I asked him, "Do your friends look up to you because you're the strongest and the tallest and the oldest?"

"Sometimes," Evan replied, scrunching up his face as if in deep concentration.

"So why do they look to you?" I wondered.

"It's hard to explain," Evan said. "I help them a lot, and when they get hurt, I usually know what to do." First he would offer to go get a grown-up, he told me. His friend "usually says no. Then I ask him what he wants me to do. Then I usually try to make him laugh, 'cause once he starts laughing, he feels a lot better."

Evan was clearly going for intelligence and compassion in his interactions with his younger friends. Humor and the ability to laugh, a human survival mechanism shown for males to be an indicator of success in later life, helped, too.

Quentin, who told me all about his idol, *Garfield* cartoon creator Jim Davis, used humor to manage conflicts among younger boys with whom he plays.

"How do you do it?" I asked him.

"I make them laugh," he said. Even though he's not an attention-seeking class-clown type, I could see how his well-developed sense of humor could help him smooth over the bumps and tussles of the playground. He learned from his moms at an early age the benefits of distraction over fisticuffs—the power of mind over muscle.

As early as possible, the single and lesbian mothers I interviewed taught their sons not to retaliate physically but to use their words instead. When a little girl on the school playground bit 2½-year-old Harrison, he cried, asked to talk to the teacher, then approached the culprit. "Look what you did," he announced, showing her the clear marks her teeth had left on his arm. "I didn't do anything to hurt you. I was just playing with my dinosaur. You shouldn't have done that." More effective, smarter, and much more acceptable than biting back.

These boys weren't angels, but they were remarkably able to relate, to convey their feelings and connect with others. "We try to give him the language to say, 'That makes me uncomfortable or anxious,' as well as permission to feel," said Henry's biological mom, Mary.

Maverick mothers' sons were also smart about how they approached situations. Joss, a 7-year-old whose extracurricular activities included science club, chess, karate, music and dance class, and clay modeling, told me that when his brother got him mad, he just wanted to bite him because "he's really the only soft thing around."

"Do you?" I asked him.

"No. I just force my mouth shut. I ignore him until it gets unbearable. Then I tell myself to solve it myself. My strategy: Tell him I'll get him something he really wants [if he backs off]."

Clearly, their mothers had taught their sons about self-control. Henry's co-mom told me about the time his little sister attacked him with her fists. While Henry was obviously not hurt, he was understandably angry. He conveyed this message to his sister and his mothers loud and clear not with blows or screams but by "putting an ice bag on his head and continuing to read."

As the boys matured, so did their verbal conflict-resolution skills. Tom and Frank, brothers ages 12 and 11, had been engaged in a heated argument for some time. Instead of escalating to physical confrontation as so many siblings—especially male siblings—do, they stuck to their oral battle. "You're not behaving appropriately," Tom finally said to his younger brother. "I thought you hated the word 'appropriate,'" Frank retorted. Dumbfounded, his older brother had no comeback. Checkmate—end of the argument.

EMOTIONAL FLUENCY

After studying these head-and-heart boys, I concluded that they exhibited an unusually high level of emotional intelligence. I spent years conducting individual interviews with these boys, interviews informed by my many years of clinical and psychoneurological testing experience in a variety of child and adolescent settings. For the first phase of my study, I utilized the Social-Cognitive and Moral Judgment Interview of Stanford University professor William Damon, Ph.D., to assess the boys' emotional intelligence as related to social issues with adults and peers. In this initial phase, I also developed an interactional (cooperative versus conflicted) scale to describe the disposition of each boy and how he interacted with adults and peers in his everyday life. I found that many of the sons from lesbian-led families had higher measures on the disposition scale and were more likely to have mothers who reported that their sons were neither verbally aggressive nor experiencing many conflicts with siblings and peers.

In other words, after countless interviews and an exhaustive review of studies on alternative parenting, I saw that these boys were different from their peers—if this were a normal EQ test, we'd call them "off the charts."

Theresa Pressman's son Dirk, 6, would ask his mother a question, and then, as she was still contemplating her answer, "his face will change and he'll say, 'You look sad. You have sad eyes,'" Theresa told me. "He'll read my eyes or a twitch in my cheek, and he knows exactly where I'm going. It's not just on negative emotions. It's anything. He registers a question. He'll register bemusement, even when you're not really smiling yet. He'll reference it; he'll talk about it. It's not as surprising with me because he sees me all the time, but he'll also pick it up in other people. He'll take cues from a facial expression or a way of sitting and read them accurately.

"You don't normally think of boys having such good antennae," said Theresa, who hoped her son would retain his emotional literacy even in a world that often discourages it in boys. "I would like him to grow up thinking of that as a strength, not an embarrassment. Friends will say to Dirk, 'Big boys don't cry,' if he falls and starts crying. It started driving me crazy. Yes, big boys do cry, and if they hurt, they should."

As these boys grew older, the cruelties they experienced in the playground and the school yard were somehow transformed into a heightened sensitivity to others. "I know to let Mom be when she's down," Kenny told me.

Not only did the sons of lesbians and single by choice moms tend to be more empathetic to others, but in a finding of mine that confirmed prior studies, they were more aware of the good and bad feelings within themselves.

This emotional literacy stemmed from a childhood of openly sharing and discussing feelings, without flinching and without cover-up. "I try to stop when I can see there's an issue and ask, 'How do you feel about that?' If that kid hit you, or if you hit that kid and you saw that look on his face, how did it make you feel?

So we talk about that quite a bit," Theresa told me. "There's [also] a lot of early categorizing of different feelings: humiliation, shame, embarrassment, anger, frustration. We work pretty hard on identifying that whole range of feelings."

The boys' ability to recognize feelings in themselves and others stemmed from their mothers' insistence that they deal head-on with emotionally challenging situations, especially when those negative emotions were directed at their moms. "Kenny said I was a sucky driver," Hannah, his mom, told me. While there was a grain of truth in her son's bantering accusation, his teasing distressed Hannah. "What you said about me really upset me and hurt my feelings," she later told him. Kenny was devastated, especially because Hannah's teasing had offended him in the past. So they talked.

"Since I teach him that it's safe to bring up whatever you feel, I had to be ready to hear about how I had hurt his feelings, too," Hannah told me. "He said I tease him a lot and that he doesn't like it. It's true that I tease, but I hadn't heard before that it bothered him. He tends to hold things in, and then they burst out of him all at once. The conversation about the sucky driving was one of those outbursts. We both cried, and I told him I wished he had told me sooner but that I was really glad he had told me at all."

One of the most striking findings of my research is that the boys raised in two-parent lesbian families and the boys that I met from single-mom families were emotionally sophisticated. Their ability to communicate with others was striking. And yet we have been told that the majority of boys are in trouble. It may be that a culture that encourages men to be tough and silent and to live in fear of any "feminizing" force is reaping what it sows: generations of violent and painfully troubled boys. Our culture reinforces the idea that a man—and even a boy—should not accept help or expect help, that he must be self-reliant in all ways.

Brain research has shown that boys are actually more empathic, expressive, and emotive at birth than girls, but according to William Pollack, Ph.D., author of *Real Boys*, the boy code that locks our sons in a culture of stoicism and reticence often socializes these attributes out of them by the second grade. "We now have executives paying $10,000 a week to learn emotional intelligence," says Pollack, when, sadly, these are actually the skills that boys are born with and are taught to live without.

As opposed to the monosyllabic nonresponse I overheard in my pediatrician's office, the boys from my study had been taught to express themselves early on. I found over and over again that these boys were in tune with their own feelings. This should be reassuring to all mothers and should fill us with hope for the future lives of boys. But my findings also made me consider the role of rigid gender distinctions in the lives of boys. Consider Carol Gilligan's work on the importance of relationships in the lives of girls, which she discussed in her groundbreaking book *In a Different Voice*. Gilligan originally postulated that teaching our sons about right and wrong broke down in distinct ways, divided between the mother's emphasis on responsibility and caring and the father's emphasis on justice and fairness. More recently, however, she and others in the moral-development field have moved beyond this singular recognition of sex differences. Gilligan now believes the two moral voices, that of fairness and that of responsibility and caring, develop in both men and women. Could it be that boys have the same potential for emotional expressiveness as girls and that our traditional message to boys that they shouldn't or couldn't communicate their feelings has stunted their development? This is worth pondering as we turn to the ways in which mothers are encouraging their sons to be themselves to the fullest.

WHEN RAISING BOYS, MAVERICK MOMS:

- Talk and talk and talk with their sons, and then talk some more. Dialogues are not linked monologues. Asking specific questions, like "What did you do in math class?" rather than the generic "How was your day?" shows involvement in life.

- Use toys to prompt discussion or initiate conversations in the car, on the basketball court, or in the kitchen while cooking together, because boys tend to shy away from face-to-face discussions.

- Listen to what their sons tell them or don't tell them, looking for messages even in silence or outbursts. Listening can reveal what kind of mothering boys need to help them become men. Sometimes it's a question of hearing and reacting to not just the words but also the feelings that trigger them.

- Encourage the recognition and display of emotions—both good and bad—as well as discussions about what caused those feelings. The resulting emotional literacy helps their sons to connect with others and to develop into caring, sensitive men.

- Allow their sons space when they need it while making themselves accessible when their sons are ready to talk.

- Foster open two-way communication in which they express their own thoughts and feelings.

- Repeatedly impart their own values—including consciously challenging gender and other stereotypes—even when their sons seem to have tuned them out.

CHAPTER SIX

THE MENTAL WORK
OF MOTHERING

"The most important thing as they're growing up is that you believe that they have what it takes to cope, to survive, to grow, to build themselves physically and emotionally to get through life. If they feel that from you, it means everything."

—*Divorced mother Helen Lewis*

DAILY CARE OF A CHILD extends well beyond the physical into the realms of empathy, emotionality, play, and nurturance. Child-rearing skills in these areas necessitate more than just being an able-bodied adult. Mothering is work that requires not only complex physical and emotional but also cognitive commitment. A wealth of evidence tells us that men and women are very different from each other on that front. In almost all families, Mom functions as the overseer, the organizer, the list maker, the keeper of inventory. Beyond overseeing practical activities, mothers are also able to look out for and interpret patterns and rhythms in the child's daily life and respond accordingly.

In my work with two-mother families, I had the privilege to observe courageous mothers on the front lines of our society. These mothers—alone and in pairs—are undertaking the emotionally and culturally fraught work of raising boys without a father in the home and doing it well. Their success depends on the recognition that as mothers, they have the innate power to raise their sons right and that they must move from disempowerment and betrayal into a renewed acknowledgment of that power.

True maternal assurance, the kind that doesn't have to prove itself, spawns a freshness and an immediacy that is expansive for both mother and child.

Pam Ingalls's love affair with Cody began the moment she saw his picture. "He's a beautiful child," she told me with pride. "Gorgeous skin. Thick, long black hair. Black eyes. Very petite in his features. Very tiny. He was only 5 pounds, 10 ounces, when he was born. . . . I think everyone immediately fell in love with him who saw the pictures. I definitely did." At last, when he was 6 months old, she was called to pick him up in Guatemala. When the baby was finally brought to her hotel, she held him, so over-come with emotion that she was unable to speak. "I had been warned that [newly adopted babies] might cry for hours or even a couple of days, being with unfamiliar people, [but] you'd never know he'd made any kind of transition. He has a very even temperament. . . . He was just a very lovable child. I'm sure that contributed to it, but I had pretty much already accepted him, through pictures. I'd gotten one video of him. He was already Cody to us."

Cody continued to wriggle his way into Pam's heart, eventually adopting his mother's personality traits, down to her penchant for organization and tidiness. When he was about 3, she came to pick him up from the church child care he always attended while she was at choir practice, only to find the teachers laughing. He and two little boys had been playing together. When the other boys went home, Cody just sat in the middle of the room, shook his head, and said, "Oh, what a mess." Then he cleaned up the whole room. "He put everything away," his teachers told Pam. He did the same thing when they visited Pam's sister, an unrepentant pack rat and a slob. As Cody went around closing cabinets and tidying up, Pam's sister looked at her and said, "Oh, my gosh, it *is* environment, not heredity!"

During the 3 years since, Pam has figured out that we can learn to use our children's eyes to see the world as a realm of possibilities and explore it with them, experience it as they do, and regain some of the wonder we may have lost as jaded adults. "I think having Cody around has given me a renewed outlook on life," said Pam, whose 7-year marriage ended well before Cody came on the scene due to her former husband's lack of family commitment. "We go to the park more. I'd never do that if I didn't have him. We sit down and talk about things. We go eat ice cream on the back porch. Taking time to do things has definitely changed me. And I'm more spontaneous. I'll say, 'Okay, let's just go do that.' One of my good friends who has helped with Cody a lot is very spontaneous. Before I got him, she knew that if we were going to do anything, she had to plan it. Now she can call and say, 'I'm going out to the farmer's market. Do you and Cody want to go?' And we'll go. I know she knows that I've changed because Cody might like to go out there and see the vegetables and the flowers. I do things now knowing that would be something that Cody would enjoy. And I find myself then enjoying it, too. Like going to the county fair. I grew up in Albuquerque in the city. We were three little girls. We never got dirty. We never got out and played with the animals and stuff. So taking him to the county fair the last 2 years and walking among the cows and sheep and chickens, and him riding horses— you suddenly see that this is kind of fun."

My research on parenting among two-mother and single-mother families engaged me intellectually and produced provocative results that I believe and hope will move the conversation about how to raise children forward in significant ways. I spent hundreds of hours with these mothers as they went about the daily jobs of mothering: making decisions, agonizing about whether or not they were right, sharing in the magnification of the moments in life with their sons. I saw the pride they took in raising these fine boys. I watched them standing back to let their sons make choices that they were afraid were wrong, intruding on choices they made that were right, worrying about being too strict or too permissive, wondering whether they said too much, too little, or just enough. I saw them suffer guilt for not being there, as well as guilt for being there too much. Whether these moms were single or partnered, however, I rarely heard them complain about the role of motherhood that they'd chosen and pursued only after painstaking planning and effort.

SINGLE BY CHOICE

Single mother by choice Denise Tauber, who's now retired and raising her 9-year-old son, Jackson, used to be pitied at her mom-and-baby group for being unmarried. Until, that is, the talk turned to the holidays and the problem every married woman had experienced in parceling out their babies' holiday time to the eager new grandparents. Either "they had an in-law visiting who was telling them they were doing everything wrong, or pressures with the husband because there wasn't dinner on the table every night at 6 o'clock, and here they are, staying home, and they have nothing else to do all day, and then finally one of them just looks over at me and says, 'Maybe you don't have it so hard after all,'" Denise said. "I was like, 'Ooh, busted.'"

Such misconceptions about the unrelenting hardships of single motherhood, and the toll that takes on their children, are common. As we talked, Denise recalled a conversation with a woman whose husband had lost his job and been forced by economic circumstances to take a consulting position for which he had to travel out of town all week long. Of course, his absence turned his wife into the de facto single mother of their young son. "Well, I can't complain to you because you always [face this]— this is your life," the woman acknowledged. Denise promptly disagreed. "This is the life I chose," she retorted. "You didn't choose single motherhood."

Yes, maverick moms sometimes have had to work harder to establish their identity as a bona fide family to others. And yes, their parenting is scrutinized more than it would have been with a mainstream family. But when it comes to mothering, mothers who have chosen to raise their children with an in-house father may have the propensity to feel victimized when that father is not emotionally or physically there for them and their children in times of need or stress.

When you're a single mom, you don't have to deal with unrealized expectations about your partner, nor do you have to cope with a partner's preconceptions or expectations. Lynn Thompson, the single mother of Malcolm and Deirdre, was happy to be unmarried with two kids. "The first year of a child's life is extremely difficult for couples because you're negotiating a whole different pattern. A lot of couples divorce in the first year. I thank God I'm not married to my ex-husband because he'd just be telling me everything to do and everything I'm doing wrong, and I really don't question myself as a mother. I feel very comfortable with my decisions. I think I'm a good mom. I get this from my friends, too. There's more conflict in the home [when there's a husband]. Not that that's a bad thing, but I personally don't like conflict. That's my own issue. I don't want my son to be afraid of conflict, but I just don't particularly enjoy it. I know it would make me tense if there was conflict going on in front of the kids."

Sometimes it's actually easier having no partner to negotiate with about parenting, even under painful circumstances. Single mothers get to do it their way, no ifs, ands, or buts. One mom I spoke with said she could think of many times she'd been to the park, the zoo, or a restaurant, given her son a quick, clean yes or no to a request, and then watched the couples fight over the same issue.

"I could be the parent I wanted to be," said Ursula Hardy, single mother of two independent boys, 12 and 10. "I could create that role and the interactions I wanted to." No discussion about parenting methodologies. No crossed signals or being played one off the other by a budding Machiavelli. For a super-organized person like Ursula, this was a major plus. No compromising on plans—at least not with her partner. The decisions, the choices, the priorities were all hers.

The single mothers I spoke with had no illusions about what it meant to parent alone. They had accepted—even embraced—single parenting after the decision had been made. I was surprised at the lack of disappointment or resentment in both the single mothers by choice and in the lesbian mom families who had thought long and hard about child raising before they had had children. As opposed to mothers who expected a partnership and, whether still married or not, wound up carrying most of the load, single moms who had chosen to parent alone expected to do it all, and the two-mother lesbian families relished their individual child-raising responsibilities.

When Denise decided the time was right to become a mother, she picked an anonymous donor very similar to the men in her family. An engineering student at the University of Michigan, he seemed to have passed on his gift for math and logic to Denise's son. Jackson had also inherited his physical prowess from the tall donor. That was also part of the plan. According to Denise, many single moms pick donors that fit their families, and they look for qualities that might offset negatives or compensate for real or imaginary deficiencies in their own genetic makeup. For instance, because she's overweight, she chose a donor who had no obvious weight problem. She further explained, "We're not super-athletic—his donor enjoys basketball and other sports, and my son actually is very physically coordinated."

Denise, who described Jackson as "smart but not nerdy," expressed her pride in him. "He is extremely good-looking and tall and not fat and doesn't have anything about him that can be picked on." Still, she remained sensitive to issues of bullying. "Not too long ago, he was being teased because he is tall! It shouldn't matter, but the fact is, if he's going to make it through adolescence, I want to do everything I can to help him make it through without Jackson targeting others or having him be one of those who's targeted."

Achieving a conscious, helpful parenting style involves ongoing effort. Denise felt the key for her was educating herself and then following through on what she had learned. "I think it's really, really sad that in a society like ours, it's so important that we all go to Lamaze classes but we don't get parenting classes." Denise took parenting seriously, gathering information about her son and acting on it both by allowing him to be who he was—spirited, slow to accept change, sensitive—and by helping him to adapt to the world as it is. "He's the type of kid that has a lot of problems with tags in his shirts and seams in his socks, and I could sit and yell at him day in and day out that it really doesn't matter that there's a seam in that sock, but it does to him," she said. "It's not going to help either one of us to sit there and argue about it every morning." Making sure from the outset that the clothes she bought were comfortable—even down to the socks—was just one way she used her own knowledge of Jackson's needs to circumvent potential problems.

Denise, who had kidney disease, was on the list for a transplant and had to spend countless hours in doctors' offices and hospitals. When she was away, her son was not only looked after but also loved by the community of friends and neighbors she had cultivated around her family in suburban Detroit. Still, "I know that Jackson worries about me."

Jackson had been told that his aunt and uncle, whom he saw regularly, would be his guardians in the highly unlikely event Denise was not able to care for him, but the question of what would happen was naturally of concern to them both. "Jackson asks a lot of questions, and I try to explain it as best I can. I try to be open. I'm one of those who think that hiding information is more scary for a child than answering their questions. I don't volunteer information, but I answer questions. We hadn't talked about it for a while, and he walks in one morning and he goes, 'You know, Mom, you don't need to worry about it anymore. I'm going to give you one of my kidneys.' And at that point I realized that I had been showing him too much of my anxiety. I explained to him that he's too young and that he needs to keep his kidneys and that it was really sweet of him to offer, but that it's not his problem and not to worry about it. I've learned to temper the way I put things so that he does not feel responsible if I'm unhappy or if things aren't going well or if I'm sick. I can't make him do too much. As he gets older, I can ask more and more, just because he's older and he's a member of the family, but not because he's the only person out there to do something."

Denise tried to anticipate potential problems. "I had him in therapy for a little while to make sure he was okay with what was going on, and he was fine." She refused to acquiesce to the notion that "it's okay if Jackson doesn't talk to me because this is how boys are." Part of their interaction involved imbuing in Jackson the qualities that were important to her and to many of the mothers I met during my research. She hoped he would grow up to be a caring, thoughtful, nurturing person. She hoped to teach him to be independent, to think for himself, to stand up for what he believed in, to have good sportsmanship and empathy, and to not try (as a male) to overpower or humiliate others. Much of the mental work of mothering is about learning how to instill these qualities in our sons.

Determined that her son not suffer because he had a single mom, she signed Jackson up for sports, even though he wasn't particularly interested in them. "I don't want to give anyone an excuse, 'Well, he's that way because he didn't have a father.' And I don't want him to also regret, 'How come I didn't get to play baseball?' These have to be his choices; they're not my choices to make. So I made him play baseball, I made him play soccer, and then it was up to him after he had tried it whether he wanted to continue."

Denise understood that organized sports could provide an important arena for the release of Jackson's pent-up energy and emotions, but they could also bring out the worst in him when not properly managed. "Everything is so competitive that by the time the kids are 7 years old, the parents are trying to stack teams so they're sure to have the winning team," according to Denise. "It's horrible. The fathers are worse, but the mothers go along with it! They won't stand up to them. We had dads teaching the kids the slide tackle illegally in soccer at 7 years old. So I've pulled Jackson, now 8, out of those. We're trying to find more noncompetitive activities. He's probably going to go to a sports camp this summer that they swear is noncompetitive, just to learn the rules of the games."

Denise realized that if she wanted Jackson to grow up into the kind of person she enjoyed having around, she had to assume the responsibility for instilling in him the qualities that were important to her. The result? By age 8, her son, known as a peacemaker among his friends' parents, was concerned about world politics, couldn't wait to be old enough to donate blood because his type— O negative—could be used by anybody, and clearly showed concern about fairness in all his interactions. As Denise demonstrated, it wasn't enough to say that a boy had a difficult temperament. "I do have a lot of power in the kind of person Jackson develops [into]. [I can influence] if Jackson's a good kid, if he cares about others, if he has a good moral center."

As a researcher, I have studied children; as a therapist, I have worked with parents and their children; and as a mother, I have raised a son. In all these roles, I have watched intently as women mother their sons. It is clear to me that no matter whether we are single mothers by choice, stepmothers, divorced mothers by choice or chance, lesbian mothers, or heterosexual married mothers, we take our mothering seriously. And we have many experiences to share.

Even though mothers have been blamed for so many of the problems their children have faced, research has given credit to their parenting styles. Recent studies have looked at differences among two-mother lesbian families, heterosexual families, and two-father families. Much of this research suggested that two-mother families managed parenting with particular effectiveness and harmony.

Analogously, studies of matched lesbian and heterosexual couples found that mothers in every category—heterosexual birth mother, lesbian birth mother, lesbian social mother—scored about the same, but they all scored significantly higher than heterosexual men on measures having to do with the care of the children. While lesbian birth mothers and heterosexual birth mothers scored about the same on all measures of parenting, the "social" mothers in two-mother lesbian couples scored significantly higher than did fathers on measures of parenting skills and qualities of interactions with children.

Social mothers spent considerably more time in important child-care activities, such as discipline and limit setting, than did fathers—including fathers of children in heterosexual couples. I found the lesbian mothers and single mothers by choice I interviewed did not use corporal punishment or harsh punitive methods when it came to correcting bad behavior. When Nathan, the boy who credits his social mom with his sports prowess, broke the bedroom door in a fit of anger, his mothers didn't ground him or take away his allowance. They sat him down and discussed alternative anger-management strategies. Then they made him pay for the damage.

Lesbian birth mothers and their co-mother partners evaluated their children's emotional states and social behaviors in almost exactly the same way. But heterosexual mothers and fathers evaluated their children differently. For example, fathers in heterosexual parenting partnerships identified fewer problems in the children than did the mothers. These findings imply that lesbian co-parents may enjoy greater compatibility with their partners and thus achieve a particularly high level of parenting skills. Indeed, the studies showed that lesbian partners enjoyed a greater level of agreement than heterosexual couples. A higher degree of consensus cut down on conflict in the home, enabling a clear message of love and support to be heard by the kids.

Research suggests that mothers—whether maverick or traditional—tend to be more invested and skilled at child care than fathers, and mothers are more apt than fathers to engage in the kinds of child-care activities that appear particularly crucial to children's emotional and social development. "I take responsibility for my son's education, for bringing him up, offering him love, affection, and support," one lesbian mother told me. She also offered up a measure of tough love when necessary. When her 9-year-old son swiped from a friend a trading card he desperately wanted, she informed him that he would have to figure out how to resolve the problem he had created. "I try to point out to him whenever I can that he's in charge and that his troubles are not mine," she told me.

OUTSIDE LOOKING IN

Who would have guessed that maverick mothers would offer so much wisdom about how to raise our sons? But on closer inspection, it shouldn't be such a surprise. By choosing to break with convention and create a family in the first place, or to accept the unanticipated hand dealt to them and forge ahead with energy and determination, these mothers were not bound so tightly to the conventions that dictate for better—and often for worse—how we define and raise our families. Aware that they were operating on the outskirts of society, many of these maverick mothers have taken a hard look at all the expectations of parents and sons. Many of them have arrived at a notion of what was truly important in many aspects of their relationships with their sons—in the quality of communication, the level of intimacy, and the commitment of time and energy they know they must make.

Are the families in two-mother and single-mother households different from mine or from other traditionally structured households? On the surface they may appear to be, but in every important way, they are not. Like ours, their children are gorgeous and charming—and misbehave. Like ours, they experience ups and downs, and they have to deal with conflict within the family and with the vicissitudes of the world. The difference I found is that these maverick moms were more deliberate in how they responded to their sons and more thoughtful about the constraints of society.

Perhaps because maverick mothers had to plan so much just to have their sons, I found their parenting to be considered on almost all fronts. One mother, for example, had consciously decided "not to try to have the perfect children, not to put that pressure on them." Another enrolled in college to let her growing son "have his space." "I never quite know if my priorities are in balance where they should be," lesbian mom Connie Carlson told me with a laugh. "I wish that somebody would send me a status report each month anonymously in the mail that says: 'Well, this month you did really good on issues A, B, and C. But you need to focus more on issues D and E. So we'll be checking back with you in a month.'"

Whether through classes or networking, many of the maverick moms I interviewed actively sought new approaches to parenting and problem solving. Concerns about how they would relate to their sons had led them to hone their mothering skills in order to take advantage of those "teachable moments," as one mom called them. Still, maverick moms have to get through every day, just like the rest of us.

Single mom Fiona's son TJ was having a tough day. Nothing pleased him; nothing his mother did kept him happy for long. He had whined and complained and kicked since morning, and she was completely fed up with him. Instead of shouting at him as they walked up San Francisco's Market Street, pushing his baby brother's stroller loaded down with groceries, Fiona suddenly said, "TJ, we have to empty your shoes. All the mad you've been feeling today has puddled in your shoes, and we have to empty it out so you don't have to carry that icky stuff around." TJ immediately sat down on the sidewalk and wrenched his shoes off. They made a big show of whacking his sneakers against the pavement, producing a satisfying shower of sand. Then the 4-year-old put his shoes back on, claiming that he'd gotten all the mad out and was okay now. "Obviously, this didn't work for long, but it got us home," said Fiona. "The triumph of figuring something like that out, of getting creative when all I wanted to do was strangle my firstborn son, has stuck with me to this day."

Naturally, such moments of inspiration are interspersed with lesser parenting times, when maverick moms, like the rest of us, plunk their sons in front of the TV to buy themselves a reprieve. And just like all working mothers, they beat themselves about the ears when they have to cut corners at work. Though divorced mother and Harvard graduate Ursula Hardy loves her environmental public interest job, "there are so many things I don't do at work because I want to be with my sons Ethan, 12, and Caleb, 10, who live half the time with me, and the other with their father," she told me. "I just don't do it. Or I make sacrifices. Or I won't do an A-plus job. A perfect example is today. Last night I didn't have my kids, so I was at work until 8:00 P.M. Tonight I technically don't have my kids, but Caleb has violin, which means I have to leave work at 5:00 P.M., which is earlier than I would normally leave, to take him to violin, since his father can't. Then Ethan has a concert at school, so then Caleb and I are going to go over there. Well, on days when I don't have the kids, I would normally be working. But I'm just not going to. As a result, certain things aren't going to get done."

The lesbian and single mothers I came to know felt just terrible about what Ursula called "a perfect bad-mother moment. Tim was in Tahoe, and I had the kids for 5 straight days. I was working full-time and had very stressful work. I was doing all the drop-off, all the pickup, all the errands. I was at my wit's end. [Ethan and Caleb] were relishing the back-and-forth arguing of siblings. I woke up, and they were already at each other, with like, 'Don't swallow your food like that!' Oh, God! I reached the limit. That night I was [going to be] putting them on a train with a friend of Tim's to meet up with him. I said, 'I am so sick of your fighting back and forth. I am so glad you are going to see your father tonight!'"

The words were barely out of her mouth when "I am thinking of all the rules that I just violated. I was horrified. The scarier thing was how effective that was. It was silence." Ursula apologized that same morning while driving them to school, acknowledging that she had said something hurtful that she didn't mean and assuring them that she liked the time she spent with them. Afterward, "I felt guilty about it for an entire 24 hours. I felt so guilty, I was spilling to anybody who would listen, 'You aren't going to believe what I just did.'" Ursula might not have realized it then, but the act of apologizing to her sons was a wonderful thing. It reminded them that she was only human, just like they were, and that you can always ask for another chance when you're in a loving family.

Ursula's conscious mothering choices outweighed her occasional lapses. She showed her preteen boys that "being a man" is really just "being a person." As a boy, "you just happen to have a penis and don't have breasts. I try to tell them that being any kind of person is how you relate to yourself, how you feel about yourself, and how you relate to other people, both men and women. Life is about the connections we make in this world. It's important to be able to show respect for others, their possessions, and respect for yourself most importantly. When kids are developing, I think self-esteem is most important. I worry much more about what they think of themselves than what they think of other people or what other people think of them. That's the key. Everything that I do is to make them feel good about themselves."

As so many of us know, that kind of positive reinforcement isn't always easy, especially when our sons push us to the limit. "I have to work hard not to give in to that knee-jerk angry response," Carol said. She is the social mom of Travis, a 9-year-old boy who, she said, "is extremely self-centered. I blame us. He's an only child, and he gets a lot of adult attention. It's like he's the only kid in the world." Like all children, he has figured out how to manipulate his parents. "Travis really pushes my buttons. He calls me 'stupid' and other mildly nasty names. He does it with Lori, too, but he doesn't put as much energy into it. He knows with me he'll get a response." Carol makes a conscientious effort to work things through, giving him a time-out and then talking it through with him. "I'm really trying to come from a calm place, but I must say, he gets to me."

Most of the maverick mothers I interviewed realized that in order to raise a son who didn't wind up with a sense of entitlement, they couldn't give in to temper tantrums or other forms of manipulative behavior. One young boy would throw himself on the living room floor and rub his face on the carpet so fiercely that he would develop a rash. "It's as if he can't understand why he would be denied something," his biological mother explained to me. "We tried to explain that he was hurting himself more than us. Gradually we realized that if we just didn't respond at all, it was the best thing. He stopped when he wasn't getting a reaction from us."

WORRYING AS AN ART FORM

Raising a child has everything to do with a parent's psychological makeup. And all kidding about Mars and Venus aside, women have a head start on some of the classic mother-associated traits, whether they like it or not. Take worry. As we've seen, in every family there is always one parent who worries about the children more than the other, and it is almost always the mother. The mother consistently performs the "psychological management" of child rearing, what I call *motherthink*. Mom is the overseer, the organizer, the list maker, the keeper of inventory. Beyond over-seeing practical activities, she is also able to look out for and interpret patterns and rhythms in the child's daily life and respond accordingly.

The maverick mothers did worrying one better. They did what I call constructive worrying, using their concerns as opportunities for growth.

Single-by-choice and two-mother families chose parenthood in an atmosphere of joy, but they also knew that their sons would face special challenges. Somehow they had to prepare their open, friendly little boys for the derogatory comment or the brush-off or noninvitation that they knew was coming. So they tried to be as present as possible to keep their sons out of harm's way.

"So far we have handled the questions and comments," another mother said. "We are learning. It's a part of our family, but it is not a major part. Every family has unique attributes. We may be fortunate that ours are more visible."

Constructive worrying also means knowing when to bite your lip and keep your fears to yourself. "My son, Jackson , is extremely assertive," Denise Tauber, whom we met earlier in this chapter, told me. "He has no problem sending his restaurant food back if it's not to his satisfaction, nor is he afraid to stand in line and pay for his own drink at a stadium snack bar." She took pride in fostering this independence. "I allowed him to cook. He could pop popcorn in the microwave probably by 4½, 5. He was actually starting to cook in the microwave a lot by 5. He could cook his steamed vegetables and salmon, and he could make a baked potato. So instead of telling him that he's too young to do things," she would allow what was safe (yes to the microwave, no to the gas-burning stove).

"I encouraged him physically. He was walking by 9 months. At parks and stuff, it was hard; he was 2½ and wanting to slide down those poles that are two stories up and he had to leap out to catch on, and I would sit there underneath, ready to catch him, but I'd let him do it. I would attempt, within reason, to allow him to do physical things. I would weigh the risks, you know, is it a skinned knee or is it a broken bone? He can climb trees, and I don't know how, but he can climb a pole to the top. I think he could probably climb a rope if he had to. He's extremely physical that way."

When Helen thought about how she was going to raise her son, Mark, she watched other mothers for inspiration as well as for lessons in what not to do. "One of the things that was a big lesson to me was observing a friend of mine who was so frightened of life that she projected that onto her little boy all the time. He had serious problems with confidence and was kept back a grade. I think that letting go of some of that [concern] is really hard, but it's important. I did make sure Mark knew the rules—you've got to learn this, this is basic, and this is safety, and you've gotta do it."

Such constructive worrying helps mothers to find a way to foster their sons' autonomy. "I want him to be independent," single mom Carole Hill told me, "and to have a strong relationship. I let my 8-year-old son go over to his friends' houses for sleepovers. I let him have a life outside of us two. I want him to know that I can function without him. He doesn't need to be my husband. He doesn't need to feel like he has to take care of me. He can go to his friend's house and know his mom isn't sitting at home, waiting for him to come home and occupy her time. I think it helps him to have that separation, to know that I have a life and he has a life outside of our relationship."

Treating their sons as full people also entailed helping them to become as well-rounded and self-reliant as possible. "My father taught me how to squirrel hunt," Mary Beth Lenardi, the single mother of Arianna, 4, and David, just 5 months, both adopted from South America, told me with some pride. "My father taught me about my car; my father taught me how to nail, hammer, saw. He said, 'You need to know.'" Mary Beth was far from worried that her son—or her daughter, for that matter—would experience the lack of a father. "The father in me will teach them because my father did me," she told me.

GOING FOR CORE STRENGTH

Mothers of these boys recognized, celebrated, and built their sons' inner and physical strength. "I think it has always been my approach to show and give love and compassion to our sons," Cora, a businesswoman, wrote to me. "As a result, I see in [my two grown sons] an appreciation for others and their thoughts and feelings. They have developed the ability to deal with others with empathy and understanding. But they are not 'wusses,' either. They are ready and willing to stand up for what they believe is right and have no trouble pushing back in discussions with their peers or with me."

The assertiveness to stand up for oneself that the maverick mothers encouraged should not be confused with the unbridled aggression that is seen in so many boys. Most moms I studied pointedly taught their sons to opt for brain over brawn and helped them develop verbal skills to deal with conflict. "I don't want Malcolm to be a kid in a corner of the playground with all the kids beating on him," said his mom, Lynn Thompson. Malcolm is only 2, but she was already working on how he handled frustrations and making sure the "no hitting" rule was consistently and gently enforced. "I want him to be able to stand up for himself and say, 'That's not cool. Let's not do that.' If he needs to be able to, I want him to be strong enough to defend himself if he's being chased, or whatever happens. I am not afraid of aggressiveness in him, but I do want him to be aware of it. In our house, we're not allowed to hit or be aggressive. I don't want him giving unsolicited punches to people. I don't hit him. You don't hit a kid when you're telling him not to hit because then they're getting two messages, and they don't understand." She prepared herself for how she'd handle playground interactions and what she'd tell her son about how people should be treated. "Maybe there'll be some cool kids, and kids that aren't cool, because that's what school is. But don't bully those kids. Bullying is never acceptable, whatever the situation. Don't let yourself be bullied, and don't bully anybody else."

Despite these mothers' best intentions, sometimes things simply spiraled out of control. As the saying goes, shit happens. Boys made the best choices they could under the circumstances, especially when it came to having problems in the sometimes brutally Darwinian preadolescent and adolescent school culture. Occasionally those choices just don't work out.

"We switched to a public school that I thought was supposed to be great," Helen told me, "and Mark didn't tell me that he was being followed and beaten up. I shouldn't say 'beaten up,' exactly, but pushed over, hit once, lying on the ground; then [the bullies would] run off." Mark was in sixth grade at the time that Helen moved him into this new school, and Helen found that he had a hard time adjusting. She continued, "So he endured, and he went months without telling me what was going on. He was very depressed. His behavior became very strange; he was cleaning up his room constantly, which was completely in contrast to his behavior before that—he was getting obsessive about it. He would start to cry over little things, and that was very unusual for him, too.

"He finally broke down one night because it was so bad. Something went wrong, some little thing he got upset about. He told me in fits and starts. And then, of course, I was *so* mad. 'Who are these kids? Where?' I was really reactive."

Helen tried helping Mark by teaching him to defend himself. Next she tried teaching Mark conflict-resolution techniques. She even had the school mediate a family conference with the troublemakers. Still, one kid continued to harass Mark.

Helen may not have been able to foresee the problem, but she sure wasn't going to tolerate it. So she finally took matters into her own hands. "Once I knew the name of this one kid, I looked up the parents in the school directory and I wrote a letter. I knew this kid's father was an attorney, I knew he would understand the language, so I wrote a letter saying their son was interfering with my son's education and if it didn't stop that I would take further action. And that kid never came within 5 feet of Mark thereafter. Mark knew about the letter, and he wasn't real happy about it, but he wasn't unhappy enough to stop me. If he had tried to stop me, I would have said, 'You've tried self-defense, we've tried going through the vice-principal, and it really is time that we do this now.' It was clear to me. You can only work with your own kid; you can't control other kids. And it's dangerous. My feeling is, I've got to stand up for my own. That's not a bad thing for a kid to see. If my kid sees that his mother will stand up for him, and protect him and fight for him, that's a good thing."

DOING IT MOM'S WAY

Not all conflicts can be solved easily. Austin was a shy, sensitive, high-needs kid, the kind who could happily save part of his allowance for the homeless and the next minute be wailing over some imagined slight. Over the years it had been hard for his two moms to stay out of arguments with him, even about trivial things. Age hadn't helped. "We've been having traumatic times with Austin lately," Kathy told me. "He's getting older, heading into puberty. He's been very emotional. He didn't want to go to a Passover seder with good friends of ours. He just decided he wasn't going to go because another friend would be bringing his daughter and there would be two girls there and he didn't want to be the only boy. I told him we go to these things as a family and that it's important to do things as a family, so we went, but we were late, and when we got there, he went crying upstairs and refused to come down. He came down for the meal and actually relaxed enough to talk to the men and had an okay time.

"Then, just the next week, I asked him to take something upstairs for me and he had a complete fit. I guess he was tired—there'd been a sleepover and a ball game, so that could've been the reason—but there's really no excuse for that kind of overreacting. He was yelling and calling me lazy and just being wretched, so it escalated and got louder and louder. He just goes into his 'I don't wanna talk about it' mode, and all we can do is wait it out."

Bianca added, "After a change of scene, he feels better and can be affectionate again. He really pushes the boundaries; he's always testing. One time I found myself arguing that he had to do what I was saying because I was older. We've invested a great deal of time and energy into making him feel that he has rights, but then, as the parent, I heard that coming out of my mouth! And I was one of those people who had a bumper sticker on my car for years that said 'Question Authority.' What a hypocrite I would be if I told Austin he had to toe the line simply because I said so. He really requires that everything be explained. Sometimes things can't be explained very well, but he insists on trying. I guess that's good because it forces me as a parent and as a person to explain myself. I used to really see it as a challenge. Now I understand that he is a very intelligent person and this is his way."

In my interviews, nonauthoritarian parenting was the rule rather than the exception. "I try to explain things to Nathan so it will seem fair, rather than just saying, 'I'm your mother and you must listen to me,'" social mom Stephanie told me.

Allowing boys to define themselves and find strength in those identities didn't mean that these moms relinquished responsibility for them. Far from it.

"If you said, 'Here's your Mother Kit. You can only pack three or four things,' what would I put in there?" Martha Lester postulated during our interview, "I would put, number one, I have to be the model, I have to embody what I want him to be, which keeps me very honest. Number two, I have to be honest with him at an appropriate level because the worst thing that you can do is say one thing that is not true because it'll screw his head up. Three, observe appropriate boundaries: 'I'm the mother. I'm not your friend. I'm not your best pal or Santa Claus. I'm your mother. There are limits to what you can do as a human being, and there are limits to life, and there are limits to your relationship with me. For one thing, you're not sleeping in my bed.' The other day he climbed into my bed, which I admit is the most comfortable bed on the planet, and he said, 'Sleep in my bed.' And I said, 'In a parallel universe, big guy. When you build a universe, you can build it that way; meanwhile, this is my universe. Go to bed.'" Clearly, a sense of humor would also be included in Martha's Mother Kit.

It isn't always easy to walk the line between being a disciplinarian and showing empathy. By disciplining with a quiet word rather than a heavy hand and by including their sons as consultants in the definition and execution of good behavior, these maverick moms model compassion and encourage open dialogue, even when more inclined to a rash, high-volume response.

When Ursula's son Ethan got in trouble with the parents of a friend, she stepped in as both The Mom and as a sympathetic listener. "Ethan was disrespectful to the parent when the parent tried to discipline her own child," Ursula remembered. "From my perspective, Ethan should have respected the parent and let the parent be the parent. But from Ethan's perspective, he was being loyal to his friend. His friend was being accused of something he hadn't done, according to Ethan. He shouldn't have gotten in trouble. Ethan felt like he needed to defend him. I listened to his reasons and said, 'I understand that you were defending your friend. Try to put yourself in the position of the parent. What would you be thinking?' I told him how I would feel if I were the parent. If my child is doing something wrong, I am the parent and my child is the child. It's important to me that I don't have somebody who is trying to interfere with my interaction with my child. 'So from my perspective,' I told him, 'you were acting inappropriately because you were interfering with what I, as an adult and a mother of your friend, was doing.'"

At the same time, Ursula was proud of her son for standing up for his friend, so they also discussed how something can be right and wrong at the same time, and how time and place are both factors. "I always use the example of table manners. Is it okay to lick your plate? Well, in my house it's okay if you get your mom's permission first. Is it okay in your grandmother's house? Absolutely not. You wouldn't even ask for permission. What about in a restaurant? That's a good example of something being appropriate in one circumstance and not another. I try to use that to show why speaking out and saying what you really feel might be appropriate somewhere but not somewhere else."

In the end Ethan wrote an apology to his friend's mom, explaining why he had piped up and apologizing for his interference. He didn't have to concede that she had been right, only that he was sorry for his part in the drama. "He is such a good friend," Ursula told me. "He will do so much for his friends. I don't want to squash that" by coming down hard on his impulse to defend his friend.

FLEXING NEW MOM MUSCLES

Sometimes, mental mothering requires that we not just talk the talk but walk the walk, no matter how challenging or uncomfortable. One night while I was at home relaxing after reading my daughter Katherine a bedtime story, the loud ring of a phone startled us both. When I picked up, my friend Bonnie, single mother of two sons, launched into a tirade about her older son, Bert. The 20-something-year-old had decided at the last minute that despite the promise he had made to his mother, he wouldn't have time to coach his 9-year-old brother Keith's basketball team. Bonnie was furious. The team was set and all the players raring to go. But without a coach, they wouldn't go far.

Finally I managed to get a word in edgewise. "Why don't you coach the team?" I asked meekly, knowing that she had recently left her law practice to spend more time with Keith. Bonnie, a Yale Law School graduate who had run a law firm successfully, supervising both male and female attorneys, stopped midsentence. The silence lasted a nanosecond. Then she proceeded to enumerate all the reasons it wouldn't work: She couldn't possibly coach, since she hadn't played basketball in years; the team would never accept a female coach; her son would be ashamed.

After further discussion, Bonnie reversed her initial position. Maybe she could handle the position. Not only did she love to watch the game; she had secretly always wanted to teach. So why not basketball? It would be fun to devise strategy and plans; she could provide a different model from last year's hypercompetitive coach.

The move proved advantageous to mother, son, and the rest of the players. The team did well (a tribute to her coaching abilities), and her son couldn't have been prouder that his mother was the first female to coach in his league. Tackling her fears and proving that she had the right stuff set an example that Keith could emulate growing up and, indeed, throughout the rest of his life.

These days we mothers get to be everything from nursemaids to coaches. That variety of roles is key to *mompower* making manpower. "One thing I think my boys saw," Frances Lee, a divorced mother of four who felt she was raising her children alone even when she had been married, reminisced, "is that I did make choices. Whether they were things they liked or not is something else again. Like leaving their father. But they did see that if I decided I needed to make a change in my life, I did. I don't think they ever got the idea that you couldn't act on something. Whether they choose to is different. But they didn't see a mom who was afraid to do anything, go outside, or make changes in her own life. I think they accept that's how I am. We've never really had a discussion about that, but I do know that [my son's] wife, Melinda, is very outgoing. She's the one who is the hard worker who leaves home, who does the traveling."

Mompower doesn't require perfect mothering. Mimi Silbert, who divorced after separating from her husband when her twin boys were quite young, can enumerate her flaws as a person and as a mother, and then assert that she is happy with the package. She feels that she has shown her sons her strengths as well and that the combination has made them stronger, better people. She admitted to me that her two boys are so good-natured, "they'd say things like 'Thank you, Mom. Dinner was delicious' every night. You don't thank mothers for dinners. Mothers cook dinners, and you don't say thank you for dinner. They're just sweet, completely generous souls, and still are. But strong-willed, not easily bendable."

THE VALUE OF VALUES

Conscious, confident mothers find plenty of ways to express their own values and to challenge outworn ideas. So many of the maverick mothers I interviewed infused their sons with a sense of social responsibility. "We talk to our son about treating people the way we like to be treated, about differences and why certain people act a certain way, and giving people another chance," one lesbian mom told me. Other mothers sent their sons to inclusive religious schools where ethics were taught and community service (like making sandwiches for the homeless) was practiced. Most emphasized to their sons how lucky they were to be more privileged than others, and regularly discussed how to treat those who were less fortunate. "We talk a lot about homeless people and why they're there, and about people with AIDS who we've had in our lives who aren't there anymore," a maverick mother explained. "We give money and food to homeless people, invite people over, give people rides, watch people's kids so they [can] do something else if they [are] having a hard time."

For Martha Lester, the divorced mom whose husband left her high and dry, sharing her values has meant continuing a story her father had told her when she was a girl. "I've been telling my son Riley, now 10, the Max stories for years. Max is a kid who was raised by people who turned out to not be his parents because his parents were locked in a tower far away, and to get them, Max has to capture three stones, and one is truth, one is respect, and one is responsibility. And those are sort of the three pillars. He knows that the three things he can do to really get in trouble are to lie, to be disrespectful to someone, and to shirk his duties." The allegory continues, with Max's bird-assistant, Petey, who is Reason. Martha's stories have all the trappings of a classic morality tale. Riley loves the story as much as Martha used to. "I make it up as we go," Martha said with a laugh. "We had a whole one about greed because he wanted a PlayStation, which I refused to get. In the story, by not taking something that was really enticing that would have only benefited him, Max got a stone in the crown. I tell it in a fable, and Riley gets it; he doesn't miss the points."

Martha knew that even her evolved storytelling was not enough. "I appreciate everything in my life because it has not come easily, and I give voice to that, hoping that Riley grows up understanding the importance of appreciation. If he can grow up with those things—respect, compassion, truth, knowing himself, valuing himself—to me that's more important than learning how to fence or speaking French. And if I don't model those things, he ain't gonna get it. I gotta walk the walk."

As a result, Riley is learning to see beyond the trappings of modern life and into the emotional lives of his peers. "Riley has figured out that with one of the richest kids in the class, his parents are never there, they're always socializing, they're always busy, they're much older parents, and he says to me, 'Jason is a lonely boy.'"

The mothers I studied could be painfully open with their sons, usually through necessity. When a boy's mother experienced extremes of either emotional or physical hardship, her son necessarily had to process them as well. She could try to shield him, but he was inevitably affected. Martha went through several life-shattering changes while Riley watched. "He saw his mother go from a huge corporate executive to this person lying on the couch in my friend's house with a suitcase, a box of toys, and 1,500 bucks and wondering, 'Okay, now what happens?' We lost everything, we lost our home, we lost our connections, I lost my career, he'd lost his father, and I had lost my husband. We were homeless for 6 months. I think he had to reach into reserves that other kids can't even fathom.

"There were times when I felt so badly that I just didn't have the energy to do what I felt a Martha Stewart mother should do. And I think he learned to live with someone who had to accept her own limitations. I always tried to articulate it on an appropriate level without burdening him with my psyche—my psyche was my business—but I would have to say, 'I'm very sad today. Can we do something quiet because I don't have a lot of energy?'"

Emotional honesty is a key building block when it comes to making head-and-heart boys into men. Ruben Gur, M.D., professor of neuropsychology at the University of Pennsylvania, concluded that men deal with emotions more on a basic animal level, whereas women will sit and talk about them. An emotional man can lash out like a wounded rhino, while an emotional woman will just talk.

When a woman is communicating with emotion, she uses expressive facial signals, body language, and a range of speech patterns. A man who switches on emotions is more likely to go into animal mode and become verbally or physically aggressive. The woman's way of dealing with emotions is, needless to say, a more desirable model for boys dealing with conflict and stress.

LISTEN UP

That doesn't mean that these boys, just like every other boy in creation, don't test their mothers, taxing both their patience and their ingenuity. Listen in again on Carol, Travis's social mom. "Right now, Lori is *it*, and I'm chopped liver," she said, acknowledging that her heavy workload as an architect, plus a part-time school schedule, impinged on how much time she had to spend with her son. Undaunted by his obvious preference for her partner, Lori—his biological mother—and by behavior toward her that at times bordered on disrespectful, Carol set limits on his back talk but at the same time reached out to Travis whenever she could. Once, she suggested that he show her around his classroom when they arrived early at school, since she hadn't seen it lately. "I'm expecting him to say *No!* because he's been treating me like dirt. But he said okay, and I thought: 'Where'd this kid come from?'" Clearly, her efforts mattered to both of them. "Even though right now I'm chopped liver," she said, "I'm still an important side dish."

Lori and Carol know instinctively what Harvard researchers have confirmed—that laughing serves as a system of defenses against adversity. The Grant study on men's development followed the lives of 268 men from the time they were college grads until middle age, some 35 years later, and examined how men coped with dreams and how they adjusted to life, whether they achieved those dreams or not. It was found that those men who had learned to laugh at themselves were among those rated "best adapted" in the study.

Listening to our sons boosts their self-esteem and shows them that they are valuable family members. But that's not always as simple as it sounds.

Austin, son of biological mom Kathy Blanchard and social mom Bianca Rollins, was infamous in his family for his "I don't wanna talk about it" moods, but his mothers persisted in listening even to his silences. The 10-year-old was all about baseball. "If you talked to him," Kathy laughed, "and you knew something about baseball, whether you were a man or a woman or a frog, he would talk to you ad nauseam about baseball." This enthusiasm translated into wanting to play baseball, even though his natural ability wasn't as well developed as that of some of his peers.

Kathy continued, "Austin played in his first baseball league last fall. It was his first experience of a coach other than us or a guy at school, and everyone played every position and it was really non-competitive. Now he's in Little League—forget it. No matter what they say about how we're all here to have fun, it's actually deadly serious. They have eliminations, and the better players get more playing time, and there's a World Series and everything."

Austin, the boy who loved baseball, hated everything about the experience. He didn't like the coach. And the coach, who didn't allow Austin to play after the team made it to the playoffs, and then wouldn't allow him to leave the dugout because he was crying, "pretty clearly didn't care for him either—or for his two mothers, for that matter." Things went from bad to worse when Bianca, swept up in the Little League drama as well, made a tactical error. She explained, "Austin told me how unfair he thought the coach had been. Instead of commiserating with him and agreeing that the coach's behavior had sucked—which it clearly had—I said something about how that's life and he'd better get used to it. Austin got very angry because he thought I was defending the coach. That's how he is. He's very quick to feel misunderstood, and that turns to anger."

Austin's anger with his mother and all things baseball didn't last, in part because his mothers recognized how deeply hurt he was as much from what he didn't say as from what he did. Finally, they convinced him to share his distress. Once they understood his perspective, instead of telling him to buck up again, they took action and managed to get him on a different team the following season.

"Parenting is more challenging than I believed it would be," Bianca confessed to me. "Some weeks I think I've got it down, and then other weeks it's like I'm in a daze. Parenting is a damn hard job. I wasn't prepared for how hard it would be. Kathy and Austin and I are learning to be a family all at the same time."

Like Bianca, the mothers in my research told me stories that pointed to their determination to be good listeners and good teachers. These single and lesbian mothers also talked about how hard they tried to avoid the traditional stance of Mother Knows Best. That's a hard row to hoe, and sometimes children need solid, no-nonsense limit setting. Even though some of these mothers may appear to have been striving for the unrealistic goal of perfect serenity, their willingness to respect their sons' feelings—no matter what they were—had a phenomenal impact on their sons' self-respect and autonomy. These are the building blocks of character. And every one of the mothers, even though they sometimes acted like the rest of us and lost their tempers and yelled, rejected the old, authoritarian view of parenting in favor of a more connected relationship.

Thinking about maverick mothers and how they are raising their sons, I began to reflect on their choices in their own lives. I bet that very few of them, when they were growing up, expected that they would raise a family without a live-in father. They didn't plan to choose a path less traveled. But once they set themselves on that path, or life put them there, they marshaled all their energy into the service of raising sons mindfully. These single and lesbian mothers are subject to the same limitations of time and patience that plague us all, but they consciously try to limit the burden their unconventional lives place on their kids. In the process, they are presenting us with a model of thoughtful parenting that we all—moms and dads alike—should take very seriously. And as you will see in the next chapter, the work of creating strong emotional bonds pays off over the course of a lifetime.

WHEN RAISING BOYS, MAVERICK MOMS:

- Build up their sons' confidence and self-esteem by promoting their independence and allowing them to test their limits.

- Exercise the power they have to influence their sons by monitoring their activities, even when that means taking the time to find other options that are less competitive and more rewarding.

- Worry constructively, using their concerns about their sons to see the patterns in their lives and provide opportunities for growth.

- Encourage their sons' humanity through their willingness to admit their own human failings.

- Recognize and teach the value of humor, a survival mechanism proven to serve as a system of defenses against adversity and an indicator of men's success later in life.

- Involve their sons in decision making and value their input, giving the boys a chance to speak their minds.

- Model the behavior they want their sons to emulate, and set examples of strength and compassion.

CHAPTER SEVEN

STAYING CONNECTED

"One thing you would not want to see is me up on a trampoline. I'm not real athletic. But I have been up there with my son."

—*Georgina Ewers, single adoptive mother of five*

DESPITE SEVERAL BEST-SELLING BOOKS about boys' need for emotional connection, mothers persist in believing that their love and protection will somehow weaken or emasculate their boys. Like a lot of mothers, I was very concerned about ensuring that my son's masculinity remained intact. I was stuck on the psychologically inspired notion that a boy has to be rescued from his mother in order to develop a sure sense of his masculinity. Women feed on young boys, according to fairy tales such as *Hansel and Gretel*, in which a cruel stepmother persuades a loving father to abandon his children in the woods so there will be more food for the two of them to eat. Ultimately a wicked witch pushes Hansel into the oven and tries to make him her dinner. Beware of engulfing hungry females, we are taught. A son must either love and be loved, or achieve. By choosing Mom, a son loses his chance at success.

Given such pervasive notions, one might conclude that maverick mothers opting to raise boys without fathers in the home would be more likely to "smotherlove" their sons, pulling them too close and encouraging neither independence nor adventure. One would be wrong. Instead, I found that for maverick mothers and their sons, "mutual recognition" was as significant a developmental goal as separation. The issue for these mothers was not how their sons could become free of them but how to actively engage and make themselves and their sons known to each other in their relationships. Whereas traditional theories stress a son's independence from his mother as a primary goal of child development, maverick mothers saw mutual knowing as important. And that has led to connections that in all likelihood will last a lifetime.

BOY TIME

Helen Lewis's son, Mark, started rearranging the furniture as soon as he could walk. "Everything was spatial," the 49-year-old hospice social worker recalled. "His speech seemed almost undeveloped compared to his cousins', and having been around girls all my life as a child [since I had three sisters], I was expecting him to be more verbal in a clear way rather than a jumble of . . . we didn't know what. By age 2, he started drawing the same-shaped object over and over again that he seemed very confident meant something, but I had no idea what it was."

The images turned out to be crude versions of the space shuttle. Just 2 years later, Mark's *Star Trek* fascination, which would last for years, kicked in. "So he was really born with a different kind of brain than I had been," said Helen, who majored in anthropology in college, favored Shirley Temple musicals, and assiduously shied away from anything that smacked of math and science. "But I just thought, 'Hey, you know, this is him, and you've got to empower that and make it a positive thing.' . . . At that phase of my life, I found it pretty interesting. He was teaching me."

Helen divorced Mark's father when Mark was just 2½. "There was a lot of turmoil, not only during that first year of separation, but at different phases as Mark went along in life, different philosophies between my ex and me. I knew it was key for me to make Mark as comfortable as possible in a social setting so he wouldn't be overinfluenced by what I saw as his dad's agoraphobic tendencies."

Helen, who was clearly thinking of the long road ahead and planning for her son's emotional and social success, believed that a big part of her entire relationship with Mark had to involve a lot more than doing the dishes and just getting through the house-work. She felt if she gave up that bond with her son, Mark was going to be raised by his peers and not by her. So she made sure that she and Mark shared pastimes and hobbies. "Even a movie or going to the trading card store, where he has to show me every card, means a lot to him—and me." Mark relished teaching her what he knew. "Mark loved to run up to me and show me some-thing he'd done or something he'd found, something he was learning about and wanted to teach me. And I tried very hard not to be patronizing—but 'Wow, how do I learn more? Tell me more about that.'"

When Mark was 13, the year after he changed from a private school and Helen had taken care of the bullies, he got into trouble in school. His grades slipped. Helen knew something was up, so she arranged a meeting with him. "I had it outside the home, at a coffee shop. There are too many environmental cues in our home that are way too 'little kid.' Taking Mark somewhere else, I made it much more an adult kind of conversation. And it's neutral. It takes Mark out of that 'Mom's looking at the dirty socks' while he's thinking, 'Oh, God, I'm going to get nagged about something.' So I took a domestic piece out of it."

The meeting focused not on how upset Helen was with Mark's behavior—which she was. As she described it, the conversation was instead on "how are we going to solve this? And really sitting down and working on the solution and less on the emotional. And then also kicking around 'How is it going to work best with this version of the picture, and how is it going to work best with that version of the picture?' Not just how Mark was going to catch up with his work but how in the bigger picture he was going to rearrange what he had been doing so that the whole rest of the year would work well for him." Her question to Mark, "How are you going to regain the respect of your teachers?" was perhaps most significant of all.

Helen and her son learned from each other, with his interests actually compelling Helen to broaden her own world. Helen showed me how much she had learned from her son over the years as she described Mark's arc from space shuttle–obsessed toddler to Air Force cadet. "When Mark was 9, I took him to this big flight convention. I was always taking him to all of these, and going to see movies about space, and kind of getting into it, too, but mostly it was feeling the need to find practical avenues for this obsession, rather than just buying everything he wanted."

Despite his passion for planes, physics, and engineering, Mark's decision to apply to the Air Force Academy came as an enormous shock for Helen. "I'm very much an ex–Vietnam peace marcher type, so just the thought of it was very hard for me," Helen confessed to me. Helen prayed that the fierce competition for academy slots would knock Mark out of the running and she wouldn't have to worry about the military implications. "But then he got in," and she had to adapt. "Here I am, I'm going to these family events, and—much to my surprise—they were very interesting. These Air Force cadets, for the most part, are in science and engineering—they're extremely bright. Strange as it felt, I was impressed by these people. And Mark was loving it." Still, when Mark lost his spot due to his asthma condition, his mother saw it as a "godsend." Mark appealed the decision, and at the time of my study, he was waiting to hear if he would be reinstated. Helen had already decided that if he got back in, she would "grit her teeth" and support his decision.

That Helen was able to handle having Mark involve himself in an arena that she personally and politically couldn't support—without losing her connection with him—is a testament to her mothering abilities. "We always kept the dialogue open. I'd say, 'Yeah, I can see that. Now, the only thing I'd worry about in your shoes is this.' And 'What do you think of that?' Instead of saying, 'Oh, this is a phase, isn't that cute,' I treated him like an adult, with respect. As much as I was tempted, I felt that it was important not to treat Mark's chosen direction as a fad. I tried my very best to see his choice as part of his growth, that it was going to have long-term, life-affecting implications for him. I took it seriously and wasn't heavy-handed or judgmental—which isn't to say I haven't had my moments—but I really tried to focus on the bigger picture, and I feel that Mark and I are closer now than we have ever been as a result. As long as Mark knows that I will be listening, and as long as I know he's going to be listening to me, I believe, hope, and pray this dialogue will continue."

Strong bonds between mothers and sons are a lifelong source of strength, independence, and a sense of connectedness. We hear this from the athletes who thank their mothers who raised them without a father. We heard it from President Bill Clinton, who routinely expressed his affection for his mother and his gratitude for her sacrifice. And we have learned from the single and lesbian mothers I studied that there are a million ways to foster genuine closeness and intimacy. Research is indicating that the more open and respectful a mother and son can be in the early years, the more robust that relationship will be in years to come.

The old-fashioned worry about smothering our sons or making them sissies should no longer concern us. But it still does. Not long ago, I was sitting in a park, watching my 11-year-old daughter play with some friends. Another mother was sitting nearby, keeping an eye on her young son. The little boy—about 4 years old, I'd estimate—took a minor tumble at the end of the slide. He stood up, looked around for Mom, and ran straight for her. I watched as he clambered into her lap, looking for a little comfort and reassurance. His mom held him lightly, but she pulled away from his embrace. "You're fine," she said. He ducked his head and dived toward her neck again, intent on physical contact. She leaned even further back, rejecting his nuzzling hug. "Go on back to the slide, now," she said. "You're a big boy!" Looking a little abashed and disappointed, her son turned away and was soon engrossed in play again. But the interaction left me wondering why she had shut him out and whether her boy was being pushed to be tough when what he needed was a hug.

Demonstrating mother love doesn't hurt our boys. Quite the reverse. "My son, Logan, is smothered in hugs and kisses," one single mother wrote me. "Raising him with so much affection and hands-on support is not turning him into a mama's boy or weakening him in any way—it's just the opposite. Logan enters new environments and greets new people assuming he is going to be adored the way he is at home. He is loving, generous, playful, and very at ease socially. He kisses strangers in the street, sits down to play with children he has never met, and laughs when another child is physically aggressive with him, turning it into a game, so that two kids who could have been hitting or crying if [the situation had been] handled differently are new friends instead."

Mothers still worry that their demonstrative mothering style will make their sons too dependent. "Ralph is 3½ years old, and Daniel is 4½ months," a mom in a two-mother family in Taos, New Mexico, wrote me recently. "I have already found myself wondering if we are too soft on Daniel, not because I think he needs to be a 'little man,' but because I hear the shouts of society saying, 'Boys need to be tough.'"

I believe that's bad news for society and for the boys themselves. Children gain strength and self-reliance from being loved and respected, not from having their needs ignored. We know that adults who have trouble experiencing—much less expressing—their feelings are at risk for high blood pressure and heart attack. It's not good for you, experts tell us, to ignore your feelings. So toughening up a 3-year-old or not hugging a crying child simply isn't a solution.

Boys are actually more fragile than girls medically as well as emotionally. Not only are boys more susceptible to birth defects and developmental disabilities; they're more vulnerable even in the womb, with more male fetuses lost in miscarriages. As children, they are more easily stressed, which means they cry more when they are upset and have a harder time calming down. And they are more emotionally vulnerable to the ill effects of extreme lack of affection. As a result, boys need more of their mothers' love, not less. All too often, they don't get it.

The myth that mothers need to pull back from their sons persists. "How can I stop my [15-year-old] son from being distant?" a mother asked an expert in a recent article. She went on to describe their previous close relationship, one where he talked openly with her and they shared the details of their lives. As an adolescent, however, her son turned away from her and began confiding in, it seemed to her, everyone *but* his mother. How had she gone from having an important role in her son's emotional life to having absolutely none?

Instead of acknowledging this mother's importance to her teenage son—or her love—the expert castigated her for wishing for an earlier time, when they had a different kind of relationship. "You're selfishly concentrating on how his maturing and reaching outside the maternal bond is affecting you, and ignoring the progress it reflects in him." This poor mother was told, in essence, that her boy's reliance on others was a sign of maturity and that his inability to respect his mother's need for more communication was in fact a good thing.

This expert's analysis that only by severing his ties with his mother could this teenager engage in the formation of his adult male identity is nothing new, though that doesn't make it any less misguided. Maturity in a boy doesn't amount to separating from his mother but rather replacing that bond—or the childish forms of closeness—with more adult forms of closeness. Dislocation, separation, or cutting off is not the way to go if your son's emotional health is of concern.

CEMENTING BONDS

The mothers I studied recognized early on that connecting with their sons often meant bucking conventional maternal gender roles, challenging societal dictums about right and wrong ways to mother boys, and creating parenting styles based on individual boys.

Marilyn Hendricks, divorced 2 years before, regularly took her 4-year-old into the wilderness or to the beach for camping expeditions. Why? That was her idea of a great time and something she wanted to share with her son. As a result, he's a trouper, and the two have become quite a team.

This particular kind of mompower is easier for some than for others. Ease, however, is not the governing criterion. Witness all those moms who stretch themselves beyond their comfort zones to provide experiences for their sons despite their reluctance, discomfort, or personal preference. They even do it with a sense of humor. "My idea of stretching myself is cooking a meal instead of microwaving a pizza," quipped Deborah Iverson, the single mother of three boys. One mother laughingly recalled the time when her child "got stuck in the chimney and I had to call the fire department to get him out. I was so far out of my comfort zone! They were real nice about it, though."

Male physicality presents a challenge for many single and lesbian moms. "There's a certain kind of energy that happens between [men and my son]," single mom Gerri Miller told me. Her 3-year-old son, Kip, was a "happy accident," but one she wouldn't trade for the world. "He likes to roughhouse a lot and [enjoys] a lot of physical contact that's a little rougher than I like to do, so I have to kind of push myself beyond my normal boundaries to do that with him. Picking him up and throwing him around. Piggyback rides. Running after him a lot. When I'm feeling like being a lot calmer, he's still 'Mom, come get me!' or 'Come and tickle me!' He asks me for it. Most of the time it's pretty fun, but he comes over to me a lot and just jumps on me. Out of nowhere. I wish there were somebody else I could foist that on more. I tend toward wanting to be a lot quieter, more analytical, more socially oriented. Sometimes he just wants to play ball or build a shooter. He's into some of these ways of looking at things and playing with things that I wouldn't have thought of and am not as inclined to do."

Whether the inclination is there or not, these moms acknowledge that they must meet their sons' needs. "Riley and I play a game at night called the kissing game," Martha Lester recalled to me, "where I'm supposed to try and get his cheek, but he hides under the blankets. And I loathe this game because I always get bonked in the nose or I have to hold him down, which I don't like to do, and somebody gets hurt. I just hate this game. So I only do it under certain conditions, not every night. Like pillow fights. I also am not a big fan of pillow fights, which he loves. But I'll tell him, 'For 5 minutes, until 8:17, we will have a pillow fight, and at 8:17 and not a minute later, we will stop.' I do it because it's something he enjoys."

Pushing themselves means just saying yes when they'd much rather say no. "One thing you would not want to see," Georgina Ewers, 51, told me with a grim expression on her face, "is me up on a trampoline. I'm not real athletic. But I have been up there with my son. Actually, a lot of parenting has been outside my comfort zone. I try to remember the rowdiness of my brother when we were growing up."

So many of the maverick mothers I spoke with knew how to find—and make—those moments of intimacy with their sons. Georgina has five adopted kids, including one "special needs" child born with Down syndrome, and is single by choice. Her 20-year career in Child Protective Services (CPS) gave her the skills and knowledge to deal with the unique challenges of adopting older children, as well as children of a different race than hers. Her daughter Mariah, a Hispanic girl, arrived at age 9 [and during my study was 20-something] when Georgina was 40. Eight years later came the baby, Elijah; then Gabrielle, age 9, who had been through nine other foster-care placements before landing on Georgina's doorstep; and, finally, two Hispanic brothers, Jorge and Miguel, ages 6 and 7, whose family of nine siblings was scattered into foster care when their grandmother died and their mother could not take care of them.

Now retired from CPS, Georgina is a full-time stay-at-home mom who isn't looking to get married. As she pointed out to me, the relationship between a mother and a father takes time and energy, and that has to come from somewhere. That explains why a counselor recently commented that her oldest child wouldn't have made it in a traditional mom-dad setting, where she would have had to compete for parental attention. She may well be right. In an interesting refutation to those family-values types who hold up the mom-and-dad configuration as the only viable family structure, a study focusing on female-headed families found that "the majority of single-mother-headed families are as successful as two-parent families in raising their children when the children are compared on measures of emotional adjustment and scholastic achievement." Also noted for their lack of conflict in child-rearing decisions, female-headed families also got along well and could rely on strong support networks.

Carl, a very verbal 4½-year-old who is the youngest of three boys that single-by-choice Deborah Iverson adopted from Guatemala, received an Elvis costume from his aunt Ann. White satin, red scarf, stand-up collar, red inset in the bell-bottoms, gold zipper up the front, and brass studs all around the top—the works. Carl loved it. "Mom, I need a guitar and a microphone," he announced. Deborah responded that he needed more accoutrements.

"What?"

"Accoutrements," Deborah answered. "Like a guitar and a microphone."

"Yeah," he agreed. "And one of those silver balls that's up in the ceiling."

When he called his aunt Ann, at his mother's urging, to thank her for the outfit, he said, "Aunt Ann, I love my Elvis costume, thank you. But I need accoutrements."

The maverick mothers I came to know emphasized not just talking to and with their children but really getting to know them as people. After the death of his grandmother, Georgina's son

Miguel had trouble communicating what he was feeling and started acting out instead. Georgina proposed that they plant a garden together. "He's been absolutely fascinated by that garden. One of the things we have to do fairly early every day is go out and check the garden. We look at the different blooms that have opened up during the night and that kind of stuff. We spend a lot of time talking as we're doing that. Something will come up, and it will be about his grandmother. I feel real close to him when he talks about her because that was such a major loss for him. I knew at the time that she died that I was going to be getting [Miguel and his brother], and I was so sorry that I could not be with him through that."

Georgina consciously encouraged both boys in their expressions of physical affection. "They're constantly coming in to get a hug or give a hug. Or to say 'I love you.' They're very affectionate children. I've tried very hard to encourage that because I don't think there have been many hugs in their life."

Maverick moms connected with their sons any way they could. "Jose liked to play basketball," single mother of two boys Maria Gonzalez told me. "He asked me one day if we could go play basketball, and I started playing with him because I think he was feeling a little bit left out. We're always talking to Eduardo, not because we don't want to talk to Jose but because Jose was so quiet at the time. Playing basketball with him was a way to spend time together and talk a little bit more, and get to know how he feels. At the time I was working all day and I was tired, but I was out there playing basketball with him. At the beginning, I thought it would be dribble, shoot, dribble, shoot, not anything joyful. When we started playing, he was different. He was fun and I enjoyed it.

"We got closer. I'll talk to him about whatever he wants to talk about. Usually, he'll talk about music. That's what I've been doing with the basketball. I don't mind. I'll do whatever. I want to be close to him."

INTIMACY BEGETS INTIMACY

Once the closeness between mother and son is established, it doesn't go away. Frances Lee's children grew up watching their mother make difficult choices. "I wasn't afraid to do anything, including making some drastic changes in my own life," Frances, the divorced mother of four grown children, two boys and two girls, told me. "I started by leaving their father, then going to law school. It was clear to me that I had to show my kids how to make their own way by making mine first." That didn't mean that she had to give up or lessen the intimacy she shared with her children.

"I hadn't seen my older son, Kevin, for a week—I'd been away, he'd been at school, it was a combination of things. But I really wanted to see him now that I was back." When she arrived to pick him up at his soccer game, it was nearly halftime. Her then boyfriend, who had tagged along for the ride, suggested that they find seats.

"No, I want to see Kevin first. I'll meet you in the stands."

"C'mon, Fran. He doesn't want to see you on the field, in front of his friends. He'll die of embarrassment," the boyfriend argued.

The halftime gun sounded, and the players began to trot back to their respective benches. Kevin caught sight of his mom, who waved and quickly started toward her son. Instead of ducking his head and pretending he'd never seen her before, as the boyfriend anticipated, the adolescent yelled, "Mom!" and dashed across the field to her, all but knocking her over with a sweaty hug. "I'm so glad to see you!"

From the start, Frances treated her sons not as males but as people. "I don't remember having any gender-specific behaviors in my mind about how a boy should be or how a boy should be treated, in terms of being treated differently from a girl," she told me. "Even as they grew up, if I was wondering how they were feeling or what was bothering them, I asked, and I never assumed that they wouldn't know or that they wouldn't respond. I didn't buy into the male stereotype, and neither did they."

Denise, the older single mom who retired from business to raise her son, told her son at least once a day that he was loved. "I have to say, 'Have I told you? I think I forgot to tell you something today.' So he says to me, in this voice dripping with sarcasm, 'I know. You love me,'" she told me with a smile. "I'm not a perfect mother by any means—I yell way too much—I don't have the patience I should with him. Still, I think all in all that we have a pretty good relationship. He's a great kid. Even when he's done something wrong, he almost always confesses. He's been getting in trouble for getting up at night and not getting his sleep, so I see him the next morning and he's got socks on, and I ask him why he's got socks on and he gets this look on his face and he says sheepishly, 'I got them on last night so I could sneak down without you hearing me walking.'"

Denise has worked on this kind of honesty since the very beginning by providing her son with, in her words, "a very child-centric" family environment, one in which she's around a lot and available to him. "He can come in and talk to me at any time, and within reason I'll stop what I'm doing," she told me. She shares her thoughts as well as her time and candidly answers her son's questions about everything from her own kidney ailment to the war in Iraq. "I think quality parenting is primarily being educated and following what you learn. [Jackson] knows he can rely on me, and he knows he can talk to me about anything," she told me. "Our family is not a true democracy, but he has every right to express his opinion. Every morning, he gets up and we have to have a cuddle. So he climbs into my bed for a while and we talk. Nighttime, he usually wants to have a cuddle, too, and we'll talk then as well. We do a lot of vacations together and spend a lot of time [together], and he has a lot of input on what we do and where we're going. I want him to feel that the world is his, is a canvas that he can make into anything he wants."

The level of emotional closeness some mothers managed to achieve with their sons surprised even them. "Mark had gone away to college, and I figured we had an adjustment to make, and so I asked him, 'Well, what would you like? Do you want me to send stuff, call more often, less often, what?' Helen told me. "And he said, 'I want you to come visit.' I was blown away. I had kind of been giving him his space—he's a grown guy; he needs to call the shots. And again, I did not want to be patronizing, saying stuff like 'Oh, I've always told him such-and-such' or 'Oh, look, his clothes are on the floor—what a surprise.' I do not like to be that way. When I am, I usually end up feeling awful. I thought it should be his call, but Mark really surprises me with 'No, it'll be really great [if you come up and visit me]. We can go out for breakfast. I want to show you this building.' And I thought, 'Well, that's cool.' I've usually taken him out to dinner with his roommate, or a friend will come along. This last time his roommate couldn't make it, so it was just him and me. I hadn't actually been out with him alone in a long time. And he said, 'I'm kind of glad for this,' and he just started telling me stuff about these relationships that he's struggled with and who he's dating."

Helen had told Mark everything he needed to know about sex at a fairly early age. But talking about intimate relationships with her grown son was a first, and she was pleased that he felt comfortable discussing friendships and romance with her. "I know he's a thoughtful guy, but he is a guy, too. One time, we were together in the car at an intersection, and there's this obviously very attractive young woman, and he's sitting in front of me, and his head is turning to watch her as she crosses the street in front of us. Later I said to him, 'FYI, I saw that, Mark.' And he burst out laughing." Helen's playful teasing of her son about his sexual interests demonstrates not only her appreciation of him as a guy with guy interests but also the ease—and the bond—they share.

PULLING SONS CLOSE

Maverick mothers work to maintain intimacy even when their sons try to push them away. Remember Quentin, the boy with a well-developed vocabulary and a love of all things Garfield? He had always been a take-charge kid. His obvious self-confidence and independence, however, didn't prevent him from being a cuddle-bunny at home. "Ever since he was little, when Sarah and I hugged each other, he would come racing over and want to be part of the hug," said Roberta. "So we would both yell, 'Group hug!' and sandwich him in the middle."

With age came self-consciousness about public displays of affection. Though Quentin still wanted to be kissed around the house, he would turn his face away if his mothers attempted to kiss him at school. "It's a guy thing," said Roberta, recalling how her son put on his "game face" even before he hit the school grounds each morning. "I think he doesn't want to be teased." So they compromised. Instead of kissing him when they dropped him off at school, his mothers would kiss him goodbye before they got there. "Do you want me to kiss you goodbye here?" they would ask some 8 to 10 blocks away. "Yeah," 8-year-old Quentin would reply. "Kiss me here." In this way, Quentin's mothers continued to feel and demonstrate affection, and Quentin continued to experience it, which was important to him, without embarrassment.

This bid for autonomy coexists with the sense of wanting to stay home with Mommy—a perfectly natural feeling. Going out into the world, risk taking, and being independent are fine, but cuddling is also nice. Many maverick mothers felt that helping their sons to lead public lives where they hid their vulnerability as needed, as well as secret lives where they could indulge in emotions, was the key to these boys' becoming—and staying—head-and-heart boys.

Though pressure for sons to separate from their mothers and shut down emotionally kicks in as early as age 8, it doesn't have to be that way. Realizing that their growing sons still really needed and wanted their mothers, the women I interviewed encouraged their sons to live in two worlds, adopting the mores of each world when appropriate. Many of the mothers I got to know encouraged their sons to alternate between cuddle-bunny at home and big boy at school. They didn't want their sons to be labeled mama's boys, but they knew how much their sons needed their hugs. "I am not at all afraid of smotherlove, so to speak. I am absolutely devoted to Victor and could have him sitting next to me on the couch for the rest of my life, probably. Our physical relationship is a little more distant—i.e., a peck on the head before bed—than in the past, but I still feel very close to him. And I like it, as does he," revealed Betsy, a chemist and a single mother with three daughters and a son. "Gee, I suppose my concern is that as he gets older, the separation will naturally increase, and that may be hard. But somehow I think we will both adjust. He will always know how much I love him, and that is the point, isn't it? I actually remember that as a nursing infant, he was the one who seemed to want to burrow back inside me, in a way. I figured that this is the way it should be! It is the beauty of having a son."

When boys like Victor and Quentin can go underground with their emotional expressions, they keep them alive in private so they can then allow a softer side to resurface as young adults. Once the rocky reef of adolescence has been passed, these boys can allow their mature selves to display "feminine" qualities.

Even the best-intentioned mother won't always get it right when trying to juggle a son's bid for self-sufficiency with his need for mothering. Linda Watkins, a single mother who adopted two Czech kids, recounted to me a funny story about her son Ivan's wanting his independence from his mother but still wanting her around. "The other day I was going to volunteer on sports day at school. I asked if he wanted me to do it. He said, 'No, you'll embarrass me.' I melted on the floor, I felt so awful. Eventually it came out that he doesn't like it when I'm yelling at baseball games or something. I get into sports. I love it, for God's sake," she relayed to me enthusiastically. "But Ivan emphatically said, 'I don't want you yelling at me to do the stuff on sports day.'

"After I stopped feeling hurt, I said, 'You've got to tell me stuff like that. If I bother you, you have to tell me and I won't do it again.' I guess normal mothers don't yell at baseball games. Next game, I didn't.

"That same game, he got hit by a pitch. All these kids were rushing up to him. I didn't say a word. After the game, he yelled at me, 'You could have acted a little concerned!' I yelled right back, 'You told me not to do anything at your games!' He starts laughing. The poor kid almost has a concussion on the plate and I'm just standing there. That's the kind of [frank] relationship we have all the time about everything. I love having that."

A boy's self-imposed ban on public displays of affection is a symptom of his coming into his own and yet still needing his mother in a different, though no less direct, way. As sons grow older, however, many mothers pull away a bit without even realizing it (some because of pressure from husbands who accuse their wives of smotherlove).

"I did catch myself holding back from kissing TJ because I had some unconscious idea that I was sissifying him. I noticed I was kissing him less and that he was tolerating that, so I upped the kiss quotient," Fiona admitted to me. "I got over it very quickly. I make sure I get and give a hug and a kiss at nearly every parting and every reunion. It's important. I do this with both sons: nonjudg-mental affection, just because you're glad to see them or you wish them well. It doesn't take much, but it has helped, I think, all of us to be a little softer. We're all happier when we show affection."

Staying close to sons means more than finding a way to keep physical affection and emotional closeness alive and well. It can also mean giving sons the space to be the little kids that parts of them still yearn to be. "TJ sat on my lap to give me a hug, then insisted that I do 'Trot, Trot to Boston' and jounce him on my knees," Fiona added with a laugh. "And he's nearly 10. Michael, 7, took turns, too, and then it turned into how high could I bounce them and how spectacularly could they crash and how much their seat bones hurt after too much jouncing. That's not anything TJ would have ever done in public. But he could still indulge the little-boy part and revel in his mother's closeness."

Development is not a straight line, and connection, like anything else, changes in different ways at different stages of boys' lives. By 14, my son Alex routinely refused to sit with us, his family, in the movie theater for fear of compromising the cool new "Drex" persona his friends had conferred on him along with the nickname. That year he also blew up at me for intruding into his room the first time he'd ever had girls over to the house. That same evening, he took out the LEGOs and cars he hadn't touched in a couple of years. Since we had enjoyed playing with them together in the past, I asked if I could join in. He was only too happy to include me, despite the fact that just hours before, he had been furious over my invasion of his personal space. At a time when we could have indulged the anger each of us felt over the event, we found a way to maintain and reaffirm our closeness instead. And with LEGOs!

At all ages, in good times and in bad, the maverick mothers I interviewed remained in their sons' lives. Single mother Cassie

Mead wrote to me about how she raised her boys through the troubled and trying adolescent years. "Despite the cynicism and criticism of my peer group," she wrote, "I continued to interject myself into their lives." Her younger son pulled away from the family for a while, and "particularly from me," Cassie confided. But "by continuing to embrace and communicate with him, despite his resistance, at least two things occurred. One is that we determined, along with the assistance of our pediatrician, that he was clinically depressed and in need of medication." Through her persistent and loving pressure, her son gave up self-medicating with marijuana and Ecstasy and started to pull out of his depression with the proper treatment.

Today Cassie asks "all the same questions I did when he was younger. 'Where are you going? Who are you going with? How can we reach you?' et cetera. All of my 'interference' in his life and insistence upon responses to my inquiries has kept me intimately involved in his life and kept him a vital and loving member of the family. I will never regret the hugs and kisses we exchange every time he leaves home for the evening, along with a promise extracted from him that he will call in an emergency and will not drive while intoxicated or take a ride from anyone who has been drinking or doing drugs."

The expressions of love we show boys, she concluded, "should not end when our sons are no longer little boys looking for consolation on the playground. Our love encourages our sons to seek our advice and guidance as they form their worldviews about going to war and waging peace."

Shifting the connection with boys in accord with their intellectual, emotional, and physical growth, as I've had to do with Alex, does not mean weakening it. If anything, adolescents and those boys readying themselves to leave the nest (even those who have already flown) need that sense of connection more than ever.

Too much independence, even when they demand it, often leads to surprisingly lonely men who are still boys at heart.

By differentiating between being a loving, involved mother who listens and treats her son with regard—rather than an intrusive one with never-ending expectations—maverick moms maintained connections with their sons even when they had left home. "Sometimes I forget I'm not talking to kids anymore," Maria Gonzales admitted to me with a laugh. "[My youngest] was wanting to stay out all night, and I was saying, 'No, no, this isn't right.' But he was 20. Eventually he came to me and said, 'Mommy, I want to move out.' It was hard for me, but it was right, so I said, 'Do it. You're ready.'

"He moved out last August. I'd never call him in the beginning, to leave him by himself. Eventually, he started calling and visiting. The other day, he went to the mountains with some coworkers, and he called me from there, saying, 'Mommy, I miss you. On the road, I was thinking of how fun it was when I came here with you.'

"I said, 'But that's good, honey. Now you'll have a different experience.'

"'Yeah,' he said, 'I'm missing you in a good way.'"

WHEN RAISING BOYS, MAVERICK MOMS:

⊙ Don't buy into trepidations about being too close to their boys, no matter what their sons' age. The combination of closeness and conversation leads to a natural and lifelong intimacy between mother and son.

⊙ Focus on problem solving rather than reprimanding.

- Frequently step out of their comfort zones to meet their sons' needs, including getting physical when it comes to roughhousing, playing sports, or, yes, jumping on trampolines.

- Connect with their sons in any way they can, encouraging physical and emotional expressions of affection even when their sons try to push them away.

- Help their sons to lead a double life on the emotional front so that their growing and publicly standoffish boys can still enjoy, in the privacy of their own homes, the mothering they secretly still crave. Allowing young males to hide their soft, vulnerable sides from the world keeps those emotions alive.

- Keep the dialogue open as their sons grow older, even when they don't agree with their sons' choices.

- Shift their connections with their sons in accordance with their sons' intellectual, emotional, and physical growth in order to stay close.

CHAPTER EIGHT

COLLECTED
FAMILIES

"A family is a collection of people who love each other and
take care of each other and help kids grow up."

—9-year-old son of two lesbian moms

THOUGH TWO-MOTHER and single-mother families push our
society to reassess its assumptions and constructions about sex,
reproduction, and parenthood, if we cut below surface, we can
see the currents and countercurrents that characterize all families.
They share the same concerns about their sons, the same pressures, and the same needs when it comes to making their families
work. That's where the similarity stops, for maverick moms have
created a vital new form of the "extended family," from sympathetic relatives to teachers and neighbors, from scoutmasters to
"seed daddies."

A close look at these self-made extended families provided me
with a redefined sense of just how valuable *nonofficial* parenting
figures can be in bringing up children with a sense of community,
security, and diversity.

IT TAKES A VILLAGE

Years ago, after Melanie Addison's 35-year-old husband died unexpectedly when her sons were 8 years, 3½ years, and 10 months old, Melanie's friends stepped in to give aid and succor to the stunned widow and her family. "I had no family here, but I had a terrific support system," Melanie, a mortgage broker, told me. "And that support system was wonderful and reached out to me in many, many ways. We had been doing Shabbat every Friday night and people would just show up, and I never quite knew who, what, or how. People reached out to the children and me individually, or to us as a family. The first holiday season we were alone, I took two of my sons to Carmel, since somebody had invited us to come and some-body else offered to watch the baby. Then the following year—I think one of the most wonderful things that happened in my life—a very close friend who used to go away with her family (her sister and family and her husband's brother and his family) included me and my family, and we've all been going there now for 30 or 40 years."

Her neighbors, older parents with two sons, also proved invaluable. Melanie remembered the time she was trying to call her oldest son in to dinner from the dead-end alley outside the house where all the kids would play. When her son continued to ignore her, the father who lived next door walked out onto his porch. "Bruce Addison, get your tush in gear—your mother's calling you!" he yelled.

Bruce did just that, just as he did anything at the encourage-ment of his mentor, neighbor Bud Franklin, whom he described as "the quintessential mensch—a wonderful human being." Franklin became a father figure who could take the boy to father-son picnics and who showed him everything from how to throw a ball to how to tie a bow tie.

Bruce eagerly told me all about the family that adopted him as readily as he adopted them. "Johnny was my age. Robert was 2 years older. Our houses were right next to one another. You know, San Francisco style, with no space. And we had decks on the back that were literally right next to one another, and there was a small railing that was just a hurdle. Johnny, Robert, and I would just hop that fence all day long. Johnny would come over for orange Popsicles from our freezer, and I'd jump over to watch cable television because my mom didn't allow us to have cable. They never felt as though their father was taking anything from them. There was never a sense of jealousy there. And I understood the relationship as well, so there was never any kind of tension either way." He had simply become part of their family, and they part of his.

In the past, the question "How was I born, Mommy?" might have caused parents to blush—but the answer was usually clear-cut. Today we live in a new world. Creating families is no longer as simple as a mom and a dad getting married, moving to the suburbs, and making a baby or two. The "facts of life" have changed radically. Already, remarkable technological advances allow us to combine egg and sperm in previously unfathomable ways. Moms can have babies that are created from their own eggs or with donor eggs. They can use a spouse's sperm or sperm donated by a friend, or procure it from a sperm bank.

Scientific breakthroughs are only a part of the story. The number of single-mother households grew 25 percent during the 1990s. Nearly half of all marriages end in divorce. Women without husbands present head up 12.2 percent of all family households. Couples remarry, creating new, extended families of stepchildren. And researchers estimate that some 5 million lesbians and 3 million gay men have become parents and are raising an estimated 6 to 14 million children.

These new families are becoming so prevalent that the subject even came up in a recent Miss Manners column. When asked by a lesbian reader expecting her first child for an appropriate response to the inevitable "Where's Daddy?" questions they would confront, Miss Manners (a.k.a. Judith Martin) replied: "With so many single mothers around, and double mothers becoming less of a novelty, it is the children of traditional couples who are going to be asked, 'Who is that man at your house?'"

As families combine, split, and recombine, they create spiraling relationships as complicated as DNA. The terms we use to describe our families are changing as fast as families are. We speak of nuclear families (mom, dad, and their kids living under one roof), immediate families (whoever is living in the household), extended families (all blood relatives, whether or not they are active members of a family), single-parent families, two-mom families, and blended families (those based on divorce and remarriage).

Today's parents in their complex configurations challenge us to ask: What is a family? I have coined a term to describe the multiplicity of families people are growing in the 21st century. I call it the *collected family*.

Collected families grow organically and naturally, through situation and circumstance. Because they are built on affinity, affection, and need, collected families don't need to depend on blood or even marriage ties. They evolve as circumstances present themselves, and they are the norm among the families I studied. This trend from nuclear families back to collected families is a return to the extended family of yesteryear, when boys could rely upon and draw from a variety of relatives of different ages, interests, temperaments, skills, and genders. In these larger family constellations, a child who is at an impasse with one parent can find the love and comfort—and sometimes even accept discipline—from another member of the clan. And that can be a lifesaver for everybody.

History gives us a good dose of reality when it comes to understanding the power of the collected family. Back in the days before antibiotics and modern medicine, a lot of women died in childbirth, leaving their babies to be raised by aunts, cousins, or wet nurses. When we didn't have the standard of living to provide a separate home for each family, many members of the family were squeezed into whatever space was available. Then there were the relatives who couldn't make it on their own. Who doesn't know of a family where somebody was taken in and cared for—a bachelor uncle, a spinster aunt (back then pejorative terms were used for unmarried women), a "slow" cousin. And think of the stories of brothers and sisters who were shipped off to new homes when their parents couldn't tend them anymore. Farms in the old days required more than one set of adults to cultivate the crops and care for the livestock. Having a variety of adults in the child's world was the norm from the beginning of time—and then things changed radically.

The postwar years ushered in a time when families no longer lived together. This change in living arrangements had many benefits, but it also gave us some real problems—look at the havoc that leaving our elders alone has wrought on society. And children lost daily contact with lots of their relatives. It might have been better for the children when a big and diverse group of grown-ups and older children was available to raise them. In addition to having someone else to hang out with when you were in trouble with your parents, there were other members of the family who were like you. It meant that if you were born a slob into a nuclear family of neat people, old Uncle Harry, a man who never cleaned anything up, would be your role model. Or if your interests were slightly off the wall, cousin Marilyn might share them. These big old families offered a much greater variety of personalities, penchants, and lifestyles to choose from.

That's precisely the dynamic the mothers I studied are creating today for their children. While a few of their collected family members may be related by blood, most come into these new families by choice. The result? A re-creation of the complex and varied families of old.

Psychologist Lawrence Kohlberg, Ph.D., known for his work in the field of moral education and his theory of moral development, theorized that a child understands how to deal with people in authority, such as parents or teachers or family friends or coaches, by engaging with a multitude of adults and learning from their relationships. Which means that the more opportunities a child has, the better off he'll be. Indeed, the number of people involved in a child's life in a caring, consistent way has been shown to be an important factor in his success. Jolie Solomon, a writer and a single mom by choice who extensively researched solo parenting, wrote, "The better the support network, the better the job the parent does, research indicates, the better the kids fare in such measures as academic performance."

As early as 1977, a 5-year longitudinal study of 1,700 poor urban high-risk first graders determined that the number of parenting persons present in the life of a child might also be a critical factor in the development of morality. The children were rated by their teachers on socialization skills with peers, as well as the capacity to follow rules and deal with authority figures. Researchers found that it was not the absence of the father but rather the isolation of the mother that predisposed children to difficulties in social adaptation. Mother-grandmother families were found to be just as effective as mother-father families in preventing social problems with peers and other adults in authority. The key to a child's ethical balance lay in having at least one other adult in the home sphere, which could be a positive influence on the child and provide help for the single parent.

From her extensive research, anthropologist Sarah Blaffer Hrdy, Ph.D., concluded that infant survival among humans and those other species of primates that bear and care for multiple babies depends on the mother's being assisted by others in the group. Raising offspring is such a difficult job that the mother is not expected to do it alone.

FAMILY 411

Children know family when they see it. Because Alexis Popescu's family lived in Austria, some 7,000 miles from her Seattle home, this single mother made a conscious effort to build a more geographically desirable collected family for her son, Declan. Not surprisingly, her core group of four or five friends has become more central to 3-year-old Declan's life than his distant grandparents are. Curious after a discussion about families that occurred at her son's day care center, Alexis, a geologist and a single mother by choice, asked Declan, "Who is your family?" The boy listed all the people central to their daily lives—Harry, their playful neighbor; Marietta, Alexis's best friend and former college roommate; Eve, a coworker and dear friend of his mother's; and his surrogate family Jan and Marty and their children, Roland and Jeanette, whom he sees most weekends and with whom he vacations. Then he added his grandparents in Austria, but they came at the end of the list.

"Do you see that a lot? People forming their own families?" I asked Janet Gast-Rainey, the single mom who introduced me to Alexis. Yes, she said, explaining that most of the people she knew didn't have blood relatives in the greater northwest Seattle area where Janet and her son, Kye, live. Janet, too, was building her own family network now that Kye, whom she described as a busy, happy "people person," was a year old. Her friend Anne-Marie was currently out of work and therefore available to take care of

Kye if he was sick, spent time at home with mother and son, or joined the family on outings to the museum, to the park to play on the swings, or for ice cream.

Janet's sister members of Single Mothers By Choice (a support and information resource for single mothers founded in 1981) and their children constituted another side of her collected family. "We have these meetings every month. It's great for me to know that there's a place where Kye can grow up with kids who are in the same situation as him. I think that will help him," she said.

Now Janet's collected family was about to expand around her 1-year-old. "Another friend of mine and her significant other are very interested in becoming more actively involved in Kye's life," she told me happily. "Her partner would have liked to have children, but she had children by a prior marriage, so he was kind of upset about that at the time. I think he's kind of interested. When I met him recently, he thought Kye was fantastic. In addition, a couple other friends will be more involved. I'll make an effort with that now in particular because Kye has just started to acknowledge people."

"Those of us who don't have a traditional family are entitled to make families however we want to put them together," said Dr. Mimi Silbert, a divorced mother of two boys. "People need to need each other." Silbert realizes that "families by definition in America have become the little meaning of the word 'family', and not the big, huge, extended, old meaning of the word 'family.'" By creating her own family structure, Silbert believed, she affirmed that "our values are real values because we've chosen them. We've fought for them. We could have had nothing, but instead we have a family. Murphy Brown is a family."

Murphy Brown is the fictional news show reporter who, thanks to then vice president Dan Quayle, became an early-1990s flashpoint around the issue of single motherhood by choice. She remained a model for Silbert and other maverick mothers for how a parent can effectively collect a family. Murphy's family included a wacky housepainter who was neither a blood relation nor a partner; a young, nerdy, overeager boss; a cast of self-absorbed newshounds; and a bartender, all of whom were committed to Murphy Brown, her son, and one another.

Murphy Brown spawned a national debate with her out-of-wedlock baby in 1992, but a scant 10 years later, when Jennifer Aniston's character on *Friends* had her baby without a husband, scarcely an eyebrow was raised. With the dominance of the nuclear family gone the way of black-and-white television sets, Americans are surely enlarging the idea of what family means. None of us raise a child by ourselves. And that's a good thing.

By revisiting and expanding the definition of primary parenting to include a host of *motherers* (that is, anyone who indulges in the act of mothering without the biological or custodial title "mother"), maverick moms are helping their sons in ways they likely never imagined. Of course, having a fallback for that new or unexpected kink that always gets thrown into the mix—like an asthma attack or a Rollerblading accident—doesn't hurt. By sharing babysitting arrangements with neighbors on the block, enrolling their kids in cooperative nursery schools, and enlisting the aid of grandparents, aunts, and friends with child care, these moms found ways to help themselves while enlarging their children's worlds.

I believe that no matter what their situation, children can profit from these self-made extended families, which is something a number of the mothers I interviewed had already figured out. "I collect people," Kristen Toles, biological mother of Justin, a boy with regularly changing hair color, told me simply.

Kids in these collected families were well aware of their unique circumstances. Quentin, then an animated 8-year-old with a thousand interests, once set out to explain his family tree: "Well, Nancy's a half mom because she's my dad's wife. But, see, my mom didn't marry my dad. Sarah is my birth mom. Instead, my dad gave her seeds. The part where Roberta comes in is that she introduced my mom Sarah to my dad. So without her there would have been no me."

Say what? It all sounded as complicated as a Gabriel García Márquez novel. A father was, as in Quentin's case, a father, but not an everyday father. A sibling was a sibling, but didn't live in the same house. Although among family members there was a profound relationship of closeness, it was profoundly new. But that didn't mean it was wrong, and as we have seen, children like Quentin benefit from maverick parenting and collected families in ways today's adults can only envy.

More and more of us can find these collected families assembling themselves among our own friends and relatives. I connect with two such families in my everyday life. My colleague Karin Ruddick's son, Van, 5, has two mothers and two fathers. Karin, a psychiatrist, and her partner, Rachel Tanner, a dot-commer, decided to form a family with two gay friends, stockbroker Craig Matthews and artist Spencer Young. Now all four parent the boy. Their various extended families have come together to share the parenting responsibilities, pleasures, and heartaches incumbent on all who step forward to bring up children. And as for Van, he's in kindergarten now, an extremely poised little boy and as warm as he is self-confident (but not adultlike, which is striking, given all the parents and grandparents he interacts with as an only son).

A GRAND SAFETY NET

These days, grandparents are increasingly filling a mothering role, thanks to their increased longevity, improved elder health, and other factors, such as the high number of mothers who work. Two years ago, when the house next to Megan O'Rourke went on the market, she convinced her mother, Leah—an army widow, still spry at 80, with an Irish do-it-yourself feistiness about her—to sell her San Jose, California, home, which had become too large for her, in order to move in next door. The arrangement was a boon to all. Grandma Leah walked James, her younger grandson, home from school every afternoon. When necessary, she picked him up from swim practice as well. Since she was the one with the piano, her 9-year-old grandson, Owen, worked on his musical skills at her house. During the day, she helped out with family chores when she was so inclined. Ditto for sharing evening meals. Striking a mutually beneficial compromise of assistance and independence, Megan knew that her mother, health permitting, was there to fill in with the boys when needed.

Biologists, anthropologists, sociologists, and demographers have been paying more attention to grandmothers and how they positively contribute to family life. Journalist Natalie Angier recently reported that researchers have concluded that the impact of grandmothers and elderly female kin in general has historically been underrated. In fact, for some cultures, the presence of a maternal grandmother is a factor critical to the survival of the grandchildren.

Grandparents are becoming the safety net for families trying to deal with the challenges of modern life. When the babysitter falls through or when school is out and summer camp is too expensive, where can a single mom park the kids? Grandmother's house. As one mom put it, "At Camp Grandma, the food is good and the tuition is free."

When a mother—whether for economic, physical, or legal reasons—cannot take care of her own children, it is often the grandmother who steps in to raise the kids. Nearly 2.5 million grandparents are primary caregivers for grandchildren. Since 1970, the number of children under age 18 living in a household headed by a grandparent has risen by a whopping 74 percent.

Of course, many of us have either lost our parents or live too far away for them to be a regular presence in our children's lives. Once again, however, a blood connection need not be necessary. Olivia Yarrow, a single mother by choice with a mathematics doctorate who was inseminated by a different unknown donor for each of her pregnancies, has not one but two sets of virtual grandparents for her two young boys, with whom they share everything from birthday celebrations to weekend brunches.

Many motherers participate in raising and civilizing our children, even if the adults are not a daily presence in the children's lives. Ever since they could talk, Monica Robinson's sons—Doug, 13, and Jonah, 9—have called their mother's best friend, Shawna Metzler, "Anya," a derivation of "Auntie." When they lived near her in Los Angeles, Shawna used to see them several times a week. Now that Monica has moved the family to Scottsdale, Arizona, Shawna makes a point of talking to her beloved boys weekly by phone, and flies out nearly every month to visit with them.

"Who is that person?" asked one of the boys' friends during a recent visit.

"She's not my aunt, and she's more than a friend," replied Doug, the older boy. "I guess she's like my second mom."

The sons of these maverick mothers have caught on to the idea that more is better, not worse, when it comes to family, and yet sometimes it's hard for them to be pioneers in this new stage of family development.

One Friday afternoon, Liam, a bright and personable third grader, brought home from school a form that his teacher told him his parents would help him to fill out. It was his family tree, complete with empty spaces for mother and father, and four spaces for grandparents. Looking at the form, Liam grew completely frustrated; he realized his family didn't fit in the assigned spaces. Liam's parents were a lesbian couple, and his father was an unknown donor.

Liam's mothers worked to persuade their son that there was nothing wrong with his family—that, instead, there was something wrong with the school form. Liam's teacher soon learned that this classic assignment was obsolete and objectionable for children from nontraditional backgrounds. Moreover, Liam wasn't the only child in his class whose family tree didn't bloom in the old-fashioned fashion. Many of his classmates had several stepparents, and an increasing number, like Liam, had two mothers or two fathers.

Liam regularly invited people to join his family. Collected family members included a friend from his mother Dawn's job and a man he calls Tio—Uncle. "Liam sees him once a month or more, and Tio spends the night at least once or twice a year," his biological mom, Katie Vernon, told me. "They go off and do things. Tio introduced him to lobster. And Liam, now 10, has convinced Tio to show him how to shave—despite his lack of even a trace of a whisker—and all sorts of stuff. They get along great. Then there's a friend of my partner Liam adores. We have an arrangement where once a week he goes down to her house and plays with her son, and then once a week they come up here, and then, about every 3 months or so, they spend the night, taking turns." In addition, Dawn, Katie's partner and Liam's social mother, belonged to a dog club, so "Liam has always gone his whole life to every one of the events, and he knows a lot of the people, and some of them are very significant to him."

DIALING IN THAT SPECIAL CONNECTION

The boys that I met with reveled in these special personal connections. Ned Warner-Collins, whom we met before, was a happy, can-do kind of boy into skateboarding and snowboarding, who wanted to be a Major League Baseball player because "I'm one of the best players on our team." He definitely knew his own mind. He liked burritos, hated eggplant and sweet potatoes ("Hate 'em, hate 'em, hate 'em, hate 'em"), and loved his mothers, graphic designer Suzanne Warner and chiropractor Amanda Collins. He also loved their friend Tracy Lawrence, a property manager with whom he had developed a special connection. "She's my best grown-up friend," he told me the first time I interviewed him. "She reads to me, and I really, really like her. She lives just downstairs."

After her romantic relationship ended, Tracy had moved into Amanda Collins's and Suzanne Warner's downstairs apartment. Initially his mothers didn't respond well to Tracy. She was so quiet whenever they got together that her silence became a family joke. "We didn't really have negative feelings about her, but we just had no feelings," Amanda, Ned's biological mom, said. "We didn't know her at all. She was just kind of like this nonentity." Ned, however, adored her. "Totally out of the blue, he just clicked onto Tracy. It wasn't because he picked up on our warm feelings for her because we really didn't have warm feelings. But she connected with him, and he really responded to that. When Ned was a baby, he'd cry if his grandmother held him. If Tracy wanted to hold him, he was totally happy. And we just kind of grew into that and grew to know her and love her."

Their bond stayed just as strong almost 10 years later. Even though Tracy no longer lived downstairs, having found a new job that included a two-bedroom apartment, she and Ned remained as close as ever. Not only did she interact with him differently than his parents do—playing with him in a more childlike, fun way—she liked to do things with him that they didn't. As a result, whenever the opportunity for her to babysit arose, Tracy and Ned were just as pleased as his parents were.

The maverick mothers in my study, aware of the benefits inherent in having a motherer on board who was not engaged in the daily family dynamics, actively sought out such relationships. Upon the birth of their son Henry, his mothers, Laurie and Mary, approached their longtime friend Daphne about being Henry's mentor. Though Daphne had originally agreed, she didn't come through at first. Instead of accepting her irregular or lackadaisical participation, however, Henry's mothers confronted Daphne. "Hey, don't get involved in this if you're not going to follow through," they told her. "You can't do that with kids. Don't fool with that."

Daphne, who was not used to being around small children and really hadn't considered how her sporadic attention (or inattention) might negatively impact Henry, rose to the challenge. The result was a thoroughly satisfying relationship for Henry and Daphne both. Daphne, a history professor, talked to the 10-year-old Henry about everything from his school yard troubles to bug collections. "She's an important safety net, someone who will always listen to him," said Henry's biological mom, Mary, who was Daphne's close friend. "When Henry gets mad, he can call Daphne and vent about how mean his mom is or how unfair." Yet Daphne could also be counted on to reinforce the lessons, rules, and responsibilities Henry's parents had inculcated in him. Somehow, hearing them from her made the message more palatable to the boy.

LET THE VILLAGE IN

Georgina Ewers, the 51-year-old mother of five adopted children, created an entire network of individuals gathered from among her friends, her family, and her church, "where I get a lot of support." Not only did the Presbyterian pastor support her in this family affair; he teased her about it. "Did you lose them?" he'd ask if she arrived at church or to visit him on her own, acknowledging that her adopted brood is indeed her family. During the time I interviewed Georgina, her sister moved in with them all, which gave Georgina another adult as a resource. But her sister was not the only one Georgina depended on. Much came from the caring community she lived in, with people and institutions that helped her bring up her children. "The support comes from different sources for different kids. Jorge is in an excellent Boy Scout troop, and his Cub Scout leader is really good about helping. We're supposed to go camping, and I'm like, 'Well, I've been camping, but somebody else has always put up the tent.' He's like, 'You bring that tent and we'll figure out how to do it.' So the support is there."

About adopting five children as a single mother, Georgina said, "I think the hardest thing for me is that I chose this for myself, so you don't have any right to ask for help. I have to watch that because the help is there. I can always find it when I need it. Sometimes it's a matter of having to look for it because people are always so worried about insulting you. I have to remember that they're dealing with that and don't want to do something that's going to make me angry or make me feel like they're trying to interfere," Georgina chuckled. "At the end of last Wednesday night's church program, for example, they were trying to decide what to do with the event's leftover food. The lady in charge of the kitchen finally approached me very tentatively and asked, 'Would you like to take this home?' It was more than most families would have been able to use in a short period of time, and because it had already been frozen once, it couldn't be refrozen. 'We'd hate to just throw it away, but if you don't want it, that's fine. We understand. We don't want to insult you.' I have ample income and certainly can feed my family and that kind of thing." She laughed, "I was like, 'Hey, I won't have to cook tomorrow night. It sounds great to me.'" Although Georgina could afford to feed her family, she appreciated having a "mini vacation" from the responsibilities of preparing dinner for her family of six. More important, she was grateful to those in her church who were sensitive to both her feelings and to the many demands of a large family like hers.

This new collected family benefits the parents involved as well as the children. A mothering mentor can counteract the tendency of women—whether single or married—to be critical of their own parenting. Sometimes we all need mentors or other members of our collected families to remind us how much we're already doing right. Terri Engler, a business consultant, began to go out of her mind "thinking something was going on with Anthony," her son, whom she described as talented, intelligent, and sweet—and also kind of kooky. "I couldn't handle it anymore, and I'd be in tears," she told me. But Fern, the mother of one of Anthony's close friends, was always there to "talk to me, tell me he was a wonderful kid, that he knew what he was doing, and that he was all right." Having that voice of sanity reassured Terri. "I really trusted what she said. She was always very calm and reached me, somehow." Terri's anxiety prevented her from assessing her son realistically, but after she talked to Fern, Terri's nervousness subsided and she "felt really good. I just didn't feel as scared anymore." Professional worries added to Terri's fears about her son. "When you're freelance, your business goes up and down. There were periods where I wondered if I could keep everything going, and then with

Anthony getting weird, it was just too much. I would go out and have dinner with Fern, and I'd feel better."

NEW BRANCHES ON THE FAMILY TREE

Communal living has become one of the newest ways to gain access to these mentors and potential co-parent figures who can both add to and facilitate family life and foster the collected family. For a single mom, such a ready-made family right in your own household could be the answer to a prayer. There are always people around to help with daily tasks and provide familial contact. When Mom has to work late, there is usually a place for the kids to go have dinner and hang out until she gets home. One set of best friends in their twenties agreed that if they hadn't married by their early to mid thirties, they would both get pregnant and share a house so they could raise their children together. Not only would this arrangement provide built-in backup for child care, but through this self-made two-parent family, the women—one a journalist and the other a pastry chef and caterer—would be able to provide each other with emotional encouragement. Moreover, their kids would profit from having two parent figures to emulate and respond to, as well as a "sibling" to play with.

But mothers don't have to rely on such tight personal connections to create a communal family unit. As a newly single mother after her divorce, Carmel Sullivan decided that sharing a house with another single mother might make a lot of sense. Not only would she feel less isolated, but she and her housemate could also share household and child-care responsibilities. So in the fall of 2000, Carmel placed a classified ad in a local newspaper and got 18 responses. Once she found her own match, she went to work trying to put other single mothers together. Two years later, she launched Co-Abode, a nonprofit Web-based matchmaking service for single moms looking to develop this new kind of family structure. The Web site, www.Co-abode.com, notes that "single moms can find compatible partners in any state to share rent, utilities and food, chores and babysitting. This allows for a higher standard of living than is possible when going it alone."

Co-housing—where a family's personal and private home is actually part of a small-scale domestic community that shares common facilities such as kitchen, dining area, laundry, and children's playrooms—is another increasingly popular choice for families looking to widen their immediate networks. There are over 40 homes nationwide and 150 in the planning stages. Though each home is self-sufficient, allowing parents to cook their own dinners in their own kitchens and dine in privacy, parents can also decide to rotate cooking duties in the communal kitchen and dine as a group. In fact, because child care is often shared, the assemblage of adults and children soon becomes a collected family, complete with any family's requisite stresses and joys.

The collected family is furthering its way into greater social recognition in the institutions that serve our children. Schools are increasingly becoming aware that family configurations these days often involve motherers in addition to—or instead of—a mother or a father. Recently, the head of an elementary school consulted me. He was interested in the ways his coed school could be more inclusive to families. Among his questions was whether "Dear Families" was a fitting salutation when addressing communications to the parent body. I responded that what he was observing—a redefinition of family—is happening everywhere. People are creating collective "parentships" to raise their children. The "Dear Families" rather than "Dear Parents" salutation on communications from school is not only a more inclusive way to communicate to the school's constituents but a more accurate description of the people who make up its members.

"We take our mothers where we can get them—and they are not always the women who gave us life," writes Lori Leibovich in an essay titled "My Other Mother." If we define family as those people we're close to, then in this age of supposed isolation, our families can grow large indeed.

"You don't even wanna know who's coming," Nathan's mom Nessa Newberry retorted with good humor when other families arriving for the school awards assembly questioned her sequestering of two whole rows. Nessa and co-mom Stephanie began collecting a family for Nathan—a sweet, usually helpful, intelligent kid who showed an early interest in writing and drawing and a later love for sports—and his little sister, Beth, since before he was born. He had a weekly babysitter, who was more a family friend than a sitter; there were the dear friends of one mom, and the childhood friend of the other. Add to that a sister-in-law, a neighbor, and other friends (called aunt and uncle) whom the family saw weekly, monthly, or a few times a year, to say nothing of biological grandparents and aunts, whom they saw less often, since they live further away. That's a lot of seats.

"It does take a village to raise a child," Stephanie explained. Stephanie, an internist, believes that the more individuals involved in her children's life, the more her children gain, since "more people provide for them. And it doesn't necessarily have to be the father or the parent that is missing. I came from a big family, and Nessa has a lot of friends, and so we have people who are involved."

Though Nathan initially felt his moms did not like boys because there was no daddy in the house, his mothers made a point of surrounding him with men. Even the children's sperm donors were part of this familial constellation. Nathan's donor, a highly religious Catholic scientist in his sixties who was also the biological father of a girl in another family (technically Nathan's half sister), lived out of state but visited Nathan's family regularly. The donor for Nathan's sister was a gay businessman younger and more lighthearted than Nathan's seed daddy. He and his partner spent all holidays with the kids and their mothers and were both available anytime help was needed.

BALANCING ACT

Different personalities, skills, approaches, and temperaments add up to different mothering strengths, no matter what a person's sex or biological connection to a child. This new kind of non-gender-based parenting helps boys to tap not only the various sides of their character but their potential as well.

Once a year, Nathan's family participated in a charity benefit—a 35-kilometer walkathon during which they raised money based on how much ground they covered. Nathan, 10, and his 8-year-old sister, Beth, had solicited a pledge of $5 per kilometer from a friend of their parents. Determined to walk as far as they could, they established 20 kilometers as a difficult but achievable goal. Concerned that her son was setting himself up to fail, Nessa suggested that he and his sister might want to lower their expectations and not push themselves so hard. "That may just be the way your body works," she told him. "You may not be able to do that."

At the same event the year before, Stephanie had challenged Nessa's approach. Nessa had suggested that Nathan—a boy who wished he were thinner because he was teased about being fat—should stop walking because his feet hurt. "Leave him alone. Let him go," Stephanie had countered. Now, taking the tricky risk of challenging her partner's parenting approach but determined that Nathan not compromise before even starting the event, she again countered Nessa's point of view.

"That's not true. You can do what you want to do," she insisted to Nathan. "If you want to do the whole 35 kilometers, you can do what you want. Yeah, maybe your feet will hurt more. But you can do what you want with your body."

Having heard both his mother's perspectives, Nathan chose the one that worked for him: He vigorously kept to his original goal of 20 kilometers, which now seemed more achievable. Nessa acceded to what their son wanted to attempt. During the event, when Nathan's sister began to flag while walking with her friends, he announced, "She should hook up with me. I'll get her through it."

Both kids made their 20-K target that day. And that evening, just before sinking into a hot tub for a well-deserved soak, Nathan put his arm around his sister. "I'm proud of you, Beth," he said. Having been protected against failure by one parent and pushed to his limits by the other, Nathan had tapped the best in himself and had learned to appreciate not only his effort but his sister's, too.

We need family for much the same reasons that we always have: support, community, and love. Today collected families—mortared not by blood, obligation, or birth and comprised not just of relatives but of neighbors and friends—provide new kinds of buttressing for children and their parents, a community through which adults and children can foster their identities and numerous opportunities for love. Such families can even function as a lifeline. A collected family web can spread out under a child, catching him or her safely when one strand of the web weakens or breaks.

In the raising of a child, the importance of connectedness to other people in the world is vital. With luck and persistence, a child's world expands to teachers, coaches, counselors, friends, and a collected family that will grow larger and larger. At the center? The mother or motherer who made—and allowed—it to happen.

"My mom gave me a chance to grow up," NCAA coach Mike Krzyzewski told me in an interview. In more than 25 years of coaching, Coach K, as he was called, participated in 15 NCAA tournaments, was voted Atlantic Coast Conference Coach of the

Year five times, and had the highest winning percentage in NCAA tournament history. He attributed his success to his hero—his mother, Emily Krzyzewski—who had given him unconditional support and unfailing love while allowing others to have their impact as well. "She had confidence in my teachers and coaches throughout. My mother never, ever would question a teacher or a coach. She allowed other people to teach me. She had confidence that I would learn from these people and adjust to good people. I think it was because of her that I never feared failure," he said.

The courage Emily Krzyzewski inculcated in her son, along with the wide range of people who also shaped his life, may help explain why Coach K had such an impact on his players and why he functioned as a leader, coach, mentor, friend—and, yes, motherer—in a collected family that he would make ever more encompassing, elastic, and robust. "We're in the process of building an inner-city family life center that's going to be right next to the church here," he told me. Called the Emily Krzyzewski Family Life Center, it would function as a collected family for the neighborhood and community.

In the end, the structure of our formal connections doesn't matter so much. It's intimacy that counts, and the responsibility that intimacy engenders. In the growing and evolving communities of caring, the potential for love for our children becomes as limitless as the sources of that love.

"The strongest thing I've ever experienced in my life is the strength of family," Coach K asserted. "It doesn't mean you're always going to win or whatever, but it does mean you're always going to be together. You have a greater chance of winning, or not just winning but doing well, if you're together. If you are successful in something and you jump up and turn around—is there somebody to hug? It doesn't have to be a genetically related person. But it's important to have somebody to jump up and hug."

WHEN RAISING BOYS, MAVERICK MOMS:

- Collect families from all the parts of their lives: blood relations, friends, colleagues, community organizations, and special groups for single moms.

- Recognize the value and importance of grandparents, whether inherited or adopted.

- Actively seek out motherers—anyone who indulges in the act of mothering without the biological or custodial title "mother"—to help in the raising of their sons.

- Counteract self-critical tendencies that so many women share when it comes to parenting by enlisting the aid of a mothering mentor.

- Allow their sons to benefit from different personalities, temperaments, and talents, in the process occasionally taking advantage of communal living arrangements that provide collected families and caretaking options.

CONCLUSION

ONLY CONNECT

Throughout my research and the writing of this book, I have come to take a stand against the recent tide of opinion and the rash of books asserting that boys must have a father in the home in order to grow to full manhood. Instead, I have found that loving, growth-encouraging parenting is what boys (and girls, for that matter) need. A good parent, whether mother or father, will enable a boy to develop to his full potential as a young man, as long as his individuality, his manliness, his courage, and his developing conscience are respectfully and fully supported.

The families I studied were all in some way on the fringes of the societal mainstream, and the sons all suffered in one way or another from the ignorance or prejudice of others. Teachers didn't accept drawings of their families; other children teased them about their families; there was a presumption that boys raised by lesbians would be sissies and that sons raised by single mothers would be automatically vulnerable to the worst elements in our society. Then there was a terrible libel against these mothers, that they have no standards or morals.

I found that this very marginalization was a source of tears and concern. But it was also a source of strength for the mothers and their sons.

The boys and mothers I studied had all the ups and downs of every family. Just like the rest of the boys on the planet, they fought, they cried, they got into trouble, they had school problems, they got furious with their parents, they didn't do what they were told. But there was something different in the quality of their relationships, both at home and in the world.

They had a wider range of interests and friendships than the boys I studied from heterosexual parents, and they appeared more at ease in situations of conflict. They developed their "boyishness" at a normal rate, but their sense of justice and fairness and their ability to express their feelings were off the charts. They admired many kinds of men, from scientists to sports heroes, and they accepted their own quirks and interests (and those around them) more readily than did boys from traditional families.

My research showed that it's the quality of parenting, not the gender of the parents, that counts. And yes, two-parent families—including both the mom-and-dad variety and the two-mom variety—work well when they work well.

Does this mean that fathers are not important? Of course not. Do I mean to bash fathers? Under no circumstances. This book describes the strengths of these maverick mothers and how their sons used emotional skillfulness as an antidote to the stigma of being raised by lesbian or single moms. The truth as I see it is that the love, the respect, and the understanding their parents offered was what made for strong and resilient young men.

I saw it every day. When I entered the laboratory of direct observation and listened to the boys, I heard the same song with different words:

⊙ Come, sit by me, Peggy.

⊙ I make them laugh.

◎ Of course I'm a boy. What else would I be?

◎ We found your glasses.

◎ We don't have a daddy. We have two mommies and a Ruffin.

◎ It was lonely, like cloud rain. You know how a rainy day makes you feel bad? It was like that.

And when I listened to the mothers I heard the same tune:

◎ We talked about it.

◎ I apologized.

◎ We needed to resolve it.

◎ He gets hugs at home.

◎ He can paint his nails if he likes.

◎ Me on a trampoline? Well, I did it.

◎ I've worked hard to find him the right role models.

This is the music of love and communication that surrounded the sons of maverick mothers. It is also the secret of sound children: You listen carefully, you respond the best way you can, you foster the children's interests, and you give them loving correction. You know what your own behavior says to them and what good observers they are.

E. M. Forster said it best 80 years ago in *Two Cheers for Democracy*: "Only connect!" This is the message of the maverick mothers. It's a lesson for us all. Mothers and fathers alike need to connect with their sons, not as clones of themselves, but as free-standing personalities. And they need to understand what their sons are going through, supporting their best instincts and teaching them how to be better men.

What kind of men will the boys I studied become? Only a fortune-teller can answer that question with certainty. But I see that the qualities they exhibited at a young age will serve them well.

From Howard Gardner's path-breaking work on the varieties of intelligence to Daniel Goleman's book on emotional intelligence, the world of social science is emphasizing the importance of inter-personal savvy in life and work. The boys I came to know already exhibited high emotional IQs. They might be a step ahead of many others when they enter the world of work.

And then there's the mountain of medical research about the importance to physical health of having intimate relationships throughout life. These boys already had an extraordinary capacity for closeness. Of course, they could shut down as teenagers (many boys do). But the chances are good that when they emerge as young men, they will once again be at home with intimacy.

These boys will bear close watching over the years to come. And like Judith Wallerstein and others, I will continue to listen to them and spend time with them as they mature. My bet is that living through all the vicissitudes of adolescence, dealing with the prejudices against their families, filling out forms that have no blanks for their family types, and surviving the torments of first love and disappointment will be very hard for these boys. But they already have a set of competencies to meet these difficulties.

We know that many successful women give credit for their courage and energy to the loving support of their fathers. I am beginning to suspect that the same dynamic between mother and son may have a similar effect.

"I've always loved and respected my mother. I thought she was a superhero," Bruce Addison, then 34, said to me, remembering those economically and emotionally challenging years when his mother raised him and his siblings on her own and worked long hours running different mortgage brokering businesses. "I've never met or read about a woman who is as powerful as she is. She'll tell you that she muddled through it and what have you, but I certainly didn't get that sense. She really lived with purpose. She instilled in me a great deal of that sense of purpose."

What a different view this is from the traditional mother bashing we know so well. Perhaps mothers have been blamed for communicating the cultural norms of the day. Those "smothering mothers" of the past were messengers of the family values of the time: Do what I tell you; go into your father's business; you have to be a doctor/lawyer/banker; no, theater isn't manly enough for you; don't cry—be a man!

By redefining manhood, mothers have the chance to redefine not only the American family but also the face of our society. "My hope is that my sons are going to be the kind of people who will understand that others haven't necessarily had the advantages they have, and not exploit or be blind to the fact that they have had a leg up, but instead use their privileges for good things," one such mother told me. "That is the kind of man who can change the world."

I'M BETTING ON QUENTIN

The first time I met Quentin, a scrappy and smart 5-year-old with the varied interests of a renaissance man and the refined sensibilities of an old-fashioned gentleman, he was still in kindergarten. He greeted me at the door of his family's Victorian home in a lumber jacket over jeans and a blue tailored oxford shirt. When his mother introduced us, he looked me straight in the eye and said, "Hello, Peggy," as poised as any grown-up.

Those remarkable qualities, which I could clearly see during our first meeting, were still very apparent when I met him again, 2 years later. Almost 8 and in the second grade, Quentin was already a fully developed person in many ways, his abundant energy focused and directed. "Look around my room. Every place you look is a toy," he exclaimed excitedly as he gave me a tour. "Take a look at this!" He proceeded to show me the tiger eye in his rock and gem collection, the bag of small plastic soccer balls he'd won at school for being a good student, drink umbrellas from a restaurant where he and his family had dined on French and Italian food, and souvenirs from the Biodome in Quebec City, where he'd actually seen a real sloth ("They're like rodents—big and wide—but they're not rodents, and they can go high in a tree"), along with monkeys, alligators, and fruit bats. He then launched into a discourse—complete with sound effects—about the bat's echo system, which he'd read about in a book. On other visits, I would learn about everything from how corn is ground and how wheat was grown during Revolutionary times to how maple syrup is made. He was like a sponge that absorbed whatever his two mothers exposed him to.

From the start, Quentin's mothers had decided to flood his life with gender-nonspecific ideas and experiences and deemphasize passive activities, such as watching television. Undoubtedly as a result, not only did their son have an expansive scope of interests (which also included music and self-taught tap dancing), but his imagination had flourished as well. Sets of little pirates and knights would trigger endless bouts of pretend games. "He's also got a couple of Barbie dolls," one of his mothers told me. Of course, "they're usually tied up."

His mother Sarah told me that the first time he set foot on his preschool playground, a day when so many children cling to their parents or take a wait-and-see attitude, Quentin marched right in without once looking back. "Who wants to come play with me?" he yelled with blustery confidence. Even at his young age, however, that extroversion was layered with remarkable sensitivity. "Come sit by me," he insisted later that year, upon noticing that a fellow classmate was feeling sad. This at the age of 4!

The lesbian and single mothers I studied were articulating a new set of family values to their sons. These lessons are as universal as they are vital, for society can benefit from their new men in the making. Sons who have been brought up to embrace diversity and inclusiveness, to communicate and to cooperate, to negotiate instead of resorting to aggression, not only will bring those qualities to their own families but will see their professional environment as an extension of their family and family values. As a result, they'll be increasingly selective about the vocations they choose, the jobs they take, the companies they work for and invest in, the communities they opt to live in. And then whatever area they touch will start to rise to the highest level of family values.

Endnotes

Introduction

p. vii [. . . of those parents were single . . .] Salamon, J. "Staticky Reception for Nuclear Families on Prime-Time TV." *New York Times*, July 30, 2001.

p. x [. . . after a divorce . . .] Wallerstein, J., J. Lewis, and S. Blakeslee. *The Unexpected Legacy of Divorce: A 25-Year Landmark Study*. New York: Hyperion, 2000.

p. xii [. . . ships semen nationwide . . .] Carson, T. "Lesbian Moms a Growing U.S. Phenomenon." Reuters, May 25, 2004.

p. xii [. . . fewer than a third favored it . . .] Cloud, J. "The Battle over Gay Marriage." *Time*, February 16, 2004.

p. xiv [. . . to grow to manliness . . .] Lamb, M. "Fathers and Child Development: An Integrative Overview." In M. E. Lamb, ed., *The Role of the Father in Child Development*. New York: John Wiley and Sons, 1981; Biller, H. "The Father and Sex Role Development" (ibid.); Radin, N. "The Role of the Father in Cognitive, Academic, and Intellectual Development" (ibid.); Biller, H. "Father Absence, Divorce, and Personality Development" (ibid.).

Chapter 1

p. 1 [. . . babies and their time lines . . .] Brazelton, T. B. *Infants and Mothers: Differences in Development*. New York: Dell Publishing, 1983.

———. *Toddlers and Parents*. New York: Dell Publishing, 1974.

p. 5 [. . . Maternal Care and Mental Health . . .] Bowlby, J. *Maternal Care and Mental Health*. Geneva, World Health Organization; London: Her Majesty's Stationery Office; New York: Columbia University Press, 1951. Abridged version: *Child Care and the Growth of Love* (2nd edition). Harmondsworth: Penguin, 1965.

p. 5 [. . . were perfectly normal . . .] ———. *Maternal Care and Mental Health*. World Health Organization Monograph Series 2, 55–99, 77, 1952.

p. 6 [. . . friendly, and well-adjusted . . .] Ibid.

p. 6 [. . . him an unfit father . . .] Bittner, C. "Basketball Mom's Unfit." www.Suite101.com, October 6, 1998; Howard, J. "A Legal Full-Court Press: Can a Single Mom—the Sparks' Pam McGee—Raise a Child and Play in the WNBA?" *Sports Illustrated*, October 19, 1998.

p. 7 [. . . it's the mother's fault . . .] Ibid.

p. 7 [. . . 7 years in prison . . .] Liptak, A. "Judging a Mother for Someone Else's Crime." *New York Times*, November 27, 2002.

p. 8 [. . . central to optimal family life . . .] http://bushlibrary.tamu.edu/papers/1992/92052000.html

p. 9 [. . . possible human arrangements . . .] Benkov, L. *Reinventing the Family: The Emerging Story of Lesbian and Gay Parents*. New York: Crown, 1994.

p. 9 [. . . things used to be . . .] Coontz, S. *The Way We Never Were: American Families and the Nostalgia Trap*. New York: Basic Books, 1992.

p. 9 [. . . working for their wages . . .] Council on Contemporary Families. www.contemporary-families.org.

p. 9 [. . . when it tripled . . .] Ibid.

p. 10 [. . . caring for dependents . . .] Coontz, S. "Nostalgia as Ideology." *The American Prospect* 13, no. 7, April 8, 2002.

p. 10 [. . . an unwanted circumstance . . .] Benkov, L. *Reinventing the Family: The Emerging Story of Lesbian and Gay Parents*. New York: Crown, 1994.

p. 11 [. . . is White women . . .] Kantrowitz, B., and P. Wingert. "Unmarried, With Children." *Newsweek*, May 28, 2001.

p. 12 [. . . a setting on the dryer . . .] Peri, C., and K. Moses. *Mothers Who Think: Tales of Real-Life Parenthood*. New York: Simon and Schuster, 1999.

p. 12 [. . . treat the children. . . .] Cowan, P. Council on Contemporary Families. www.contemporaryfamilies.org.

p. 12 [. . . in a single-mom family . . .] Herzog, E., and C. Sudia. "Children in Fatherless Families." In B. E. Cadwell and N. H. Ricciuti, eds., *Review of Child Developmental Research* 3:141–233, Chicago: University of Chicago Press, 1973; Amato, P. A., and B. Keith, "Parental Divorce and Child Well Being: A Meta-Analysis." *Psychological Bulletin* 110:26–46, 1991; Marsh, H. W. "Two-Parent, Stepparent, and Single-Parent Families: Changes in Achievement, Attitudes, and Behaviors During the Last Two Years of High School" *Journal of Educational Psychology* 82, no. 2:327–340, 1990; Cashion, B. G. "Female-Headed Families: Effects on Children and Clinical Implications." *Journal of Marital and Family Therapy* 8:77–85, 1982; Kissman, K., and J. Allen. *Single-Parent Families*. Newbury Park, CA: Sage Publications, 1993.

p. 13 [. . . boys were without fathers . . .] Ricciuti, H. "Single Parenthood and School Readiness in White, Black, and Hispanic 6- and 7-Year-Olds." *Journal of Family Psychology*, September 1999.

p. 13 [. . . after the divorce . . .] Wallerstein, J., J. Lewis, and S. Blakeslee. *The Unexpected Legacy of Divorce: A 25-Year Landmark Study*. New York: Hyperion, 2000.

Chapter 2

p. 18 [. . . to more general conclusions . . .] Coles, R. *Children of Crisis*. Boston: Little, Brown and Company, 1967.

p. 19 [. . . measure of statistical analysis . . .] Rasch, G. *Probabilistic Model for Some Intelligence and Attainment Tests*. Chicago: University of Chicago Press, 1980; Ludlow, L. H., and S. M. Haley. "Rasch Model Logits: Interpretation, Use, and Transformation." *Educational and Psychological Measurement* 55:967–75, 1995.

p. 19 [. . . development in their sons . . .] Walker, L. J., and J. H. Taylor. "Family Interactions and the Development of Moral Reasoning." *Child Development* 62, no. 2:264–83, 1991.

p. 20 [. . . or standardized measures . . .] Damon, W. *The Social World of the Child*. San Francisco: Jossey-Bass, 1977; Drexler, P., "Moral Reasoning in Sons of Lesbian and Heterosexual Parent Families: The Oedipal Period of Development." *Gender and Psychoanalysis* 6, no.1, 2002.

p. 20 [. . . children of heterosexuals . . .] Patterson, C. *Lesbian, Gay, and Bisexual Identities and Youth: Psychological Perspectives*. Oxford University Press, 2001; Perrin, E., et al. "Technical Report: Coparent or Second-Parent Adoption by Same-Sex Parents." *Pediatrics* 109, no. 2:341–44.

p. 20 [. . . Social and Emotional Development . . .] Robinson, D., "Experts: Gays No Threat as Foster Parents," *Arkansas Times Record*, March 24, 2004; Lamb, M. (ed.), "Mothers, Fathers and Childcare in a Changing World," in J. Call, E. Galenson, and R. L. Tyson, eds., *Frontiers of Infant Psychiatry* 2, 343–62, New York: Basic Books, 1984.

p. 21 [. . . of their caregivers . . .] Silverstein, L. B., and C. F. Auerbach. "Deconstructing the Essential Father." In H. L. Tischler, ed., *Debating Points: Marriage and Family Issues*, 25–33, Upper Saddle River, NJ: Prentice Hall, 2001.

p. 23 [. . . The relationships vary . . .] Ehrensaft, D. "Alternatives to the Stork: Fatherhood Fantasies in Donor Insemination Families." *Studies in Gender and Sexuality* 1, no. 4, Hillsdale, NJ: The Analytic Press, 2000.

p. 24 [. . . were social saboteurs . . .] Silverstein, O., and B. Rashbaum. *The Courage to Raise Good Men*. New York: Penguin Viking, 1994.

p. 24 [. . . were so remarkable . . .] Stacey, J., and T. Biblarz. "(How) Does the Sexual Orientation of Parents Matter?" *American Sociological Review* 66, no. 2:159–83, April 2001.

p. 25 [. . . color from coming out . . .] Boykin, K. *One More River to Cross: Black and Gay in America*. New York: Anchor, 1996; Cantu, L., "Entre Hombres/Between Men: Latino Masculinities and Homosexualities." 224–46, in P. Nardi, ed., *Gay Masculinities*, Thousand Oaks, CA: Sage Publications, 2000.

p. 29 [. . . in heterosexual families . . .] Patterson, C. "Children of Lesbian and Gay Parents." *Child Development* 63, no. 5, October 1992.

p. 30 [. . . substantiates my observations) . . .] Kinsey, A., W. Pomeroy, and C. Martin, *Sexual Behavior in the Human Male*. Philadelphia: W. B. Saunders, 1948; Kinsey, A., W. Pomeroy, C. Martin, and P. Gebhard, *Sexual Behavior in the Human Female*. Philadelphia: W. B. Saunders, 1953; Michael, R., J. Gagnon, E. Laumann, and G. B. Kolata. *Sex in America: A Definitive Survey*, Boston: Little Brown, 1994; Diamond, M., and K. Sigmundson. "Sex Reassignment at Birth: Long-Term Review and Clinical Implications." *Archives of Pediatric Adolescent Medicine* 151:298–304, 1997.

Chapter 3

p. 34 [. . . into the world with us . . .] Diamond, M. "Sexual Identity, Monozygotic Twins Rated in Discordant Sex Role and a BBC Follow-Up." *Archives of Sexual Behavior* 11: 181–86, 1982; ———, and K. Sigmundson. "Sex Reassignment at Birth: Long-Term Review and Clinical Implications." *Archives of Pediatric Adolescent Medicine* 151:298–304, 1997; Hamer, D. H., S. Hu, V. L. Magnuson, N. Hu, and A. M. L. Pattatucci. "A Linkage Between DNA Markers on the X Chromosome and Male Sexual Orientation." *Science* 261:321–27, 1993; LeVay, S. "A Difference in Hypothalamic Structure Between Heterosexual and Homosexual Men." *Science* 253:1034–37, 1991.

p. 48 [. . . as having higher status . . .] Levant, R. F. "Toward the Reconstruction of Masculinity." *Journal of Family Psychology* 5 (3, 4):379–402, 1992; Hare-Mustin, R. T. and J. Marecek. "Gender and the Meaning of Difference." In Rachel T. Hare-Mustin and Jeanne Marecek, eds., *Making a Difference: Psychology and the Construction of Gender*. New Haven, CT: Yale University Press, 1990.

p. 48 [. . . like gender, innate . . .] "Born to Be Gay." *The Independent*, October 15, 2003; Hamer, D. H., S. Hu, V. L. Magnuson, N. Hu, and A. M. L. Pattatucci. "A Linkage between DNA Markers on the X Chromosome and Male Sexual Orientation." *Science* 261, 321–27, 1993; LeVay, S. "A difference in hypothalamic structure between heterosexual and homosexual men." *Science* 253:1034–1037, 1991.

p. 49 [. . . heterosexual or homosexual development . . .] Friedman, R. *Male Homosexuality: A Contemporary Psychoanalytic Perspective*. New Haven, CT: Yale University Press, 1988.

p. 51 [. . . is genetically determined . . .] Brookey, R. A. *Reinventing the Male Homosexual: The Rhetoric and Power of the Gay Gene*. Bloomington: Indiana University Press, 2002.

p. 51 [. . . gay or lesbian themselves . . .] Patterson, C. "Children of Lesbian and Gay Parents." *Child Development* 63, no. 5, October 1992; Robinson, D. "Experts: Gays No Threat As Foster Parents." *Arkansas Times Record*, March 24, 2004.

p. 51 [. . . children of straight parents . . .] Patterson, C. "Children of Lesbian and Gay Parents." *Child Development* 63, no. 5, October 1992.

p. 56 [. . . health and educational outcomes . . .] Allgood-Merten, B., and J. Stockard. "Sex-Role Identity and Self-Esteem: A Comparison of Children and Adolescents." *Sex Roles* 24:129–40, 1991; Orr, E., and E. Ben-Eliahu, "Gender Differences in Idiosyncratic Self-Images and Self-Esteem," *Sex Roles* 29:271–96, 1993.

p. 56 [. . . for violent behavior . . .] Pleck, J., F. Sonnestein, and L. Ku. "Problem Behaviors and Masculinity Ideology in Adolescent Males," in *Adolescent Problem Behaviors: Issues and Research*, 165–186, R. Ketterlinus and M. Lamb, eds., Hillsdale, NJ: Lawrence Erlbaum, 1994; Stein, J., M. Newcomb, and P. Bentler. "The Effect of Agency and Communion on Self-Esteem: Gender Differences in Longitudinal Data." *Sex Roles* 24:129–40, 1992.

p. 56 [. . . at boys' hearts . . .] Real, T. *I Don't Want to Talk about It: Overcoming the Secret Legacy of Male Depression*. New York: Scribner, reprint 1998.

p. 56 [. . . data, Jeanne Block . . .] Block, J. H. *Sex Role Identity and Ego Development*. San Francisco: Jossey-Bass, 1984.

Chapter 4

p. 67 [. . . day with his children . . .] Yeung, W. J., J. F. Sandberg, P. D. Kean, and S. L. Hofferth. "Children's Time with Fathers in Intact Families." *Journal of Marriage and Family* 63:136–54, February 2001.

p. 69 [. . . fill in those we can . . .] Peri, C., and K. Moses. *Mothers Who Think: Tales of Real-Life Parenthood.* Celeste Fremon essay "Boys without Men." New York: Simon and Schuster, 1999.

p. 84 [. . . her own expressions . . .] Bright, S. "Exploding the Daddy Myth," http://www.hip-mama.com; Silverstein, L. B., and C. F. Auerbach. "Deconstructing the Essential Father," in H. L. Tischler, ed., *Debating Points: Marriage and Family Issues*, 25–33, Upper Saddle River, NJ: Prentice Hall, 2001.

p. 85 [. . . being seen in psychotherapy . . .] Herzog, J. *Father Hunger: Explorations with Adults and Children.* Hillsdale, NJ: Analytic Press, 2001.

p. 86 [. . . *The Courage to Raise Good Men* . . .] Silverstein, O., and B. Rashbaum. *The Courage to Raise Good Men.* New York: Viking Penguin, 1994.

p. 87 [. . . with their own children . . .] Real, T. *I Don't Want to Talk about It: Overcoming the Secret Legacy of Male Depression.* New York: Scribner, reprint 1998.

p. 90 [. . . Kindlon . . . and . . . Thompson . . .] Kindlon, D., and M. Thompson. *Raising Cain: Protecting the Emotional Lives of Boys.* New York: Ballantine, 1999.

Chapter 5

p. 95 [. . . one's own experience . . .] Main, M. "Recent Studies in Attachment: Overview, with Selected Implications for Clinical Work." In M. Goldberg and C. Kerr, eds., *Attachment Theory: Social, Developmental, and Clinical Perspectives,* pp. 407–474. Hillsdale, NJ: The Analytic Press, 1995.

p. 95 [. . . their sense of "objectivity" . . .] Seligman, S. "Attachment, Intersubjectivity and Reflective Functioning." Paper presented at the Second Annual James Grotstein Conference. Los Angeles, June 2002.

p. 117 [. . . this boy code . . .] Pollack, W. *Real Boys: Rescuing Our Sons from the Myths of Boyhood.* New York: Henry Holt, 1998.

p. 118 [. . . popular sentiment or prejudice . . .] S.N.E. v. R.L.B., 699P.2d876 Alaska Supreme Court, 1985; Dooley, D. S. "Immoral Because They're Bad, Bad Because They're Wrong; Sexual Orientation and Presumptions of Parental Unfitness in Custody Disputes." *California Western Law Review* 26: 418, 1990.

p. 121 [. . . with a paternal authority . . .] Freud, S. (1900). *The Interpretation of Dreams, Standard Edition,* 4 and 5, London: Hogarth Press, 1953; —— (1905), "Three Essays on the Theory of Sexuality," *Standard Edition,* 7:123–243, Hogarth Press, 1953; —— (1908). "On the Sexual Theories of Children," *Standard Edition,* 9:205–226, Hogarth Press, 1959; —— (1924). "The Dissolution of the Oedipus Complex," *Standard Edition,* 19:171–79, Hogarth Press, 1961.

p. 121 [. . . moral attitude toward others . . .] Piaget, J. *The Rules of the Game.* London: Routledge and Kegan Paul, 1932; —— (1932) *The Moral Judgment of the Child.* New York: Free Press, 1965.

p. 124 [. . . of emotional intelligence . . .] Goleman, D. *Emotional Intelligence: Why It Can Matter More Than IQ.* New York: Bantam, reprint 1997.

p. 125 [. . . confirmed prior studies . . .] Patterson, C. *Lesbian, Gay, and Bisexual Identities and Youth: Psychological Perspectives.* Oxford University Press, 2001; Mitchell, V. "The Birds, the Bees . . . and the Sperm Banks: How Lesbian Mothers Talk with Their Children about Sex and Reproduction," *American Journal of Orthopsychiatry* 68:400–409, 1998; O'Connell, A. "Voices from the Heart: The Developmental Impact of a Mother's Lesbianism on Her Adolescent Children." *Smith College Studies in Social Work* 63:81–99, 1994.

p. 127 [. . . taught to live without . . .] Pollack, W. *Real Boys: Rescuing Our Sons from the Myths of Boyhood*. New York: Henry Holt, 1998.

p. 127 [. . . on justice and fairness . . .] Gilligan, C. *In a Different Voice: Psychological Theory and Women's Development*. Cambridge, MA: Harvard University Press, reissue 1993.

Chapter 6

p. 129 [. . . emotionality, play, and nurturance . . .] Ehrensaft, D. *Parenting Together*. New York: The Free Press, 1987.

p. 129 [. . . but also cognitive commitment . . .] Ruddick, S. *Maternal Thinking*. Boston: Beacon Press, 1995.

p. 129 [. . . and respond accordingly . . .] Ehrensaft, D. *Parenting Together*. New York: The Free Press, 1987.

p. 138 [. . . to their parenting styles . . .] Winterbottom, M. R. "The Relation of the Need for Achievement to Learning Experiences in Independence and Mastery," in J. W. Atkinson, ed., *Motives in Fantasy, Action and Society*. New York: D. Van Nostrand Co., Inc., 1961.

p. 138 [. . . particular effectiveness and harmony . . .] Chan, R. W., B. Raboy, and C. J. Patterson. "Psychosocial Adjustment Among Children Conceived Via Donor Insemination by Lesbian and Heterosexual Mothers." *Child Development* 69: 443–57, 1998.

p. 138 [. . . with the care of the children . . .] Chan, R. W., R. C. Brooks, B. Raboy, and C. J. Patterson. "Division of Labor among Lesbian and Heterosexual Parents: Associations with Children's Adjustment." *Journal of Family Psychology* 12, no. 3: 402–419, 1998.

p. 139 [. . . to be heard by the kids . . .] Flaks, D. K. et al., "Lesbians Choosing Motherhood: A Comparative Study of Lesbian and Heterosexual Parents and Their Children," *Developmental Psychology* 31, January 1995; Chan, R. W., B. Raboy, and C. J. Patterson, "Psychosocial Adjustment among Children Conceived via Donor Insemination by Lesbian and Heterosexual Mothers," *Child Development* 69: 443–57, 1998.

p. 139 [. . . emotional and social development . . .] Fustenberg, F., and A. Cherlin. *Divided Families: What Happens to Children When Parents Part*. Cambridge, MA: Harvard University Press, 1991; Simons, R., ed., *Understanding Differences between Divorced and Intact Families: Stress, Interaction, and Child Outcomes*. Thousand Oaks, CA: Sage Publications, 1996; Brewaeys, A., I. Ponjaert, E. V. Van Hall, and S. Golombok. "Donor Insemination: Child Development and Family Functioning in Lesbian Mother Families." *Human Reproduction* 12: 1349–59, 1997.

p. 144 [. . . life and respond accordingly . . .] Ehrensaft, D. *Parenting Together*. New York: The Free Press, 1987.

p. 151 [. . . execution of good behavior . . .] Kindlon, D., and M. Thompson. *Raising Cain: Protecting the Emotional Lives of Boys*. New York: Ballantine, 1999.

p. 157 [. . . with conflict and stress . . .] Gur, R. C., L. H. Mozley, P. D. Mozley, et al. "Sex Differences in Regional Cerebral Glucose Metabolism during a Resting State." *Science* 267: 528–53, 1995; Erwin, R. J., J. C. Gur, R. E. Gur, et al. Mawhinney-Hee, J. Smailis. "Facial Emotion Discrimination: I. Task Construction and Behavioral Findings in Normal Subjects." *Psychiatry Research* 42: 231–40, 1992; Natale, M., R. E. Gur, R. C. Gur. "Hemispheric Asymmetries in Processing Emotional Expressions." *Neuropsychologia* 21: 555–65, 1983.

p. 158 [. . . "best adapted" in the study . . .] Vaillant, G. *Aging Well: Surprising Guideposts to a Happier Life from the Landmark Harvard Study of Adult Development*. Boston: Little, Brown and Company, 2002.

Chapter 7

p. 162 [. . . his chance at success . . .] Silverstein, O., and B. Rashbaum. *The Courage to Raise Good Men*. New York: Viking Penguin, 1994.

p. 163 [. . . mutual knowing as important . . .] Benjamin, J. *Like Subjects, Love Objects*. New Haven and London: Yale University Press, 1995; Weingarten, K. *The Mother's Voice: Strengthening Intimacy in Families*. New York: Guilford, 1997.

p. 168 [. . . lost in miscarriages . . .] Gilbert, S. *A Field Guide to Boys and Girls*. New York: HarperCollins, 2000.

p. 168 [. . . extreme lack of affection . . .] Ibid.; Pollack, W. *Real Boys: Rescuing Our Sons from the Myths of Boyhood*. Henry Holt, 1998; Taitz, S. *Mothering Heights*. New York: Berkley Publishing Group, reprint 1994; Bassoff, E. *Between Mothers and Sons: The Making of Vital and Loving Men*. New York: Plume Books, reprint 1995.

p. 169 [. . . in fact a good thing . . .] McGraw, P. C. "Would You Like Some Cheese with That Whine? How to Get Back on the Road, Help Those You Love, and Stop Kidding Yourself." *O, The Oprah Magazine*, July 2001.

p. 172 [. . . and scholastic achievement." . . .] Cashion, B. G. "Female-Headed Families: Effects on Children and Clinical Implications." *Journal of Marital and Family Therapy* 8:77–85, 1982.

p. 178 [. . . display "feminine" qualities . . .] Steinberg, J. *Adolescence* (5th ed.). San Francisco: McGraw Hill, 1999.

Chapter 8

p. 186 [. . . of all family households . . .] United States Census 2000, http://factfinder.census.gov/servlet/GCTTable?_bm5y&-geo_id501000US&_box_head_nbr5GCT-P7&-ds_name5DEC_2000_SF1_U&-_lang5en&format5US-9&-_sse5on

p. 187 [. . . that man at your house?' . . .] Martin, J. "Miss Manners." *San Francisco Chronicle*, March 15, 2004.

p. 189 [. . . learning from their relationships . . .] Kohlberg, L. *The Philosophy of Moral Development*. New York: Harper & Row, 1981.

p. 189 [. . . important factor in his success . . .] Freedman, M. *The Kindness of Strangers: Adult Mentors, Urban Youth, and the New Volunteerism*. San Francisco: Jossey-Bass, 1993.

p. 189 [. . . measures as academic performance . . .] Kellam, S. G., M. E. Ensminger, and R. J. Turner. "Family Structure and the Mental Health of Children: Concurrent and Longitudinal Community Wide Studies." *Archives of General Psychiatry* 34, vol. 9:1012–22, 1977.

p. 189 [. . . a 5-year longitudinal study . . .] Angier, N. "Weighing the Grandma Factor." *New York Times*, November 5, 2002.

p. 194 [. . . survival of the grandchildren . . .] Ligos, M. "Child Care Woes Can Make for a Sticky Summer." *New York Times*, April 27, 2003.

p. 195 [. . . caregivers for grandchildren . . .] United States Census Bureau. www.census.gov

p. 195 [. . . whopping 74 percent . . .] Gore, A., and T. Gore. *Joined at the Heart*. New York: Henry Holt, 2002.

p. 201 [. . . make a lot of sense . . .] Groves, V. "Co-Abode Matches Up Single Moms to Share Households." *Women's E-news*, April 14, 2003.

p. 202 [. . . in the planning stages . . .] Paoli, R. "Home at Last." *San Francisco Chronicle*, November 23, 2003.

p. 203 [. . . "My Other Mother" . . .] Peri, C., and K. Moses. *Mothers Who Think: Tales of Real-Life Parenthood*. New York: Simon and Schuster, 1999.

Index

Adoptions, by social mothers, 23
Affection, fostering mother-son closeness, 167–68, 173, 179–80
Aggressive behavior in sons, mothers blamed for, xiv, 6
Anger, expressed by sons, 104–7
Assertiveness of sons, maverick mothers encouraging, 147–49

Background of author, vi
Blame on mothers
 for aggressive behavior in sons, ix, 6
 for crimes by accountability, 7
 in custody fights, 6
 origin of, 4–5
 persistence of, 5–6, 13–14
 in single-mother and two-mother families, ix, 7–8
Boy code, 117, 127
Boyishness
 example of, 36–40
 expressed by choice of playthings, 41–42
 origin of, 30, 34–35, 40–41, 42
 ranges in expression of, 45–48
 role of mothers in forming, 44–45
Boy power, definitions of, 34–35, 44
Bullying, 147–49

Caregivers, outside, used less by lesbian mothers, 20
Child care skills, of mothers vs. fathers, 139
Co-Abode, 201–2
Co-housing, 202
Collected families. ?See also$ Extended families
 advantages of, 189–90, 192, 204–6
 characteristics of, 187
 children's response to, 192–93, 195–96
 in co-housing arrangements, 202
 in communal living arrangements, 201
 disadvantages of losing, 188
 examples of, 190–91, 193, 195, 196, 197–98, 203–4
 in history, 188
 mothering mentors in, 200–201
 role of grandparents in, 193–95
 sensitive to mothers' feelings, 199–200
 in shared house arrangement, 201–2
 social recognition of, 202
 TV depiction of, 191–92
Communal living arrangements, 201
Communication skills
 of boys, society's low expectations of, 99–100

 of sons of maverick mothers
  encouragement of, 101–4
  example of, 99
  rewards of, 103
Conflict-resolution skills, of sons of maverick mothers, 123–24
Crimes by accountability, blamed on mothers, 7
Custody fights, mother's career as factor in, 6

Decision making, involving sons in, 108–9
Differences of people, discussed with sons, 120–21
Divorce, and effect on children, assumptions about, 13
Donor fathers
 considerations in choosing, 134–35
 as part of collected family, 203–4
 role of, in children's lives, 23
 sons' interest in, 69–72

Economic factors, influencing success of child, 13
Emotional closeness with sons
 advantages of, 31, 103, 168
 as children vs. adults, 169
 enabled by noncompetition for parental attention, 171–72
 mothers' concerns about, xi, 62, 67, 68
 permanence of, 110, 174–77
 in public vs. private, 177–80
 requiring mothers to leave their comfort zones, 169–71
 shift in, as sons grow up, 180–82
 through affection, 167–68, 173, 179–80
 through openness and communication, 165–67, 172–73, 175–76
 through problem solving vs. reprimanding, 164–65
 through shared interests, 163–65
Emotional honesty, of maverick mothers with sons, 156–57
Emotional intelligence
 loss of, in boys, 136–37
 of sons of maverick mothers, 124–27
Emotional savvy of sons of maverick mothers, 30
 examples of, 96–98, 107–8
 qualities associated with, 94–96
Extended families. See also Collected families
 example of, 185–86
 motherers in, 192, 195
 role of, 184

sharing values with sons, 118–19,
154–55
teaching social responsibility to sons,
154–55
Mentors, for maverick mothers, 200–201
Moral attitudes, of lesbian mothers vs. heterosexual parents, 19
Moral development
in boys, 127
extended family aiding, 189
in sons of lesbians, 19, 20, 21–22, 35,
121–22
Motherers, in extended families, 192, 195
Mothering
benefits of maternal assurance in, 130–31
for instilling qualities in sons, 136–38
roles required in, 129, 132, 144, 152–54
Mothers
blamed for child's problems, 3–5
child care skill of, 139
conflicting with fathers, 133, 139
nontraditional (*see* Lesbian mothers;
Maverick mothers; Single mothers)
prejudices against, viii–x
spending adequate time with children, 67
studies on parenting styles of, 138
worry and angst of, 1–3
Mutual recognition, in mother-son relationships, 163
Myths about traditional nuclear family, 8–12

Parenting, good, author's definition of, xiv,
208, 209
Parenting styles
of maverick mothers, 140–44, 149–52
of single mothers by choice, 135–38
in two-mother families, studies on effectiveness of, 138–39
Prejudice
against lesbian mothers, xi–xii
example of, 14–15
means of coping with, 113–14
mothers preparing sons for, 116–18
sons responding to, 112–13, 114–16
against single mothers, x–xi

Reflection, as marker for secure self, 95
Role models for boys, 60–61
for development of morality and
masculinity, 121
found by mothers for their sons, 80–81
found by sons of maverick mothers,
60–61, 63–64, 65–66, 78–80,
89–90
psychological benefits of, 87
selectivity in choosing, 67–68

sources of, 60, 66, 78–80
sports figures as, 69, 73–78

Self-expression, involving sons in, 108–9
Sensitivity, of sons of maverick mothers,
95–98, 110–12, 125
Sexual orientation
development of, 48–49
of sons of lesbian mothers, 31–32,
49–51
Single mothers. *See also* Maverick mothers
acceptance of role as, 134
benefiting from lack of partner, 133–34
characteristics of, 11, 27
considerations of, in choosing donor
father, 134–35
misconceptions about, 14, 132–33
parenting styles of, 135–38
prejudice against, x–xi
statistics on, 11, 186
stereotypes about, 7–8
Social mothers
adoptions by, 23
definition of, 19
role of, 23
studies on parenting styles of, 138–39
Social responsibility, taught to sons,
154–55
Socioeconomic status, as predictor of child
welfare, 8
Sons of maverick mothers
anger expressions of, 104–7
assertiveness encouraged in, 147–49
author's conclusions about, 208–10
communication skills of, 99, 101–4
conflict-resolution skills of, 123–24
decision making and self-expression of,
108–9
defining terms of relationships, 66, 95
development of masculinity in, 19,
28–30, 34–35, 40–43
development of sexuality and sexual orientation in, 31–32, 49–51
differences of people discussed with,
120–21
emotional closeness with (*see* Emotional
closeness with sons)
emotional honesty with, 156–57
emotional intelligence of, 124–27
emotional savvy of, 30
examples of, 96–98, 107–8
qualities associated with, 94–96
expectations for, 27–28
father-son relationships of, 23, 71–72,
88–89, 203–4
desire for, 69–71, 73, 83–85, 86

Sons of maverick mothers *(cont.)*
    finding male role models, 60–61, 78–80,
        89–90
        examples of, 61–66
        selectivity in, 67–68
        in sports figures, 69, 73–78
    future of, 211, 214
    gender roles expressed by, 82
    importance of listening to, 158–59
    independence fostered in, 28, 145–46
    moral development in, 19, 20, 21–22, 35,
        121–22
    open-mindedness of, 53–54
    perceptions of, about fathers, 90
    respecting and appreciating their
        mothers, 166, 211–12
    responding to intolerance
        as burden of responsibility, 112–13
        ease and naturalness in, 114
        mothers' concern about, 113–14
        mothers' help with, 116–18
        self-consciousness in, 114–16
    as role models for others, 122–23
    sensitivity of, 95–98, 110–12, 125
    social mothers and, 23
    social responsibility taught to, 154–55
    taught about gender stereotypes, 118,
        119–20
    values shared with, 118–19, 154–55
    "womanly traits" vs. competitiveness in,
        90–91
Sports figures, as role models for boys, 69,
    73–78
Stereotypes
    gender, 55–56
        maverick mothers challenging, 118,
        119–20
    about single-mother families, 7–8
    about two-mother families, 8

Studies of author on maverick mothers
    conclusions about, xv–xvi, 208–14
    interest in, xv
    issues explored by, 25–26
        creation of family environments, 31
        development of masculinity, 19,
            28–30
        effect of nurturing environment, 30
        moral development, xi, 19, 21–22, 35
        mother-son closeness, 31
        stigma, 30
    origin of, xii, xiii–xiv, 26–27
    as reflected in this book, xiv
    research design in, xv, 18–29, 20
    source of subjects in, 21–22
    typical families represented in, 22,
        24–25
    as unique, 18

Traditional nuclear family
    alternatives to, 186–87
    competition with fathers in, 90
    conservative support for, xii, 8, 12
    decreasing numbers of, vi–vii, 11
    dysfunctional father-son relationships in,
        87–88
    myths about, 8–12

Unwed motherhood, myth about, 9–10

Values, shared with sons, 118–19, 154–55
Violence, affecting boys, ix, x, xvi, 35, 56,
    67, 126

Working mothers, early study on, 5
Worrying
    constructive, of maverick mothers,
        145–46
    of mothers, 144